Towards Capitalist Restoration?
Chinese Socialism After Mao

Also by Michel Chossudovsky

Poverty in Venezuela (in Spanish)

Is the Canadian Economy Closing Down?
(with F. Caloren and P. Gingrich)

Unemployment on a World Scale
(in Italian, with E. Alvrater, S. Amin,
A Gunder Frank and H. Jaffe)

Towards Capitalist Restoration?

Chinese Socialism After Mao

Michel Chossudovsky

St. Martin's Press New York

Scholarly & Reference Division,
St. Martin's Press, Inc., 175 Fifth Avenue, New York, NY 10010

First published in the United States of American in 1986

Printed in Hong Kong

ISBN 0-312-81134-9
ISBN 0-312-81135-7 (Pbk.)

Library of Congress Cataloguing-in-Publication Data
Chossudovsky, Michel.
Towards Capitalist Restoration?
Bibliography: p.
Includes index.
1. Communism–China. 2. Capitalism–China.
3. China–Economic policy–1976– . I. Title.
HX418.5.C488 1986 335.43′45 86-6684
ISBN 0-312-81134-9
ISBN 0-312-81135-7 (Pbk.)

To Natacha

Contents

List of Tables

Acknowledgements

The author and publishers wish to thank the following who have kindly given permission for the use of copyright material: Foreign Languages Press for excerpts from *Selected Works of Deng Xiaoping*, *Resolution on Certain Questions in the History of Our Party*, *Selected Works of Mao Zedong* and *China's Socialist Economy* by Xue Muqiao; Monthly Review Foundation for excerpts from *China Since Mao* by Charles Bettelheim © Monthly Review Press (1978); M. E. Sharpe, Inc. for excerpt from 'Strengthen the Party's Leadership' by Li Hsueh Feng, *Chinese Law and Government*, no. 1 (1980); Every effort has been made to trace all the copyright-holders, but if any have been inadvertently overlooked the publishers will be pleased to make the necessary arrangement at the first opportunity.

Preface

This book originated from earlier research conducted in 1980 on China's 'open door' to foreign capital and the consequences of the relocation of a sizeable portion of South-East Asia's low wage export industries to yet cheaper supplies of labour in socialist China. This early penetration of the Chinese economy by Hong Kong and foreign capital was not limited, however, to the border areas of Guangdong province (see map p. xiii), it extended, through subcontracting agreements with state enterprises, to major cities in China's industrial heartland. The 'open door' to foreign capital was also accompanied by special rights to the overseas Chinese bourgeoisie to own property and develop industrial and commercial undertakings within the People's Republic.

In 1981 I joined the Centre of Asian Studies of the University of Hong Kong, where my earlier research interests on the 'open door' policy evolved towards a more global assessment of the far-reaching social, economic and institutional changes unfolding in China since the death of Mao Zedong and the downfall of the so-called 'Gang of Four' in October 1976. Field research conducted in 1981–2 during several visits to China confirmed that the transition towards capitalist agriculture was well under way, particularly in the more affluent regions, as a result of the new farm contract system adopted by the Chinese Communist Party (CCP) Central Committee in 1978. Further field research conducted in 1983 enabled me to assess the speed at which these reforms had taken place: the initial movement toward private household farming characterised by the fragmentation of collective landholdings was followed by the institutional collapse of the people's commune and the concentration of farmland in the hands of the rich peasantry.

The 1984 establishment of extraterritorial 'development zones' in many of China's former treaty ports constituted an important new phase in China's relationship to the world capitalist economy. The influx of foreign capital was also intended to provide the necessary impetus in the 'modernisation' of China's factory system through the adoption of 'scientific' methods of personnel management, the setting up of American-style business schools and the embodiment of western models of enterprise management.

These developments also coincided with important shifts in China's foreign policy and considerable diplomatic intercourse between Beijing and Washington in the sphere of strategic and military relations. Joint ventures in defence production were signed, top level consultations between the CCP Central Committee's Military Affairs Commission and the Pentagon were established, and US military advisers were invited to contribute to the 'modernisation' of the People's Liberation Army (PLA). Ronald Reagan's speech, in the Great Hall of the People, praising the virtues of free enterprise in China's 'modernisation' during his 1984 visit to China was followed by the US Head of the Joint Chiefs of Staff, General John Vessey's, visit to Beijing for consultations with the CCP Politbureau and senior members of China's defence establishment.

Against the unfolding of these events, the post-Mao reforms represented a major reversal of the policies of socialist construction of the 1950s and 1960s. In retrospect, the pre-1976 economic and social transformations were precarious and short-lived, in that they did not result in permanent changes in the fabric of Chinese society. To understand the ease with which these transformations were reversed and undone after Mao required a careful re-examination of the struggles and confrontations of the 1950s and 1960s which were ultimately conducive to the *abandonment* of the attempt of socialist construction after 1976. On the other hand, an understanding of the post-Mao process required a comprehension of the economic and social system in existence prior to 1949, for whereas the post-Mao political project signified the abandonment of socialist construction, at the same time it rehabilitated or 'restored' many features of the 'old' social and political order in existence prior to 1949 during the Kuomintang period.

I am indebted to Charles Bettelheim, André Gunder Frank, David Harris and Wolfgang Rosenberg who commented on earlier versions of the manuscript. Hosea Jaffe was largely instrumental in motivating my initial research interest on China's 'open door' policy. My father, Evgeny Chossudovsky, provided critical comments and encouragement throughout this endeavour. Edward Chen, Steve Chin, Claude Comtois, Elaine Kurtenbach, C.K. Leung, Claire Hollingworth, Hiromi Yamamoto, and many friends and colleagues at the University of Hong Kong contributed to my understanding of post-Mao China. I am also indebted to many people in factories, rural townships, universities and research institutions for their assistance and warm hospitality during my visits to China.

Financial assistance from the International Development Research Centre (IDRC) and the Social Sciences Humanities Research Council of Canada (SSHRC) is gratefully acknowledged. The views expressed in this book do not necessarily represent those of the IDRC or SSHRC. I am also indebted to Ginette Rozon, Louise Clement and Chi Hoang of the Social Sciences Faculty Research Secretariat of the University of Ottawa for their assistance in the typing and editing of the manuscript.

Aylmer, Québec MICHEL CHOSSUDOVSKY

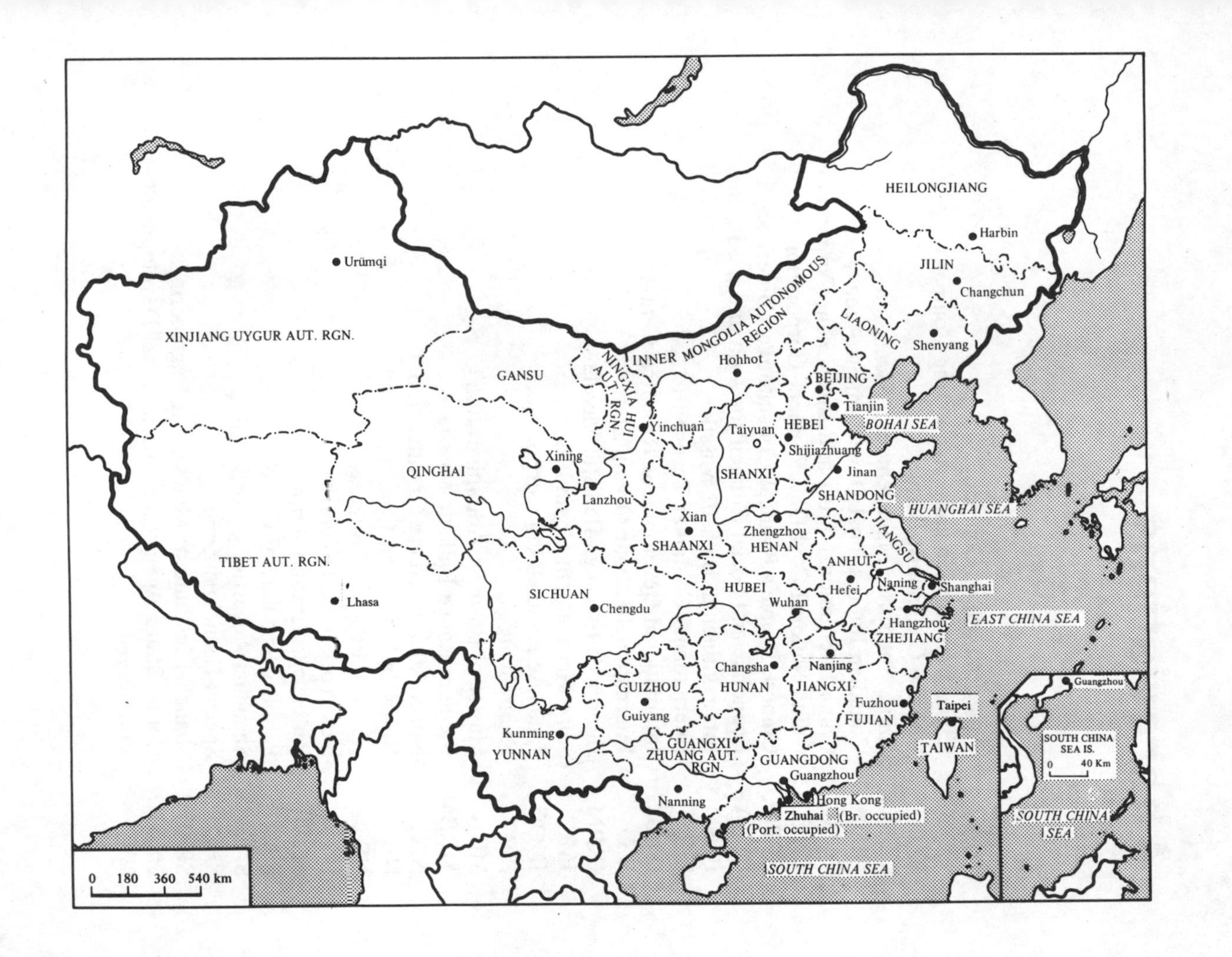
HEILONGJIANG
Harbin
JILIN
Changchun
LIAONING
Shenyang
Urümqi
XINJIANG UYGUR AUT. RGN.
INNER MONGOLIA AUTONOMOUS REGION
Hohhot
NINGXIA HUI AUT. RGN.
GANSU
BEIJING
Tianjin
BOHAI SEA
Yinchuan
Taiyuan
HEBEI
Shijiazhuang
Xining
QINGHAI
SHANXI
Jinan
Lanzhou
SHANDONG
HUANGHAI SEA
Xian
Zhengzhou
JIANGSU
SHAANXI
HENAN
TIBET AUT. RGN.
ANHUI
Naning
Shanghai
HUBEI
Hefei
SICHUAN
Lhasa
Chengdu
Wuhan
Hangzhou
EAST CHINA SEA
ZHEJIANG
Changsha
Nanjing
GUIZHOU
HUNAN
JIANGXI
Fuzhou
Taipei
Guiyang
FUJIAN
Kunming
TAIWAN
GUANGXI ZHUANG AUT. RGN.
YUNNAN
GUANGDONG
Guangzhou
Nanning
Hong Kong
Zhuhai
(Br. occupied)
(Port. occupied)
SOUTH CHINA SEA
0 180 360 540 km
Guangzhou
SOUTH CHINA SEA IS.
0 40 Km
SOUTH CHINA SEA

Abbreviations

AMC	American Motor Company
CCEC	China Construction and Engineering Company
CCP	Chinese Communist Party
CEMA	China Enterprise Management Association
CIDA	Canadian International Development Agency
CITIC	China International Trust and Investment Corporation
CNCDC	China National Coal Development Corporation
CPPCC	Chinese People's Political Consultative Conference
ESCAP	Economic and Social Council for Asia and the Pacific
ICBM	Intercontinental Ballistic Missile
ICT	International Container Transport
IDRC	International Development Research Centre
ILO	International Labour Organisation
IRBM	Intermediate Range Ballistic Missile
JMC	Joint Management Committee
JNOC	Japanese National Oil Corporation
KMT	Kuomintang
MBA	Master of Business Administration
MRBM	Medium Range Ballistic Missile
NATO	North Atlantic Treaty Organisation
NIC	Newly Industrialised Country
NPC	National People's Congress
NYSU	New York State University
PLA	People's Liberation Army
PRC	People's Republic of China
SAC	Shanghai Advertising Corporation
SEZ	Special Economic Zone
SIME	Shanghai Institute of Mechanical Engineering
USAID	United States Agency for International Development
VW	Volkswagen

Introduction

The economic and social reforms adopted in several stages since the downfall of the so-called 'Gang of Four' in October 1976 exhibit a consistent and coherent pattern which is not one of 'revision' but of major upheaval in the foundations of Chinese socialism. The post-Mao leadership under Deng Xiaoping has formally reversed and undone many achievements of the Chinese Revolution. This volte-face in relation to the policies of socialist construction of the 1950s and 1960s may at first appear confusing. One thing is replaced by its opposite: collective agriculture is displaced in favour of private commercial farming, economic self-reliance gives way to the 'open door' to foreign capital, individual entrepreneurship replaces the mass movement as the essential instrument of socialist construction, and so on. What was adopted in the name of socialism is now reversed and undone also in the name of socialism.

In rural China the People's Commune is dismantled alongside the privatisation of the means of production and the restoration of the rich peasant economy. In the state industrial sector, democratic management, which had developed during the 'Great Leap Forward' and the earlier years of the Cultural Revolution is undone: the new 'scientific' management structure involves a clear social demarcation between those who work and those who supervise the work of others. In accordance with the regime's new interpretation of the principle 'to each according to his work', the organisation of the factory is increasingly geared towards 'individualised' work and rewards and labour discipline and the social subordination of working people to the material requirements of industrial production.

Confiscated residential property of the 'patriotic national bourgeoisie' is returned. The state has reinstated property rights to members of the national bourgeoisie who left China at Liberation or during the Cultural Revolution and who are now returning to China to contribute to the motherland's 'Second Long March toward Socialist Modernisation'. Alongside the reforms of the state sector, private corporate ownership by the 'patriotic national bourgeoisie' and 'patriotic overseas Chinese' is restored in several areas of the Chinese economy. The system of economic planning is undermined in favour of profit maximisation, the liberalisation of commodity prices and the free interplay of market forces. The leaders of China's 'modernisation' are a new generation of managers and engineers:

an entreprenurial élite class of mandarins and decision-makers has replaced the masses of workers and peasants as the 'agents of socialist construction'.

Foreign and overseas Chinese capital is invited to 'contribute to China's socialist construction', by setting up joint ventures and corporate subsidiaries; extraterritoriality is restored by transforming China's pre-Liberation treaty ports into 'socialist' free trade zones in which foreign entreprises can trade and invest entirely along capitalist lines. Enterprise management is reformed and American business schools are invited to set up Master of Business Administration (MBA) programmes in China's key universities.

In the area of foreign policy the communist party leadership has directed its efforts towards a strategic rapprochement with the US, including provisions for the purchase of US conventional and strategic weapons, logistical support and training of the PLA by US military advisers, as well as American investment and joint ventures in China's defence industries. With the unfoldment of Sino-US relations, China has considerably softened her condemnation of US imperialism and American intervention in the Third World. From a historical position of supporting progressive social and economic change in the Third World, insurgent movements in countries such as Thailand, the Philippines and Malaysia have been weakened as a result of Beijing's (Peking) desire to establish 'friendly' relations with several of the world's most authoritarian and repressive regimes.

In health and education the tendency is to restore privilege and social hierarchy in the structure and coverage of social services. In all respects, these changes are consonant with those adopted in industry and agriculture: the educational system is characterised by *social and educational apartheid*, the élitist system of key schools – which channels students from primary school to university into separate 'ability groups' – is rehabilitated alongside an entirely separate system of rural schools. The health care system is reformed by restoring the legitimacy of private practice and by downgrading grass-roots primary health care in rural areas which developed during the Cultural Revolution.

The reforms are internally connected and hang together as the constituent elements of a coherent political project. In all its essential features this political project presents itself in opposition to revolutionary socialism. Beneath the internal coherence of these measures, however, lies the complexity of analysing the political transition, namely in correctly identifying the system from which these reforms have emerged and evolved, as well as the nature of the economic and social system which is unfolding in the post-Mao period. These reforms can indeed be misunderstood if the socialist system in existence prior to 1976 is viewed as socially and economically monolithic, characterised by the absence of class conflict and having in the main achieved the objectives of 'socialist transition'. Our understanding of this period has, in this regard, been unduly influenced by a large body of literature on the Cultural Revolution and the Great Leap which has highlighted the achievements of the mass movement without fully assessing the forces of social inertia and political resistence to radical economic and social change. Whereas the post-1976 political process formally reverses the policies of socialist construction of the previous period, the post-Mao reforms are also the expression of historical continuity in that they rehabilitate many features of the pre-1949 economic and social order. It is, therefore, important to critically evaluate, in the light of the post-Mao reforms, the extent to which the socialist transformations of the 1950s and 1960s actually resulted in fundamental and permanent changes in the inner fabric of Chinese society.

The debate is further confused by the fact that the post-Mao reforms are supported by Marxist-Leninist rhetoric and are presented by the party leadership in the name of the proletariat as a new phase of socialist construction characterised by the necessary 'modernisation' and development of productive forces. Whereas the leadership remains formally committed to 'scientific socialism', the concept of 'modernisation' and 'socialist construction' which underlies these reforms is more consonant, however, with 'the principles of anglo-saxon liberalism, that is, the actual practice of these reforms points in the direction of 'Third World modernisation', based on the rehabilitation of the 'old social order' alongside the free entry of foreign capital, the development of western consumerism and the reinsertion of the Chinese economy into the capitalist international division of labour. In many respects this was the model of dependent capitalist development in existence prior to 1949 against which the Chinese people waged a long and arduous struggle. A struggle which is all the more significant in that the 1949 Revolution represented, after the Second World War, an alternative political avenue open to the contemporary Third World to break the ties of feudalism and colonial dependency and construct a new society based on broad and progressive social and economic reforms. In many respects China was able to achieve, from a position of economic backwardness and underdevelopment and in the aftermath of a protracted Civil War, what few countries in the Third World were able to achieve: the changes of the 1950s and 1960s were both fundamental and dramatic in transforming the structure of ownership in industry and agriculture and bringing about far-reaching changes in the material and social livelihood of close to one quarter of humanity.

The 'old' Confucian social order of the Republican period was not crushed, however, simply as a result of Liberation and the economic and social reforms of the early 1950s. The 1949 Revolution, although the outcome of a long-standing struggle since the late 1920s, emerged from the particular historical circumstances of the War of Liberation against Japan and its aftermath. It mobilised diverse and conflicting class interests in a broad nationalist and reformist movement. Many of the social groups which integrated the communist party at Liberation, although supportive of some of the earlier reforms of the new democratic period, were by no means genuinely committed to a socialist political project based on the alliance of the proletariat and the peasantry. Moreover, the policies of the early 1950s, while formally representing the necessary basis for socialist construction (that is, in the form of agrarian reform, the development of state industry, and so on), in many respects *also* unleashed the forces of capitalism: in the countryside, land redistribution in the early 1950s had initially promoted the development of commercial farming and the rich peasantry; the early reforms of the system of industrial management maintained, under the formal disguise of the 'Soviet model', the Confucian managerial hierarchy and structure of authority prevalent in the state sector during the Republican period and Japanese occupation. The taking over of the Kuomintang-run enterprises and the formation of a state-owned sector did not in themselves create the necessary conditions for a fundamental change in social relations at the factory level.

The historical record of the Chinese Revolution until 1976 is indeed complex in that it highlights the significance of the radical reforms of the Great Leap and the Cultural Revolution without fully bringing to the forefront the powerful counteracting social forces at work. These forces – which express the continuity of the 'old' social and institutional order – were ultimately decisive in the demise of the 'revolutionary line' and the reversal after Mao of many of its most important achievements. An analysis of the post-Mao reforms must, therefore, take as point of departure the social and political struggle which has unfolded historically since Liberation, namely, the historical roots of the post-Mao political project which are to be sought in the social contradictions of the pre-1976 period.

Many books and articles on China have been produced by conventional western scholarship. This body of literature, which is supportive of the general direction of the post-Mao reforms, echoes almost *verbatim* the CCP Central Committee's condemnation of the Cultural Revolution and 'the insiduous influence of the "Gang of Four" '. Its assessment of the Cultural Revolution and the post-Mao period conveys little in terms of a genuine understanding of the deep-seated social struggle and confrontation underlying an important period of Chinese history. This predominant western 'scholarly' viewpoint, which ironically coincides both with those of the CCP Politbureau, the western press and US foreign policy, describes the post-Mao leadership as having 'restored order' and 'eliminated the anarchy of production' prevalent during the 'disastrous years' of the Cultural Revolution. Such an opportunistic interpretation will not stand up when the history of the post-Mao period is written, because it denies the very existence of social struggle and reduces our understanding of what constitutes a significant political and social process to an incomplete, partial and biased historiography of the events themselves. This graphical description of particular political events invariably centres on the 'excesses of the Left' and the so-called 'Lin Biao and Jiang Qing Counter-revolutionary Cliques' without analysing the fundamental social and political context in which confrontation between the two 'lines' unfolded. The question is not whether these excesses occurred or not (indeed they did); the question is one of correctly representing history as a process rather than in identifying – to use a simple analogy – the political significance of the French Revolution in terms of the events which led up to the capture of the Tuileries by the 'Paris mob' and the subsequent guillotine execution of Louis and Marie-Antoinette. This is precisely the tone of historical debate – namely the absence of historical debate – which has been set by the post-Mao regime, that is, the creation of an atmosphere of falsehood which distorts the process in its totality by highlighting the interplay of political personalities and condemning Mao and his followers for their 'excesses', while at the same time downgrading the historical significance of the economic and social transformations which were put forward during the Cultural Revolution.

It is for this reason that the record of the post-Mao reforms has to be established so as to provide an understanding both of the historical evolution of Chinese socialism and its failures as well as of the political process which ultimately led up to the defeat of the revolutionary line in 1976. Moreover, it is important to carefully establish the *actual* economic and social consequences of post-Mao 'modernisation' in relation to what the leadership claims to have achieved in terms of improving the material and social livelihood of the masses. Our analysis in later chapters confirms that these claims are grossly exaggerated. The dynamics of the post-Mao reforms, including the leadership's commitment to 'combating equalitarianism' in favour of efficiency, profit and economic growth, reverses a fundamental economic process which was geared towards the provision of basic human needs and what Wilfred Burchett and Rewi Alley entitled *China, The Quality of Life*. This is important because, in a country where the balance between subsistence and poverty remains extremely precarious, the regime's narrow economism, characterised by a shift towards socially differentiated patterns of consumption and earnings – as opposed to the provision of food, housing and essential social services for the masses – will most certainly result in the familiar Third World route of poverty and underdevelopment alongside the unfoldment of small 'modernised' pockets of social privilege, affluence and western consumerism.

It is in the foregoing context that the post-Mao reforms will be examined in subsequent chapters. This book focuses on the economic and social reforms in parallel with an analysis of the political and ideological changes unfolding in the post-Mao period. Chapter 1 centres on the political transition following the 1976 *coup d'état*, and the development of new power relations in the inner-ring of the communist party leadership. This shift in the structure of power alongside major political purges in the party, state apparatus and the PLA directed against Maoist partisans, was decisive in creating the requisite political circumstances for the adoption and carrying out of the CCP Central Committee's reforms in agriculture, industrial management, foreign trade and investment, and so on, examined in the subsequent chapters.

By far the most important of the reforms are those adopted in the rural sector. Chapter 2 examines the process of land reform and collectivisation from its inception in the liberated areas prior to 1949, and identifies the historical background against which the collective structures in agriculture were dismantled and undone after 1976. Chapter 3 examines the transition towards private commercial farming and the restoration, after Mao, of the rich peasant economy from the initial carving up of collective landholdings under the household responsibility system, to the subsequent policies of land concentration and privatisation of the means of production.

The reforms in industry and the system of economic planning are examined in chapters 4, 5 and 6. Chapter 4 discusses the unfolding of state capitalism in industry through the demise of the 'mass movement', the political purges of factory leaders and the adoption of so-called 'scientific' models of industrial management. Chapter 4 also examines the development of management education characterised by the setting up of American style business schools concurrently with the influx of foreign capital. Chapter 5 focuses on the restoration of a 'free' market for wage labour and the new practices of hiring and firing which accompany the reforms in enterprise management. Chapter 6 centres on the restoration of the market mechanism, the promotion of so-called 'socialist competition', and the partial collapse of the system of central economic planning. These reforms have far-reaching effects on the structure and pattern of economic growth.

Chapters 7, 8 and 9 focus on the 'open door' policy, the penetration of the Chinese economy by foreign capital and the consequences of China's reintegration into the structure of the capitalist international division of labour. Chapter 7 examines the structure of extraterritoriality in historical perspective and the development of the 'open door' policy after Mao. Chapter 8 centres on the specific institutional and legal provisions regulating the entry of foreign capital as well as the development of extraterritorial development zones and trading areas in designated coastal cities and ports. It also analyses the process whereby foreign capital penetrates and gains control over several important areas of Chinese industry. Chapter 9 examines the integration of China's manpower reserves into the 'international reserve pool' of cheap Third World labour and the subordination of its natural resource base of conventional and strategic raw materials to the needs and requirements of world capitalism. The implications of such a reintegration are far-reaching not only for China, but they also modify in a fundamental way the structure of the international division of labour.

Chapter 10 focuses on some of the geopolitical implications of China's 'open door' policy, namely the development of Sino-US strategic relations, the rapprochment between Beijing and Washington in the areas of defence and military relations, the development of an 'open door' in the area of military technology and the influx of foreign capital into China's defence industries. This strategic rapprochement with the United States is indeed consonant both with the 'open door' to international corporate capital as well as with the general direction of the reforms within China itself.

The last chapter examines the leadership's political project in relation to the problematic of 'capitalist restoration'. The analysis focuses on the nature of the economic and social system which is unfolding and the extent to which these changes are characteristic of a process of capitalist restoration.

1

The Political Transition

Deng Xiaoping's Rise to Political Power

This chapter focuses on the political process leading up to the consolidation of a new leadership group within the Chinese Communist Party in the aftermath of the 1976 *coup d'état*. Whereas this 'political transition', which was instrumental in the adoption and implementation of the Central Committee's economic and social reforms, is pinpointed here as coinciding with the events of 1976 which led to the demise of the so-called 'Gang of Four', the 'Rightist line' within the party had gained considerable impetus since the late 1960s, and many f the economic and social changes were, in fact, present at a much earlier stage as a result of the confrontations of the Cultural Revolution and its aftermath. The political form of the Shanghai commune was abandoned and replaced by the revolutionary committees set up after 1967. These committees and other organs of revolutionary power, such as the workers' management groups set up in the first years of the Cultural Revolution, were, however, gradually encroached upon by the party bureaucracy.[1] By 1971, the revolutionary committees in the factories had in practice been superseded by unelected party committees which reinstated the authority of the factory cadres and engineers.

The events surrounding Lin Biao's unsuccessful plot to take over power in an armed uprising in 1972, his mysterious death in an airplane crash over Mongolia, and the campaign to repudiate Lin Biao after his death, were conducive to further changes in the structure of political power: 'Rightists' within the party used the 'repudiation of Lin Biao' to consolidate their position in the party. Shortly after the Tenth Party Congress was held in Beijing in August 1973, Deng Xiaoping – who had been denounced as a 'Rightist' at the outset of the Cultural Revolution – was reinstated in the Central Committee Politbureau. Attempts were also made within the Party 'to reverse the verdict' on Liu Shaoqi, the main contender of the 'capitalist road' during the first years of the Cultural Revolution. In the factories the rehabilitation of the authority of the managers and engineers was accompanied, in many cases, by a wave of repression directed against the workers' movement. This repression was instigated by the state and party bureaucracy, and supported by the security forces.

Major changes were also taking place in China's foreign diplomacy and trade relations with the Kissinger and Nixon visits to China in 1971 and 1972 respectively, and the signing of the Shanghai Communiqué with the US in 1972. These initial overtures are important because they established the basis for the formulation of several features of the 'open door' policy prior to its official adoption in 1978.

In autumn 1973 the 'Left' responded with the *dazibao* (big character posters) campaign directed against Confucianism and élitism in education. In early 1975 a further campaign was launched by Mao, designed to examine the practical meaning of the dictatorship of the proletariat and to what extent the proletariat actually exercised power.[2] This was followed early in 1976 by the campaign against Deng Xiaoping who was accused of stirring up a 'right deviationist wind' in education and the economy.[3] And on 10 March 1976 Mao opened a campaign directed against the reversal of 'correct verdicts' passed during the Cultural Revolution: 'You are making the socialist revolution and yet you do not know where the bourgeoisie is, it is right here in the Communist Party'.[4]

Against the unfoldment of these events, the death of Mao Zedong in September 1976 and the *coup d'état* of October, which led to the downfall of the group of Four (the so-called 'Gang of Four') are historical landmarks in the evolution of the class struggle because they created the requisite conditions for the reorganisation of the Communist Party apparatus and the 'restructuring' of the seat of political power within the Central Committee. The death of Zhou Enlai in January 1976 is equally significant because Zhou was viewed as an intermediary between the 'Left' and the 'Right'. Faithful on the one hand to Mao, he attempted to master-mind the 'cohabitation' of the 'bourgeois' and 'proletarian' lines within the party and sought to maintain a form of populist class alliance between the two 'lines'. Zhou Enlai's conciliatory role and position within the party was, none the less, ambiguous, both in his staunch support of Deng Xiaoping as well as his endorsement of several features of the so-called 'capitalist road'.

The political situation further evolved after Zhou Enlai's death with the campaign directed against Deng Xiaoping. In April 1976 Deng (who was Zhou's protégé) was ousted from the Politbureau by the group of Four, apparently at Mao's personal request. Vice-Premier Hua Goufeng was appointed to succeed Zhou Enlai as Premier and Vice-Chairman of the Chinese Communist Party. From April 1976 to Mao's death in September, secret meetings were held between Deng Xiaoping, provincial Communist Party leaders from Guangdong, Sichuan and Fujian and senior military cadres of the PLA.[5] Immediately after Mao's death Deng Xiaoping returned to Beijing to seek the support of Premier Hua Guofeng against the Gang of Four and the radical faction within the CCP.

Notwithstanding these developments, Hua Guofeng's leadership did not externally appear in the late months of 1976 as implying the return to power of Deng Xiaoping and the 'bourgeois line'. In fact, shortly after Mao's death, Hua reaffirmed the achievements of the Cultural Revolution, attacking 'those in power taking the capitalist road' and explicitly stating that the Cultural Revolution had 'smashed the schemes of Liu Shaoqi, Lin Biao and Deng Xiaoping. . . . [It is necessary] to deepen the struggle to criticise Deng Xiaoping and repulse the Rightist deviationist attempt to reverse correct verdicts'.[6]

Beneath the anti-Deng rhetoric, however, there was evidence of tacit political collusion between the Hua and Deng factions both prior and after the October 1976 *coup d'état*, largely because many of those within the CCP and the PLA, who had collaborated with Hua and who had been instrumental in eliminating the group of Four, were also supporters of Deng Xiaoping and the 'bourgeois line'. It is, therefore, incorrect to view the Deng and Hua factions as competing political and ideological alternatives.

The *coup d'état* of 6 October 1976 was carried out by Hua, and Defence Minister Ye Jiangying who was in control of the Armed Forces. Whereas Deng Xiaoping was not visibly involved, he had been active in seeking the support of 'anti-Maoists' both within the party and the PLA. Hua relied on the security forces and the military leaders of North China in arresting the group of Four:

> During these operations Mao Yuanxin, a nephew of Mao Zedong was killed as was Ma Xiaoliu head of the Peking's workers' militia. On October 8, in the most dubious of circumstances, some members of established leading bodies having been deprived of their liberty and others having been threatened with arrest, Hua Guofeng had himself 'appointed' chairman of the Central Committee and Chairman of the Central Committee's Military Affairs Commission while retaining the post of prime-minister. . . From October 10 on, a campaign was launched against the Four who were accused of 'revisionism' and of 'weaving plots and intrigues'. . . [O]n October 21 great demonstrations [were] announced to 'acclaim' the 'appointment' of Hua and to 'celebrate the crushing of the Gang of Four'. Thereupon in complete conflict with historical truth it was declared that Mao had been against the Four. On October 28, Zhang, Yao and Wang were stripped of all their functions in Shanghai: criticism of Deng Xiaoping, however, remained officially on the agenda.[7]

Criticism against Deng Xiaoping stopped at the end of November 1976.[8] Ye Jiangying was instrumental in the formal rehabilitation of Deng Xiaoping in meetings held with the Central Committee in March 1977. From March 1977 to late 1978 the CCP leadership was split between 'moderate Maoists' who backed Premier Hua Guofeng and 'Rightist' supporters of Deng Xiaoping. The 'Deng faction' consisted of veteran party leaders such as Hu Yaobang, Wan Li, Chen Yun, Bo Yibo and Peng Zhen (the controversial mayor of Beijing who was the target of the student and workers' movement during the Cultural Revolution), as well as a group of younger 'pro-western' technocrats.[9] The veteran party group had been closely associated with former Premier Liu Shaoqi (Mao's principal opponent in the CCP and the major proponent of the so-called 'capitalist road') and Deng Xiaoping since the mid-1950s, when Deng was General Secretary of the Communist Party.

The opposition between the Hua and Deng factions should not be considered, however, as a struggle between 'Left' and 'Right' within the CCP because in addition to 'moderate Maoists' (the so-called 'whatever group'), Hua Guofeng had the support of a group of economists and technocrats known as 'the petroleum group', because of their important role in the development of China's petroleum industry.[10] This group can by no means be identified as 'Leftist' because several of its members had been sympathetic to the liberal-reformist policies of Liu Shaoqi. Hua Guofeng's leadership should, therefore, be understood in the context of political transition, ultimately conducive to the consolidation of the 'Rightist' line and the reorganisation of the political organs of the party and state apparatus.

The balance of power gradually came to shift in favour of the Deng faction. Deng was reinstated as Vice-Premier and PLA Chief of Staff in 1977. By late 1978 he was in control of the Central Committee prior to the historic Third Plenary session of the 11th CCP Central Committee during which a number of major policy reforms were adopted. These meetings of late 1978 are important because they not only denoted a major shift in communist party ideology, but also because they established the political basis for the development of the 'open door' policy to foreign capital, the decollectivisation of agriculture and the rehabilitation of a socially hierarchised 'scientific' management structure in industry. The decisions of the 1978 Third Plenary of the Central Committee – while reasserting at a rhetorical level the party's commitment to Marxism-Leninism-Mao Zedong Thought – denote, in this regard, a fundamental shift in the direction of economic and social policy even in relation to the resolutions adopted a year earlier at the Eleventh Party Congress and a few months earlier at the 1978 meetings of the National People's Congress.

The Purges

In 1978 a campaign was launched in *Renmin Ribao* (People's Daily) against so-called supporters of the 'Gang of Four'. In fact this campaign was also intended to contribute to the political demise of Hua Guofeng. During 1978 eight provincial communist party First Secretaries were dismissed and replaced by adherents of Deng Xiaoping.[11] Hua Guofeng's political power and influence was ended with events surrounding the Central Committee Work Conference and Plenary and the big character poster campaign of late 1978 on Beijing's *Xidan* 'Democracy Wall' which criticised Mao Zedong and denounced Hua's handling of the Tian' anmen Square demonstration of April 1976.[12]

At the Fifth National People's Congress (NPL) in June 1979, many of the 'capitalist roaders' had not only been rehabilitated but appointed to positions of power in the party and state organisation. Peng Zhen, former mayor of Beijing during the Cultural Revolution and a long-time advocate of 'rightist' policies, was named NPC Vice-Chairman, economist Chen Yun (the main ideologue of economic liberalisation), Yao Jilin and Bo Yibo were elected Vice-Premiers.[13] A few months later, Peng Zhen was appointed to the Central Committee Politbureau (and later Chairman of the NPC) along with Zhao Ziyang. Twelve other prominent 'capitalist roaders' and former close associates of Liu Shaoqi were appointed to the Central Committee. In February of the following year, Liu Shaoqi (who died in prison during the Cultural Revolution) was rehabilitated and four leaders of the 'whatever faction' of moderate Maoists: Wang Dongxing, Chen Xilian, Wu De and Ji Dengkui were ousted from the Central Committee Politbureau.[14] Wang, once Mao's bodyguard, was considered a major threat to Deng Xiaoping. Chen was commander of the Beijing military region and Wu De was former mayor of Beijing.

From late 1978 the conditions were ripe for the further consolidation of the 'bourgeois line' in the party through the implementation of political purges and so-called 'streamlining' of the party, state bureaucracy and PLA. The streamlining affected party and government officials at the central and provincial levels and was extended to the rank and file through a policy of combating 'Leftist ideological contamination'. Central Committee 'guidelines' for conducting these purges were, in this regard, extremely explicit, calling, on the one hand, for 'stern legal action against those who prove incorrigible' and identifying political opponents with common criminals on the other hand. In the words of Deng Xiaoping:

> Towards the latter, we must not be tender-hearted. . . In some places, the measures taken against them are far from effective or stern. The people will resent it *if we tolerate these remnants of the Gang of Four, counter-revolutionaries and other criminals. We have recently taken measures to crack down on them with only preliminary results. We must continue to strike resolutely at various kinds of criminals*, so as to ensure and consolidate a sound, secure public order. We must learn to wield the weapon of law effectively. Being soft on criminals only endangers the interests of the vast majority of the people and the overall interests of our people.[15]

In parallel with the purges in the party and state organisation the regime clamped down on several of the more outspoken underground newspapers. Dissidents were arrested, demonstrations and big character posters critical of the party's policies were banned. In March 1979 the communist party put a ban on all posters and publications considered to be 'opposed to socialism and the leadership of the Chinese Communist Party'.[16] In 1980 the authorities once again cracked down on unofficial journals and publications, stating that every publication had to be backed by a recognised organisation.[17] In early 1981 twenty of the main editors of unofficial journals were arrested. Deng Xiaoping's 'guidelines' on the freedom of speech were, in this regard, most explicit:

> *It is absolutely impermissible to propagate freedom of speech, of the press, of assembly and of association in ways implying that counter-revolutionaries may also enjoy them*, and it is absolutely impermissible to make contacts with counter-revolutionaries and other criminals unbeknownst to the Party organisation. . . Party organisations at all levels down to the branches must be firm and show no hesitation or ambiguity about fighting counter-revolutionaries, saboteurs and all other kinds of criminals. . . By dealing sternly with these criminals now, we will be giving some kind of education, not only to the overwhelming majority of offenders, but to the whole Party and people.[18]

Amnesty International reports, with regard to the question of freedom of expression, that most of the 'Democracy Movement' activists are now in prison. Some were tried secretly in 1982 and sentenced to prison terms ranging from 10 to 15 years on so-called 'counter-revolutionary' charges.[19]

The repression of political opponents was further 'legitimised' through major changes introduced in 1979 in the Criminal Law and the Law of Criminal Procedure pertaining to so-called 'counter-revolutionary offences'. The new Criminal Law provides *inter alia* for imprisonment of individuals 'guilty of counter-revolutionary propaganda and agitation', 'organising or taking part in a counter-revolutionary group', and so on.[20] The new Criminal Law, which came into force in January 1980, also lists 14 so-called 'counter-revolutionary offences' punishable by death. Since then new legislation has been adopted introducing the death penalty for a further 23 offences.[21]

These arrangements virtually give the regime *carte blanche* to arrest, imprison and/or execute political opponents or dissidents to the party line. Moreover, in addition to the statutes of the new Criminal Law, provisions were also implemented in November 1979 to facilitate so-called 'administrative detention' for people considered to have 'anti-socialist views'. These provisions allow for detention without charge or trial for the purpose of 're-educating them through labour'.[22] Under these regulatory provisions, which lie outside the formal jurisdiction of the Criminal Law, individuals can be detained for up to four years on simple police order 'without being charged or having access to any judicial process'. 'Special labour camps exist for those held under this legislation'.[23]

In early 1982, the communist party magazine *Hongqi* (Red Flag) stated that supporters of the 'Gang of Four' still held positions of authority and called for the purge of remaining 'Leftists': 'We must be resolute in removing those who persist in opposing or boycotting Party policies. . . Opportunists who sneaked into the Party with clandestine motives and ambitious people who made trouble and engage in sabotage must be eliminated from the ranks'.[24] A 'second phase' of 'streamlining' party and state organs was thus initiated by the Central Committee Politbureau in January 1982. Although this streamlining programme stressed the importance of retiring veterans and retraining middle-aged cadres, it should, none the less, be considered as a continuation of the political purges initiated in early 1978. This 'second phase', however, rather than cracking down in a piece-meal fashion on known political opponents, was geared towards the consolidation of state and party structures by undermining and breaking up the complex 'networks' of potential political opposition within the state and party bureaucracies. These networks are based on a system of political patronage in which junior cadres are protected by cadres higher up in the administrative hierarchy. Consolidation of political power by the 'Right' necessitated, therefore, a massive reshuffling and restructuring of these networks of authority at different levels. The purpose of this process was not, therefore, to displace specific individuals but to undo entire networks of political power within the party and state systems.

The number of people affected by these measures was reported to be of the order of several million (in actuality the number was much smaller):

> [S]treamlining organisations constitutes a revolution. Of course, it is not our intention to overthrow anyone but to transform the organisational structure of our Party and State. . . My [Deng Xiaoping] second point is that this problem concerns several million people. At the central level we want to cut staff by one-third. At the lower levels, I think that more than one-third should be trimmed. If we were to cut only one-fourth, that still would be five million people. . . . Generally speaking, this plan will affect several million cadres at the higher, middle and lower levels. If we include enterprises and institutions that are also to be streamlined, even more people will be involved. In Party, government and mass organisations alone they will number four to five million. . . This process will inevitably affect a number of persons who belong to one faction or another, triggering their factionalism and causing complications. But come what may, we must stick to our guns in this revolution, standing staunch and unshakable. A little trouble is nothing to worry about.[25]

At the January 1982 meetings of the Politbureau, Deng Xiaoping also called for the streamlining and reorganisation of the central state organs and those bodies of the party immediately under the Central Committee:

> The programme for Party organs directly under the Central Committee is not concrete enough. Let me be blunt: there may not be enough revolutionary spirit in the programme. I don't mean that we should dismantle the 'big temple' of the organs directly under the Central Committee, but there are too many 'small temples'. . . The trade union, youth and women's organisations can [also] take this opportunity to draw up plans for trimming their staffs.[26]

As a result of the demotion and cutting back of staff, the streamlining policy opened the way for promoting – through the system of political patronage – individuals firmly committed to the 'Rightist' line. In turn, these promotions were conducive to major changes in the various networks of political authority discussed earlier:

> My fourth and last point is that in this revolution [streamlining] *we must pay attention not only to cutting back staff by several million and that this matter must be handled well. But promotion is the primary issue*. Selecting and promoting the right people to the leadership of ministries and their departments and bureaus is the most important thing. This is also true in the army. Promotion is primary, cutbacks are secondary. We must make the best choices 'selecting the virtuous and appointing the able' as the saying goes. This embraces the three qualifications of good political quality, competence and experience.[27]

This statement could not be more explicit in its ultimate political intent. This major reorganisation of leading state and party organs constitutes the essential basis for consolidating political power through 'organisational trimming' on the one hand, and promotion of the 'virtuous' of 'good political quality' on the other hand.

Further to the Politbureau January decisions, the Central Committee announced in March 1982 that the administrative structure of government ministries would be reorganised, and the size of the Civil Service in the central government would be cut by 30 per cent and from 50 to 75 per cent at the senior level. In the reorganisation that followed in the spring of 1982, which led to the *formal reassignment* (partly through reshuffle, partly through demotion) of two-thirds of the ministers and vice-ministers and the sacking of hundreds of senior government officials in the ministries, the political power structure was again substantially modified in favour of the 'Rightist line' by weeding out those who were considered politically undesirable. In Beijing municipality alone 200 000 government employees were (according to official reports) said to have been relieved of their duties, demoted or reassigned. Similar measures were carried out at the provincial and municipal levels; according to *Xinhua* (China News Agency) those relieved of their posts in 1982 'will undergo training before they can return to work'. Some reports suggested, however, that thousands of senior and mid-career civil servants had been reassigned to manual labour in factories.

In early 1984 Party Secretary Hu Yaobang announced that whereas the 'ongoing consolidation drive will make the Communist Party stronger and more capable of leading the Chinese people to realize modernisation' it was also intended to eliminate those 'people who rose to political power during the Cultural Revolution and who are still behaving badly. . . Degenerates and law-breakers constitute only about one per cent of the total membership, that is about 400 000'.

The shake-up of the Party and State bureaucracy initiated by Deng in early 1982 came to its completion at the September 1985 'Special Conference' of the Chinese communist party. The 'voluntary resignations' of prominent communist party veterans at the Conference had been carefully orchestrated by the leadership well in advance. These resignations enabled Deng to reshuffle the composition of leading bodies of the party and bring into the Politbureau and Central Committee a new wave of pro-Western technocrats firmly committed to economic liberalisation and the 'open door' policy. Six new members, most of whom were already occupying leading positions in the government were brought into the Politbureau. These included Li Peng and Tian Jiyun who had been appointed Vice-Premiers two years earlier, Hu Qili, a former Communist Party Youth President and a likely successor to CCP General Secretary Hu Yaobang, and Qiao Shi, head of the party's organisation department and a close protegé of Deng Xiaoping. Several prominent Maoist members of the Military were removed from the Politbureau and no new appointments from the Military were made thereby significantly downgrading the influence of the People's Liberation Army in the Party's 'inner circle'.

The 'crack-down against crime'

In the nationwide 'law and order' campaign against crime initiated in 1983, tens of thousands of people were arrested and several thousand were executed.[28] Although the crack-down was directed against delinquency, economic crimes, criminal gangs, robbery, and so on, political opponents were often identified with common criminals and executed for 'counter-revolutionary' activities. According to some press reports, the number of executions during the first three months of the campaign was in excess of 5000. Amnesty International reports in this regard that:

> In many cases groups of convicted offenders were paraded in public in the streets or during mass rallies. They were all shot later the same

day. . . Executions of groups of 15 to 40 persons continued during the following months throughout the country. Many of those executed were reported to have been unemployed young people between 18 and 40. Most of those executed appeared to have been convicted of murder, rape or robbery, *but people were also executed for a wide range of offences. For example, two men were executed in Guangzhou on 5 September 1983 after being convicted of hanging a banner with a 'counter-revolutionary' slogan from a hotel window* and of plotting to set up a radio station and two subversive organisations.[29]

Along with the crack-down on crime, trial procedures under the new Criminal Law were speeded up 'if there is a presumption of guilt before trial':

> In order to speed up trial procedures, in such cases, this decision allowed courts to bring defendants to trial without giving them a copy of the indictment in advance and without giving advanced notice of the trial or serving summonses in advance.[30]

This speeding up procedure was described as 'necessary' because it 'hinders' efforts to 'frighten' other potential criminals.[31]

Streamlining the People's Liberation Army

After his reinstatement as PLA Chief of Staff in 1977, Deng initiated the 'streamlining' of the Military. In his December 1977 address to the Military Commission of the Central Committee, he called for 'the consolidation of the Army' to be accomplished in parallel with that of the leading bodies of the party and state organisation:

> On the whole, the movement to expose and criticise the Gang of Four is proceeding well in the Army. In most units it is developing soundly and in depth, but in some it has yet to be deepened. . . Beyond all doubt we must crack down resolutely on the unrepentant diehards among the sworn followers of the Gang of Four. But we should deal leniently with those followers of the Gang and participants in its factional activities who are willing to make amends and thoroughly expose the crimes of the Gang and its faction – once what they say proves to be true. We must not entrust important jobs to persons who have made grave errors and whose attitude remains bad; they should be deprived of their current rank and perquisites.[32]

In his statement to the Military Commission, Deng Xiaoping proceeded to identify and describe, in a 'witch-hunt' type fashion, the categories of individuals either to be excluded from the Army or not to be recruited or nominated to important posts. These included, *inter alia*: 'persons who exercised a fascist dictatorship and acted tyranically', 'persons who serve their own interests through trickery and swindling', 'persons who are keen on factional activities', 'skilled political tricksters or specialists in "knifing" people'.[33] Deng, however, warned the Military establishment 'that it is not enough' merely to repress those visibly involved 'in the plots of the Gang': 'For there is another category of persons who have little or no connection with the Gang of Four but who are, nevertheless, politically unsound and ideologically anti-Marxist'.[34] In 1981 the NPC Standing Committee adopted 'Provisional Regulations of the People's Republic of China on Punishing Servicemen who Commit Offences against their Duty'. These provisions, which include the death penalty for a number of so-called counter-revolutionary offences, constitute the legal framework for eliminating both active and potential political opponents in the Armed Forces. The death sentence applies *inter alia* to 'sabotage', 'spreading rumours undermining Army morale', 'disobedience', 'false reports', 'harming civilians', and so on.[35]

At the higher echelons of the PLA many senior officers were purged, Deng supporters were appointed to key military posts, and old 'Maoist' PLA cadres were forced into retirement. The purges in the PLA were less successful than those in the party and state bureaucracy: there was strong opposition among PLA veterans to Deng's 'de-Maoification' policy. Despite frequent confrontations between Deng and senior (Maoist) PLA leaders, sweeping changes in the PLA hierarchy were carried out between 1978 and 1982. By 1981, ten out of eleven of the commanders of China's military regions and all 11 political commissars in the military regions had been replaced by Deng supporters. In 22 out of China's 28 province-level military districts, new military commanders were appointed.[36]

A further process of restructuring of the PLA hierarchy was initiated in June 1984 shortly after Defence Minister Zhang Aiping's visit to the United States, and the visit of several US military delegations to China. The emphasis was on 'streamlining' as well as 'modernisation', using foreign military training and technology and US military advisors in the PLA.

Mao Zedong and Mao Zedong Thought

In parallel with the consolidation of political power by the 'Right', the party's official rhetoric gradually shifted towards a major 'reassessment' of Mao Zedong and Mao Zedong Thought. The 1981 Central Committee *Resolution on Certain Questions in the History of our Party* constitutes, in this regard, not only an ideological turning point in its condemnation of the

Cultural Revolution and the role of the so-called 'revisionist Jiang Qing – Lin Biao Clique' but also in its 'assessment' of Mao's personal 'errors' in initiating and leading the Cultural Revolution.[37]

Although Marxism – Leninism – Mao Zedong Thought is retained as the *formal* ideological pillar of Communist Party discourse, the CCP's so-called *Authoritative Assessment* of comrade Mao's 'Left error' is consistent with the general direction of political, economic and social change since 1976:

> Chief responsibility for the grave 'Left error' of the Cultural Revolution does indeed lie with comrade Mao Zedong. *But after all it was the error of a great proletarian revolutionary*. . . Mao Zedong's prestige reached a peak and he began to get arrogant. . . He gradually divorced himself from the masses. . . Comrade Mao Zedong was a great Marxist and a great proletarian revolutionary, strategist and theorist. It is true that he committed gross mistakes during the Cultural Revolution, but if we judge his activities as a whole his contributions to the Chinese revolution far outweigh his mistakes.[38]

What these passages convey is that there is a rupture or discontinuity in Mao Zedong Thought, a 'transition' from 'correct' positions to 'Left error'. On the other hand, Mao Zedong Thought is still viewed in the *Authoritative Assessment* as 'the valuable spiritual asset of our party. . . *the crystallization of the collective wisdom of our party*' which suggests that *Mao Zedong, in committing his 'left error' was in overt violation with Mao Zedong Thought*.[39] But this document was not meant to be consistent and coherent. On the one hand, it identifies a major turning point in the consolidation of a new political ideology; on the other hand, its ambiguities reflect the fact that, despite major purges directed against so-called 'Leftist deviationists,' major divisions and opposition to the present leadership were still prevalent within the communist party in 1981.

Despite its inconsistencies, however, the party's new ideological discourse constitutes a first step towards the *de facto* demise of Mao Zedong Thought. Whereas Mao is criticised for his 'left error', the renewed emphasis on the role of Sun Yatsen and the 1911 Revolution – including the attempted diplomatic overture to the Kuomintang – are intended to gradually discredit Mao Zedong and to some extent also downgrade the *relative* historical significance of the 1949 Revolution. Whereas Mao's 'left mistakes' are brought out, none of Sun's 'errors' are assessed, nor is the historical significance of the 1911 Wuchang Uprising critically evaluated. All this clearly indicates that the present leadership is not only interested in discrediting the Cultural Revolution: its so-called *Authoritative Assessment* is a first step towards a comprehensive *re-writing* of a major portion of twentieth century Chinese history.

It is also significant that the *Resolution on Certain Questions* emphasised the historical importance of so-called 'former capitalists in "socialist construction"': 'The changes [of the early 1950s] were too fast . . . We failed to do a proper job in employing and handling some of the former industrialists and businessmen'.[40] In the words of Deng Xiaoping: 'Most of the former capitalists no longer exist as a class and have been transformed into working people earning their own living'. Former capitalists, whose property and interest payments were restored after the Cultural Revolution '*have a real patriotic desire to build a strong national economy*':

> When the government turned over this large sum [of money] to the former capitalists, it made three requests, don't spoil your children, don't disrupt the state economy; and don't let this interfere with your personal ideological reform. What the Shanghai capitalists did with the money reveals both their patriotism and faith in the Party and State leadership. They pooled their funds and established the Patriotic Construction Company to build much needed factories and housing for the city.[41]

Former capitalists are said to have knowledge, skills and the 'spirit of entrepreneurship' which are needed in the construction of socialism. Their 'patriotism', puts 'socialist construction' *above* their personal or class interests. The laws of profit and accumulation are subordinated to the 'transition to socialism'.

With the *de facto* demise of Mao Zedong, the theoretical categories of Marxist thought are distorted, turned upside-down and divorced from the realm of practical reality. References to Marx, Lenin and Mao are increasingly used to support the CCP's new analytical categories. It is argued that: 'according to Marx, capitalism must preceed socialism', *therefore*, a policy of so-called 'limited' restoration of capitalism 'reinforces' the construction of socialism and upholds Marxism. These statements are put forth dogmatically by the party establishment without debate or critical assessment of their theoretical and practical implications.

The CCP's Rapprochement with the Kuomintang

The development of a new party ideology opened the way in 1981 for the communist party's attempted rapprochement with the Kuomintang (KMT). Taiwan President Chiang Ching Kuo, Mrs Chiang Kaishek and top Kuomintang leaders were invited to visit the mainland; Chiang Kaishek's ashes 'from their temporary resting place in Taiwan, can be buried in the family cemetery in Fenghua, Zhejiang province' where, according to *Renmin Ribao* (People's Daily): 'The tombs of Chiang Kaishek's parents and first wife Mao Fumei are being renovated'.[42]

Although this attempted rapprochement had little in terms of short-run political implications, it clearly identified the party's ideological position and confirmed the leadership's economic and political orientation:

> Why can we not have a third period of cooperation between the Kuomintang and the Communist Party . . . Taiwan industrialists and businessmen in Taiwan are welcome to invest and engage in various economic undertakings on the Mainland and their legal rights, interests and profits are guaranteed.[43]

The 1981 overture to the Kuomintang, however, went beyond the realm of diplomatic rhetoric, for whereas on the one hand the communist party was the theatre of major purges directed against supporters of Mao Zedong, on the other hand the leadership approved (in 1981) the appointment of several prominent 'former nationalists' to the Chinese People's Political Consultative Conference (CPPCC). These included Jia Shizhai, the former KMT Deputy Secretary-General of the so-called 'North China Bandit Suppression Headquarters', set up during the Civil War to organise mass repression and massacres of communist partisans.[44] While the CPPCC is a consultative body with no decision-making powers, these appointments not only give formal legitimacy to the KMT, they also provide clear confirmation of the CCP's 'united front' ideology.

While Taipei's response to Beijing's 1981 'nine-point proposal' for China's reunification was notoriously inflexible, the current of opinion in Taipei intellectual and business circles is, on balance, in favour of the economic and social reforms implemented on the mainland. In the words of (Kuomintang) Premier Sun Yunsuan:

> If the political, economic, social and cultural gaps between the Chinese mainland and free China [Taiwan] continue to narrow, the conditions for peaceful reunification can gradually mature. The obstacles to reunification will be reduced naturally with the passage of time.[45]

Beijing's position subsequent to the joint declaration reached with the British government regarding the status of Hong Kong after 1997 is that Taiwan would also be reintegrated into the People's Republic of China (PRC), that is, as an autonomous region or province, while retaining a fully-fledged capitalist system. In turn, under the 1982 Constitution and Deng Xiaoping's commitment to the principle of 'one country, two systems', Hong Kong and Taiwan capitalists were granted special rights to invest and own capital on the mainland. The rehabilitation of the (overseas

Chinese) *expatriate bourgeoisie* as a property-owning class within the People's Republic of China is, in this regard, not only an integral part of the leadership's political project but also a major element in the unfolding of social class relations in the post-Mao period. The role of the expatriate bourgeoisie will be discussed in the following chapters in the context of the reforms in industry and foreign trade.

Concluding Remarks

Massive purges, and the repression of political opponents initiated after the downfall of the group of Four, represented the cornerstone upon which rural and urban grassroots organisations as well as party and state bodies at different levels were subordinated to the party monopoly and brought into conformity with the regime's political project. The purges were, in turn, accompanied by major changes in the Criminal Law and in various other legal provisions in the civilian and military sectors regulating the treatment of so-called 'counter-revolutionaries'. These changes in the legal statutes provided the post-Mao regime with the required 'legitimacy to repress' and eliminate political opponents from the Central Committee down to village and factory level organisations. New legal provisions were adopted in relation to the death sentence for so-called 'counter-revolutionary offences'; the particularly harsh provisions applying to members of the Armed Forces allow for the application of the death penalty to virtually any presumed act of insubordination.

In addition to the repression and elimination of political opponents, the regime has attempted to break up the networks of political power in the state bureaucracy through a policy of massive firings and demotions initiated by the Central Committee in early 1982.

In the sphere of ideology, the regime has stressed its adherence to Mao Zedong and Mao Zedong Thought while at the same time condemning Mao for his role during the Great Leap and the Cultural Revolution. This ambivalence should not be the source of confusion in identifying what the new leadership actually stands for: the regime's commitment to Mao is the concrete expression of political opportunism instigated and instrumented by Deng Xiaoping himself. Mao's leadership is essentially considered to be 'correct' before 1957. Whereas his writings of the 1950s and 1960s are censured by the regime and removed from bookstores across China, Deng Xiaoping has called for the study of Mao Zedong Thought, and its 'development' beyond Mao and in opposition to Mao: 'In many respects, we are doing things Comrade Mao suggested but failed to do himself, setting right his erroneous opposition to certain things and accomplishing some things he did not.'[46]

In parallel with the regime's formal adherence to Mao Zedong, Maoists are purged, imprisoned and executed essentially for their loyalty to the principles of revolutionary socialism as put forth by Mao. Along with the purges, the development of a new political order within the state and party systems after October 1976 provided the party leadership with the institutional and legal framework to formulate and implement the economic and social reforms initially put forth at the historical 1978 third plenary session of the 11th CCP Central Committee. The weeding out of political opposition and the consolidation of the networks of authority at different levels in the party and state bureaucracy constituted the basis upon which the reforms in agriculture, industrial management, foreign trade, and so on, were carried out at different levels. The following chapters proceed with an analysis of these reforms and of the economic and social system which is unfolding in the post-Mao period.

2

Land Reform and Collectivisation

Introduction

Present policies of decollectivisation carried out since the death of Mao Zedong and the fall of the group of Four take place against a long-standing struggle between opposing factions within the Chinese Communist Party with regard to agricultural policy. The 'rectification movements' carried out at various times since Liberation, and more particularly by Liu Shaoqi in the aftermath of the Great Leap Forward, represented important setbacks in the construction of socialist agriculture. Past 'rectification' policies, however, were unable to destroy the basis of the collective economy in the countryside.

Decollectivisation policies after Mao should, therefore, be distinguished from their historical antecedents and from previous 'rectification movements' because, in the aftermath of the Cultural Revolution, there exists no articulate political opposition (either within the party or outside it) which is capable of mobilising mass dissent to the dominant 'Rightist' faction in the CCP. This means that whereas present policies are in some respects comparable to those carried out under Liu Shaoqi, they represent, alongside the reforms in the system of planning, factory management, the 'open door' policy to foreign capital, and so on, a coherent and cohesive programme intended to destroy the very basis of collective agriculture. The origins of decollectivisation after Mao are, none the less, to be found in the process of collectivisation itself. In this context, this chapter focuses on the Agrarian Revolution and the process of collectivisation carried out in various stages since the inception of the Land Reform Movement. The next chapter outlines the process of decollectivisation and the rehabilitation of the rich peasant economy after Mao.

Both the early policies of land confiscation and distribution adopted prior to Liberation, as well as the Land Reform Movement of the early 1950s, consisted in breaking up feudal land holdings while maintaining the status of the middle (and to a lesser extent) rich peasantry. The formation of mutual aid teams and elementary producers' co-operatives was carried out while preserving the private ownership of farm machinery and draught animals. The process of collectivisation *per se*, consisting of the creation of producers' co-operatives of the advanced type, was implemented in various stages after the mid-1950s leading up to the collectivisation campaign in 1957 and the formation of People's Communes initiated by the Great Leap Forward movement in 1958.

From the early 1950s major political opposition to collectivisation developed from within the ranks of the leadership and communist party. In rural areas the social basis of this opposition was characterised by the resistance of the rich peasants and former landlords, many of whom had 'wormed their way' into the ranks of the local communist party organisation at Liberation. The mass movement towards the formation of advanced producers' co-operatives and subsequently People's Communes was in fact opposed by many of Mao's 'followers' within the CCP. Edgar Snow, in this regard, recalls that the 'Rightist' faction in the Honan Provincial Communist Party had attempted to force a number of large scale co-operatives to split up.[1] Moreover, the traditional attachment to land by the smallholder was very strong, and many individual farmers resisted the transfer of land ownership to the collective. Rapid collectivisation was said to have caused considerable loss of material incentive and desertion from the land by the more prosperous peasants.

Decollectivisation after Mao does not, therefore, emerge in a historical vacuum. The precarious foundations of socialist agriculture characterised by the *de facto* maintenance of the rural class structure *within* the formal institutional framework of the People's Commune will be conducive after Mao, to the re-emergence and consolidation of the rich peasant economy. Our discussion of the Land Reform Movement in this chapter, is, therefore, intended to place, historically, the process of decollectivisation, and to identify the precise nature of the transition to capitalist farming since the adoption of the so-called 'agricultural responsibility system' by the Third Plenary of the CCP Central Committee in late 1978.

The dismantling of the People's Commune after Mao – while destroying the very basis of socialist agriculture – is also the expression of historical continuity in relation to previous attempts by the rich peasants, former landlords and their representatives within the communist party organisation to undermine the process of collectivisation. The roots of decollectivisation are, therefore, contained within the organic structure of the collective economy itself, because the development of socialist agriculture in many areas of China (and particularly in the more affluent farming communities) maintained a (latent) social structure based on a clear demarcation between the rich, middle and poor peasantry. While feudal landlord holdings were eliminated through confiscation and land redistribution, the collectives were, in a sense, superimposed upon an incipient capitalist agricultural base which had developed as a result of feudal decline during the Kuomintang Republican period. In this regard it should also be understood that the Land Reform Movement consisted initially in transforming feudal land ownership into private ownership by the peasantry. This, in many cases, favoured the *de facto* development of capitalist farming.

Land Tenure and Class Relations Prior to 1949

The structure of land tenure, ownership and rural class relations is described in Alfred Lin's study of Guangdong province based on Chen Han Sheng's first survey of land tenure conducted in the early 1930s under Chiang Kaishek.[2] Here, extreme concentration of ownership by a landlord class coincides with a process of fragmentation of land use by individual tenant households. With the exception of a small sector of rich peasants, large landholdings, however, did not exist as the landlords were essentially 'rentiers'.

Surveys on land distribution in Guangdong conducted in the 1930s differentiate between independent cultivators (*zi geng nong*), semi-tenants (*ban zi geng nong*), tenants (*tian nong*) and hired labourers.[3] Tenant holdings (*tian nong*) represented 75 to 80 per cent of arable land and up to 90 per cent in the more populated and productive agricultural regions close to Guangzhou. Alfred Lin suggests that tenancy was positively related to commercialisation of agricultural output.

Chen Han Sheng's survey mentioned above confirms that 77.4 per cent of the rural population of Guangdong were tenants or semi-tenants and 10.6 per cent were hired labourers (landless peasants). In a subsequent survey Chen estimated the distribution of land-ownership using Mao's categories on 'How to Differentiate the Classes in Rural Areas'.[4] As suggested in Table 2.1, the landlord class, which represented two per cent of the rural population, owned 53 per cent of the land. The landlords were rentiers whereas the rich peasants practiced individual capitalist farming based on hired wage labour. The middle peasants constituted 20 per cent of the rural population.[5]

The tenant relationship was characterised by three distinct forms: (1) share-cropping (*fen zhi*), (2) a fixed rent in kind (*shiwu ding'e zhi*) and, (3) a fixed cash rent (*ding'e qian zhi*).[6] Republican records confirm that fixed rental payments were more prevalent than crop-sharing. The exaction of a fixed cash rent developed in the early twentieth century with the expansion of commercial agriculture. In Guangdong it was most prevalent in the Guangzhou delta region where landholdings were owned by absentee merchants residing in the city. In all three cases Lin's study confirms that land rent was oppressive not only because of its high rate but also because

TABLE 2.1 *Distribution of landownership among the various rural classes in Guangdong in the early 1930s*

Rural classes	Total no. of households	% of total households	Land owned in mu	% of total landowners
Landlords	100 000	2	22 360 000	53
Rich peasants	220 000	4	5 460 000	13
Middle peasants	1 090 000	20	6 550 000	15
Poor peasants & hired labour	4 040 000	74	8 080 000	19
All classes	5 460 000	100	42 540 000	100

NOTE One mu equals 0.1518 acres.
SOURCE Alfred Lin, 'Agrarian Crisis in Pre-Communist China', in S.S.K. Chin and C.K. Leung (eds), *China, Development and Challenge*, vol. 1 (Hong Kong: Centre of Asian Studies, University of Hong Kong, 1979). Data based on Chen Han Sheng's survey.

of the practice of paying rent before harvest (*yu zhi*) and paying rent deposits (*ya zhi*).[7]

Other investigations on land tenure and rural class relations were conducted in Jiangxi, Shaanxi and Zhejiang and other provinces. In Jiangxi another survey conducted in the 1930s suggests that a sizeable portion of land was controlled by the rich peasantry: 30 per cent of the land was owned by the rich peasants (5 per cent of the population) and 40 per cent by the landlords (1 per cent of the population); approximately 10 per cent of the land was in co-ownership between landlords and rich peasants. In other words, the landlords and rich peasants who made up six per cent of the population, owned 80 per cent of the land. In Shaanxi province an investigation conducted in 1942 in Mizhi County identified the following structure of land tenure: landlord households, which represented 2 per cent of the population owned approximately 64 per cent of the land, rich peasants (3 per cent of the population) and well-to-do middle peasants, (4.6 per cent of the population) owned respectively 12 and 11 per cent of the land.[8] These surveys, as well as data on land tenure for other provinces (for example, surveys for Sichuan and Zhejiang), are consistent with the patterns observed in Guangdong in Chen Han Sheng's study.

The late Qing and early Republican periods were characterised by the rapid development of commercial agriculture and cash crops. Prior to the nineteenth century, cash crops did not compete seriously with grain production.[9] The shift in land-use patterns is associated with the opening up of foreign trade after the Treaty of Nanjing, and the development of export-oriented cash crops in the coastal provinces. Cash crops were also encouraged through the development of commercial agricultural outlets and the payment both of land rent and grain tax in money form. From the early 1920s the shift in land-use patterns not only reduced the production of grain staples, thereby aggravating food shortages, but the peasants also became increasingly dependent on merchant middlemen. International instability in major export crops was conducive to frequent dislocations in the patterns of agricultural production and land use. Duty-free imports of foreign rice in the 1920s further accentuated the shift in land-use patterns and the dependency on foreign grain by forcing down the price of domestically produced rice.

The Agrarian Revolution

In the early 1930s, following the establishment of the Jinggangshan Mountain base, Mao Zedong outlined the principles of the Agrarian Revolution: *Relying on the poor peasants and farm wage-labourers, uniting with the middle peasants, restricting the rich peasants, protecting the medium and small industrialists and businessmen and liquidating the landlord class.*[10] The seat of the Chinese Revolution from the beginning was based primarily in the countryside characterised by the struggle of the peasantry against feudal exploitation. The War of Resistance against Japan and the War of Liberation proceeded alongside the Land Reform Movement implemented prior to 1949 in the liberated areas.

When Sun Yatsen advocated 'Land to the Tillers' in the early 1920s, the strongest endorsement was from the communist faction in the Kuomintang. In 1927, when the communists broke with the Kuomintang, the first Chinese soviets were established in Jiangxi and a land reform programme involving the expropriation of landlords as well as rich peasants was initiated. In the process of land redistribution, land was denied to the landlords and poor land was given to the rich peasants.[11] These early programmes constituted the basis of the Land Reform Movement initiated in November 1943 as a result of Mao's 'Get Organised' appeal to the peasantry.[12]

In May 1946 the communist party issued a directive on the Land Question (May 4th Directive) which supported the wartime practice of rent reduction and limited the expropriation of landlord holdings:

> Individual areas under CCP control put forth their own land reform programmes which ranged from a voluntary land contribution from landlords and land redistribution through government purchases to downright confiscation. Within a year or so about 60 million peasants were reported to have conducted some form of land reform which was usually designed to coordinate closely with para-military operations

(Mao type of guerilla war) and agricultural production (through cooperative production teams).[13]

The Land Reform Movement was led by the peasants themselves under the leadership of the communist party in the form of the Popular Peasant Congress and the Poor Peasant Corps composed of poor peasants and farm labourers.[14] The Land Reform Movement had a profound impact on the rural social class structure with about one hundred million peasants obtaining land in the liberated areas. The peasantry took an active role in the War of Liberation. In fact, the People's Liberation Army adopted defensive strategies involving evacuation and withdrawal from urban areas into the countryside. Mass participation of the peasantry was not only a necessary basis of PLA military operations, but the very foundations of the revolutionary movement.

In the countryside the struggle was against the landlords; in urban areas, on the other hand, Mao Zedong's 'policy concerning industry and commerce' was one of moderation and preservation of the urban capitalist base: 'Precautions should be taken against the mistake of applying in the cities, the measures used in rural areas for struggling against landlords and rich peasants and destroying the feudal forces'.[15] Capitalist industry was to be preserved, 'patriotic' capitalists and workers were to organise joint committees for the management of production 'so as to attain the objectives of giving *consideration to both public and private interests, benefiting both labour and capital* and supporting the war'.[16] From the inception of the Land Reform Movement during the Civil War, the rich peasants were in principle put on the same footing as the landlords. The 'Resolution on the Land Question' adopted by the Central Bureau of the Soviet Area in August 1931 proposed 'to confiscate the land of the landlords and the rich peasants'.[17]

The position of the communist party *vis-à-vis* the rich peasantry, however, evolved considerably throughout the Civil War. In 1949 the 'Decisions on Provisional Measures Concerning Suburban Rural Land' adopted by Tianjin Municipality, for instance, stipulated that 'land managed by the old-type rich peasants themselves should be left to them while the part of land rented out should be requisitioned'.[18] The 'Directive on the Question of Suburban Rural Land in the Old Liberated Areas' similarly stipulated that 'land rented out by the old type rich peasants should be confiscated' while 'the proprietory rights and rights of use should remain unchanged with regard to the land of the old type rich peasants cultivated by hired labour'.[19] In other words, the rich peasants were restricted only inasmuch as they acted as rentiers. These and other provisions purported to preserve capitalist agriculture based on hired farm labour.

In its 'Directive on Agrarian Reform in the Newly Liberated Areas' of October 1949, the North China Bureau of the CCP Central Committee stressed the importance of distinguishing between 'rich peasants who have built up the family wealth through their own labour from the rich peasants in general'.[20] In practice, this distinction was difficult to make. This policy none the less contributed to the preservation of the rich peasant economy under the protection of the 'Rightist' faction in the CCP. A further provision implemented in 1949 prior to Liberation consisted in preserving the ownership status of 'all land which was cultivated with machinery, or large orchards and pastureland managed with advanced facilities and methods'.[21] This provision was also intended so as not to undermine the productive base of the rich peasant economy.

Land was not always confiscated and distributed to the poor peasants and hired labourers. In many rural areas, feudal landlord holdings were sold by the landlords and/or transferred to well-to-do peasants. This meant, in some cases, that the rich peasantry *increased* the size of its landholdings as a result of the Land Reform policies. Prior to Liberation, feudal landholdings were often transferred through so-called 'voluntary land contributions by the landlords' as well as 'redistribution through government purchases'.[22]

After 1949 policies pertaining to the rich peasantry were the result of the political struggle between opposing factions within the Chinese Communist Party. Mao Zedong's position was one of moderation essentially so as to *temporarily* preserve the productive base of the rich peasant economy. Land confiscation and distribution, however, (which essentially established ownership rights for the peasantry) was to be followed by collectivisation. Otherwise, capitalist agriculture would develop because the rich peasants had the capacity to appropriate and accumulate wealth. Namely, a reformist type policy of redistribution without collectivisation would, inevitably – and Mao was very clear on this – be conducive to the development of capitalist agriculture.

After 1949 the rich peasant economy gained in impetus largely as a result of policies emanating from the anti-Mao faction within the communist party. These policies essentially consisted in 'preserving' rather than 'restricting' and 'weakening' the rich peasantry as had been the case in the earlier stages of the Land Reform Movement prior to Liberation.

The communist party's present assessment of the historical role of the rich peasantry is worth mentioning since it represents, in a sense, the ideological basis for 'justifying' the rural policies adopted after Mao. Du Jing, writing in *Social Sciences in China* (September 1982) states:

> that as a result of the victories of the War of Resistance against Japan and the War of Liberation, *the rich peasants had changed politically* from the landlords' ally to a neutral force. The preservation of their economy would help to further neutralise them, and thus make it easier to isolate

> the landlords and abolish them as a class . . . Preservation of the rich peasants helped arouse their enthusiasm for production, relieved the middle peasants fear of expropriation and gave free rein to their initiative in production . . . As it has been proved by facts, to preserve the rich peasant economy during the period of rehabilitation of the national economy did not constitute any danger nor did it present an obstacle to the steady development of the socialist transformation of private ownership of the means of production in the countryside.[23]

The rehabilitation of the rich peasantry after Mao, in the context of decollectivisation, is consistent with the liberal reformist policies in support of the rich peasantry proposed by the 'Rightist' faction of the CCP in the early 1950s and after the Great Leap Forward.

The Agrarian Revolution in China and Soviet Russia

The structures of land tenure and social classes in pre-revolutionary China are fundamentally different from those which existed in Tsarist Russia. In Russia, as in China, the structure of rural class relations came to determine the precise nature of the worker-peasant alliance as well as the subsequent development of urban-rural relations under socialism. In this context it is instructive to briefly compare Chen Han Sheng's survey on land tenure and Mao Zedong's categories on 'How to Differentiate the Classes in Rural Areas' on the one hand, with Lenin's categorisation of the Russian peasantry in *The Development of Capitalism in Russia* on the other hand. Lenin's analysis was based on the *Zemstvo* statistics and Posnikov's data for Southern Russia.[24] Contrary to the structure of land tenure in China, during the Republican period, characterised by a feudal relationship and the predominance of poor peasants, Russian agriculture in the late nineteenth century was made up of an important sector of well-to-do peasants involved in commercial farming and representing approximately 30 per cent of the rural population.[25] Moreover, 60 per cent of the well-to-do peasantry, accounting for more than half the agricultural production, employed both regular farm labourers as well as day labourers.[26] In China, on the other hand, commercial farming involving wage labour was at a comparatively much lower level of development, that is, poor peasants were largely tenants.

In other words, the process of proletarianisation of the Russian peasantry was quite advanced as a result of feudal decline and the development of a sizeable sector of commercial agriculture in the second half of the nineteenth century. Also, in Russia the October Revolution was essentially urban-based whereas in China the worker-peasant alliance was the cause and motivating force of revolutionary activity. The overthrow of the

Kerensky provisional government on 25 October 1917 was essentially the result of a well-led armed insurrection supported and integrated by the urban working class. Nevertheless, this insurrectionary form was conditioned by the evolution of class relations between February and October 1917 and more specifically by the *spontaneous* eruption of peasant revolts across the Russian heartland.[27] Contrary to China, however, these revolts were not forcefully led by the communist party.

The alliance of the urban bourgeoisie and the well-to-do peasantry (which was the basis of political power during the Kerensky government) collapsed with the October Revolution. In the aftermath of October 1917, however, the Bolshevik party, which was poorly organised in the countryside, was unable to develop the worker-peasant alliance based on the poor peasantry and farm labourers.[28] The poor peasant committees in Russia were few in number and politically ineffective. Moreover, the division of landlord holdings had *de facto* reduced the number of poor peasants, thereby increasing that of the middle peasantry.

Initially, and contrary to China's experience, the Bolshevik's policy was directed against both the rich and middle peasantry. Lenin recognised subsequently in 1919 that the party's earlier position regarding the middle peasantry was mistaken. Lenin stressed the importance of 'developing our relations with the middle peasants on the basis of a firm alliance and so preclude the possibility of a repetition of those mistakes and blunders we have repeatedly made in the past. These blunders estranged the middle peasants from us'.[29] The failure of the Bolsheviks to mobilise the middle peasantry, that is, in alliance with the poor peasantry, however, was conducive from the early 1920s, to the development of a rural petty bourgeoisie composed of the middle strata of the peasantry. Collectivisation in the 1930s in Russia *did not*, therefore, have an articulate class base in the countryside, and generally did not have the support of the peasantry. Rather than constituting a process of social change in the countryside, collectivisation was a means of extracting the economic surplus from the agricultural sector (through repressive procurement policies) so as to support the urban industrial base.

In contrast to the experience of Soviet Russia, Mao stressed the alliance of the poor peasants with the middle peasants as a means of combating feudal exploitation and, to a lesser extent, the rich peasantry. Mao's position in the early 1950s, however, was one of moderation, sensitive to the underlying practical realities:

> At present the 'left' deviations consist chiefly in encroaching on the interests of the middle peasants and national bourgeoisie . . . making no distinctions in the treatment of big, middle and small landlords, or of landlords who are local tyrants and those who are not, not leaving the landlords the necessary means of livelihood as required by the principle of equal distribution.[30]

Land Reform After Liberation

In June 1950 the Agrarian Reform Law calling for the confiscation of landlord holdings and their redistribution to tenant farmers and landless peasants was promulgated. This programme was a continuation of that carried out prior to 1949 in the liberated areas. Mao's categorisation of rural social classes provided the theoretical and practical basis for implementing the Agrarian Revolution. Initially the programme consisted in confiscating feudal landholdings, and by 1952 700 million (106 million acres) of land had been redistributed to 300 million peasants.[31] As described in Alfred Lin's study, the middle peasants represented an important sector of the rural population. Mao Zedong's position regarding the role of the middle peasants was in this regard consistent with that formulated prior to Liberation in the liberated areas. In 1955, in the editorial notes on *Socialist Upsurge in China's Countryside*, Mao emphasised that:

> It is essential to unite with the middle peasants, and it is wrong not to do so. But who should the working class and the Communist Party rely on in the rural areas in order to unite with the middle peasants and achieve socialist transformation in the entire countryside? Surely none other than the poor peasants. That was the case in the past when the struggle was waged against the landlords to carry out agrarian reform, and that is the case today when the struggle is being waged against the rich peasants and other capitalist elements to achieve the socialist transformation of agriculture. In both these revolutionary periods the middle peasants wavered in the initial stage. Only when the middle peasants see clearly which way the wind is blowing and only when victory in the revolution is in sight will they come on the side of the revolution.[32]

Whereas the tenant relationship had been broken as a result of land distribution, the form and nature of the system of individual economy was not substantially modified. Labour productivity was low, the majority of small individual producers with an average 10 mu (1.52 acres) per household were barely able to produce and reproduce their own subsistence. The fragmentation of landholdings and the small scale of production were obstacles to the creation of an agricultural surplus, that is, the agricultural surplus was generated essentially by the rich and middle peasants. In the absence of collectivisation directed towards modifying the underlying social relations, as well as setting the foundations for the socialist modernisation of agriculture, the rich peasantry would consolidate its position.

Moreover, the scale of output of individual smallholdings made the application of farm machinery extremely difficult, and prevented investments in infrastructure, irrigation and water conservancy. The structure of private farming and individual household work had to be broken as a necessary pre-condition for the modernisation of agriculture. The maintenance of the individual economy characterised by *individual* rather than *collective* work and the private ownership of the means of production represented the basis upon which a capitalist rich peasant economy would develop.

A second phase of Agrarian Reform was initiated in December 1952 with the formation of mutual aid teams, and subsequently with the development of semi-socialist producers' co-operatives. Xue Muqiao describes this process as follows:

> To put the soil to better use, it was necessary to link up the patches belonging to different households. This was done through the formation of elementary cooperatives in which the peasants, while retaining private ownership of their land, pooled it together for common use and management. Draught animals and big farm implements also remained under private ownership but were used jointly by the co-op members. Thus the income was distributed according to work as well as investments in the form of land, draught animals and farm implements. The income from land-ownership was known as 'dividends on land'. All this meant that some members appropriated the fruits of labour of others on account of their possession of means of production. But as the elementary cooperatives developed their collective economy, they accumulated more and more public property and increased the proportion of income which the peasants earned by work. This made it both necessary and possible to abolish the dividends on land and other means of production and change over to the advanced form of agricultural producers' cooperatives by transferring land, draught animals and farm implements to public ownership with compensation to the owners.[33]

The mutual aid teams developed as a result of patterns of co-operation which existed historically in China's traditional agriculture. However, 'the pooling of several work teams paved the way for a new development when there was a land-pooling campaign in which thirty to fifty households pooled their land, implements and cattle'.[34] This campaign was conducive to the development of farming co-operatives of a semi-socialist nature. The first stage consisted in the formation of elementary agricultural producers' co-operatives and subsequently led to the consolidation of advanced producers' co-operatives.

The formation of mutual aid teams was completed by 1953, and by 1956 92 per cent of peasant households belonged to elementary producers' co-operatives and 63 per cent to socialised co-operatives of the more advanced type in which members collectively owned the land. Upon completion of the collectivisation campaign in 1957 there were 760 000 to 800 000 co-operatives each with an average of 160 families or 600 to 700 persons.[35]

In February 1958 the National People's Congress initiated the Great Leap Forward Movement. The formation of People's Communes involving a higher stage of socialisation of rural production was initiated. The mass movement to create People's Communes consisted initially in the amalgamation of existing advanced producers co-operatives into larger integrated units. The movement started in Hebei, Henan and parts of Manchuria and subsequently spread to other parts of the country. By the end of 1958 there were 26 000 communes covering 98 per cent of the rural population.[36] The communes were to take over the administrative functions of the villages, collect taxes, operate schools, medical facilities, and so on. Private property of land, houses, farm implements belonging to households and/or producers' co-operatives was appropriated by the commune. Moreover, the commune was responsible for agricultural procurement, fulfilling state quotas and assigning work and production quotas.

The commune was characterised by three levels of organisation: *commune, brigade* and *production team*. The former advanced producers' co-operatives were to become production brigades. In turn, the elementary producers' co-operatives were to become production teams in the three level commune structure. The *production team*, composed of 30 to 40 households, was the basic production unit of the commune responsible for specialised agricultural work. Members of the team were paid in terms of work points. The *brigade* level was responsible for irrigation, water conservancy, flood-control works and farm machinery for the production under its jurisdiction. It also managed small-scale industries, a primary school and a primary health care unit. The brigade was administered by a *revolutionary committee* elected by the membership.

The *commune*, which regrouped several production brigades, was in principle to become an integrated political-economic unit of self-government. On the production side, the commune was responsible for large scale agricultural infrastructure and investment projects and it managed the large farm machinery and the large factories. The commune integrated the functions of collective agricultural production with those of local government: it was responsible for running secondary and technical schools, health clinics, cultural activities, security and military affairs, and so on. Moreover, it was responsible for trade and commerce, banking and marketing of agricultural output.

The communes were viewed as decentralised and self-reliant units of state power run and administered by the peasants. The revolutionary committee of the commune was in principle elected democratically by commune members. Whereas this system of commune management was intended to prevent the emergence of a bureaucratic structure and a permanent managerial class, in many cases, the Party bureaucracy dominated the political process at the local level.

Collectivisation and the 'Rectification Movement'

Policies implemented after 1958 and in the early 1960s were only partly based on the genuine need to 'rectify' the rapid pace at which collectivisation had taken place and consolidate the initial achievements of collectivisation. The set-backs in the formation of the People's Commune were used by Mao's opponents in the communist party to restore many features of individual household farming. Whereas the basic structure of the People's Commune was maintained, many of its essential features were reversed and undone, the average size of the commune was reduced, individual household farming within the communal structure was emphasised and free market sales were restored.

The so-called *Four big freedoms* – that is, the freedom to buy and sell land, practice usury, employ wage labour and practice private trade – had been advocated in 1955 at the Seventh Central Committee by Teng Tsu Hui as a policy to be used in the 'transition period'.[37] The 'Four freedoms', firmly opposed at that time by Mao Zedong, were again advocated by Liu Shaoqi in the aftermath of the Great Leap. Mao Zedong, in the political struggle against the Liu faction, considered the 'Four freedoms' as the pillars of bourgeois reform in agriculture which supported the consolidation of a class of rich peasants:

> That formulation was wrong and was a veritable bourgeois programme in nature, a capitalist programme, not a proletarian one . . . Therefore, the 'four big freedoms', under which no restrictions are placed on hiring labourers, trading, money-lending and renting out land, must be called into question.[38]

Poor agricultural performance in 1960–61 was attributed by Mao's opponents to a 'hasty process of collectivisation' and the 'failures' of the Great Leap movement. The movement to create People's Communes had important disruptive effects on agricultural output, the economic downturn in 1960–61, however, was also the consequence of bad weather which produced several consecutive poor harvests and the withdrawal of Soviet technical aid.

A critical reappraisal of the rapid changes which had taken place during the Great Leap was indeed necessary to correct imbalances and consolidate the process of collectivisation. This reappraisal, however, was not possible because the debate was very much interwoven with the struggle between political factions and the attempt by Liu Shaoqi to reverse the mass movement towards collectivisation.

In December 1958 Mao Zedong gave up his position as Chairman of the People's Republic although retaining his position as leader of the communist party. Liu Shaoqi was elected Head of State in 1960. The leadership was polarised and factionalised; formal policies implemented during the 1960–63 period were largely controlled by the Liu faction. The 'three freedoms and one responsibility' were advocated. The 'three freedoms' were freedom to develop a free market, freedom to develop small enterprises which operate according to a profit-loss calculation, freedom to increase the size of private household plots. The 'one responsibility' was fulfillment of output quotas by the collective.[39]

From the Great Leap to the Cultural Revolution

The communist party leadership had been divided since the mid-1950s, when the first purges and centralisation measures adopted by the CCP leadership during the Korean War consisted in getting rid of Mao supporters at the provincial and local levels. As a result of these purges Mao Zedong was relegated to the 'second line'; Liu Shaoqi and CCP General Secretary Deng Xiaoping, were largely in control of the party apparatus.

Mao's strategy from the Great Leap to the Cultural Revolution consisted in stirring the support of the masses and grassroots party militants against the 'Party Empire' led by Liu Shaoqi. The 'dislocations' of the Great Leap enabled the party 'first line' composed of 'Rightists' to restore several features of the individual economy. Whereas some of the measures adopted were indeed necessary to 'rectify' and consolidate the achievements of the Great Leap, the 'Rightists' were actively engaged in promoting the rich peasantry. Mao Zedong responded by encouraging the association of poor peasants and by promoting big character posters' campaigns in the cities directed against the inner-party leadership. Liu Shaoqi's response was to issue the 1964 directive ordering the control of the poor peasant associations by the District Party Committees.[40]

At the Central Committee Work Conference in 1962, Liu Shaoqi openly criticised Mao and his followers for the 'errors' committed during the Great Leap which 'had led the Chinese economy to the brink of collapse' due to the loss of 'material incentive' and 'individual initiative' which resulted from 'a hasty process of collectivisation'.[41] In fact, material incentives, even at the height of the Cultural Revolution were never abandoned: in Dazhai production brigade, which served as a model for other communes, the work point system allowed a ratio of 11 to 5 between the highest and lowest earnings.[42]

Despite the setbacks of the Great Leap, the communes were maintained. Joan Robinson attributes the successful harvests from 1962 to 1967 to the very existence of collective agriculture:

> There has been a succession of ever-improving harvests since 1962 to make the harvest of 1967 the greatest in the recorded history of China,

though the weather was favourable, there is no doubt that high spirits contributed something extra . . . Recovery started in 1962, and the fruits of the huge effort of investment made in 1958, began to show that the Great Leap was not a failure after all, but the Rightists were reluctant to admit it.[43]

The Cultural Revolution

The Cultural Revolution was initially sparked off as a movement against 'bourgeois ideology' in culture and arts. In 1965 the struggle sharpened and transformed itself into a major mass movement by students and factory workers against 'persons in authority taking the capitalist road':

> Although the bourgeoisie has been overthrown, it is still trying to use the old ideas, culture, customs and habits of the exploiting classes . . . At present our objective is to struggle against and overthrow those persons in authority who are taking the capitalist road, to criticise and repudiate the reactionary bourgeois academic 'authorities' and the ideology of the bourgeoisie.[44]

It is impossible to describe here the complex sequence of events of this period. Although the Cultural Revolution was essentially urban-based, leading in 1967 to the seizing of political power in Shanghai by proletarian mass organisations, it revitalised the class struggle in the countryside against the rich peasants and former landlords, and temporarily reversed Liu Shaoqi's attempts to destroy the People's Commune.

The formation of revolutionary mass organisations in the universities and in industry was followed by that of revolutionary committees in the rural communes:

> The organ of power leading the great cultural revolution in the countryside shall be the cultural revolution formed of poor and low-middle peasants. These committees shall be elected democratically by congresses of poor and low-middle peasants . . . The leading groups in charge of production after being consolidated or re-elected through discussion among the masses, shall be responsible for the work of production, distribution, purchase and supply: The cultural revolution in the countryside should be conducted by means of free-contending, free discussion, free airing of views, big character posters and great debates i.e. the practice of extensive democracy . . . It is permissible to organise groups of revolutionary students to go to the countryside for the purpose of establishing revolutionary ties.[45]

The Cultural Revolution in the countryside was directed against former landlords and rich peasants. Dazhai production brigade was to constitute the model of collective work and social distribution of income in the 'Learning from Dazhai' movement.

In fact, the Cultural Revolution failed to achieve a major shift in social class relations in rural areas – that is, the political and social strife which prevailed in the cities directed against the party and state organisation, did not result in a similar and significant mass movement in the countryside. This was partly a result of the 'social distance' between urban and rural China and the lack of communication between the proletarian mass movement in the cities and the peasants. Contrary to the revolutionary civil wars and the War of Liberation against Japanese occupation in which the peasantry played a key strategic role, the Cultural Revolution only managed to mobilise a small minority of the peasantry.

In the countryside the Cultural Revolution is described as one of 'moderation' (*La révolution culturelle modérée*).[46] The 'seizing of power' in the countryside was defined in the directive of 4 December 1967 reprinted in several Red Guard newspapers: This 4 December directive, while encouraging the 'seizing of power' in certain districts which were under the control of 'those who had adopted the capitalist road', essentially recommended the maintenance and consolidation of the production team as the basic political and economic unit. It also recommended the maintenance of private plots. It was not necessary to seize power at the level of the production teams because 'in brigades where it is necessary to seize power efforts should be made to establish a new group of peasant cadres at the local level'[47] Indeed, the 4 December directive was intended against 'the unnecessary seizure of power'.

The Cultural Revolution brought about major achievements in the rural health care system. Primary health care was to be provided by the 'barefoot doctor' at the level of the production team. The health care system was to be decentralised involving an important transfer of medical personnel from the cities to the countryside. Major changes were also brought about in the system of rural schools. It is worth noting, in this regard, that many of the progressive reforms in rural health and education were reversed after Mao. The barefoot doctors' system was disbanded after 1978 in an effort to 'modernise' the rural health care system. The provision of health care after Mao is increasingly linked to 'the ability to pay' of its recipients. The state has withdrawn its financial support to rural health and education and has called upon rural cadres to finance these sectors through 'voluntary contributions by the peasantry'.

The Cultural Revolution also made considerable progress in the drive towards mechanisation; collective work projects carried out during the late 1960s contributed to improved irrigation, water conservancy and flood control. Considerable growth in agricultural output was achieved according to CIA statistics – which in any event tend to underestimate (rather than overestimate) economic achievements during that period. 'Taking grain as key link' was stressed in an effort to promote self-sufficiency in basic food staples at local and regional levels. Considerable impetus was given to the development of commune-run factories managed by the peasants as opposed to government appointed managerial cadres.

Concluding Remarks

This chapter has outlined the various phases of the Agrarian Revolution from its inception in the liberated areas prior to 1949 to the Cultural Revolution. Our essential purpose was to place the process of decollectivisation after Mao – to be examined in the next chapter – in a useful and relevant historical perspective.

In spite of its significant achievements, collective agriculture was adopted without modifying in a permanent and fundamental way the rural social class structure prevalent in the mid-1950s. This meant that despite its success in changing the material and social livelihood of the peasantry, particularly in the poorer agricultural regions, the People's Commune unfolded under very difficult circumstances and in the context of a major struggle against the 'old' social order in the countryside. The Land Reform Movement of the early 1950s created, through land redistribution, the requisite conditions for the emergence of capitalist agriculture. Namely, the rich peasant economy unfolded in parallel with the decline of feudal agriculture. These early reforms were, therefore, conducive, from the early 1950s, to economic and social polarisation characterised by the concurrent development of capitalist farming alongside the consolidation of the individual poor peasant economy:

> What exists in the countryside today [mid-1950s] is capitalist ownership by the rich peasants and a vast sea of ownership by individual peasants. As is clear to everyone, the spontaneous forces of capitalism have been steadily growing in the countryside in recent years with new rich peasants springing up everywhere and many well-to-do middle peasants striving to become rich peasants.[48]

The social transformation of agriculture was intended by Mao and his followers, to counteract the initial impact of land redistribution and eliminate the incipient development of capitalist farming. These reforms, however, were incapable of eliminating the rich peasantry as a social class. Namely, the prevailing social class structure was to some extent reproduced within the People's Commune. This signified that, inasmuch as the social class structure in the countryside had not been modified in a permanent way, the organic structure of collective agriculture could be reversed and undone as a result of a shift in political power relations within the party leadership. The next chapter identifies the mechanics of this reversal and the nature of the transition from the People's Commune to capitalist farming in the post-Mao period. It should, however, be understood that the requisite social conditions for this reversal were present in the countryside well before the 1976 *coup d'état* and the subsequent adoption of the household responsibility system at the Third Plenary meetings of the 11th CCP Central Committee in late 1978.

3

The Decollectivisation of Agriculture

Introduction

Counter-revolutionary tendencies have been present from the very inception of the Land Reform Movement. The policies of decollectivisation after Mao have their counterpart in the early 1950s and in the aftermath of the Great Leap. The movement to restore private household farming, however, only became fully cohesive after the downfall of the group of Four and the initial period of purges in the communist party conducted during 1977–9. The latter were conducive to the political demise of Hua Guofeng, the return and rise to power of Deng Xiaoping and the consolidation of a corporate bureaucratic leadership firmly committed to the 'Rightist' line. The evolution of agricultural policy since 1977 is, therefore, intimately related to the power struggle during the years of the Cultural Revolution and in its aftermath.

This chapter examines the household responsibility system adopted in 1978, and the subsequent collapse of the People's Commune, the privatisation of land use and the restoration of private ownership of the means of production. The concentration of land and farm machinery in the hands of the rich peasantry is accompanied by the development of commercial cash crops, the liberalisation of agricultural markets, and the penetration of the Chinese economy by international agro-business. The tendency is towards economic and social polarisation characterised by the unfoldment of 'modern' commercial capitalist farming by the well-to-do peasantry alongside the parallel consolidation of a dependent, socially subordinate and fragmented poor peasant economy.

At the Third Plenary session of the Eleventh Central Committee of the Chinese Communist Party in late 1978 two major documents entitled 'Some Questions Concerning the Acceleration of Agricultural Development (Draft)' and 'Regulations on the Work in Rural People's Communes (Draft for Trial Use)' were presented. The first document constituted a general ideological statement on the so-called 'failures' of collective management in the past and the 'excesses' of the Great Leap and the Cultural

Revolution. The second document was more explicit because it contained concrete regulatory principles:

> Economic organisations at all levels in the People's Communes must carry out the principles of 'from each according to his ability', 'to each according to his work', 'more pay for more work', 'less pay for less work' and 'equal pay for equal work between men and women', strengthen norm management, pay wages according to quantity and quality of work, establish necessary reward-penalty systems and criticise egalitarianism.[1]

Whereas the system of fixing output contracts to households *(bao chan dao hu)* and individual farming (*fendian dangan*) were explicitly prohibited in the 'Draft for Trial Use', the final document adopted with substantive amendments by the Central Committee in September 1979 gave *de facto* legitimacy – at the ideological and policy levels – to the implementation of *bao chan dao hu*. Hua Guofeng was known to be firmly opposed to 'the household responsibility system'. The initial formulations of the Central Committee were modified through subsequent stages (for example, Central Committee Document, no. 75). The elimination of Hua Guofeng from political power alongside major purges in the party and bureaucratic apparatus at different levels, including the structure of local government, laid the political basis for carrying out the agricultural reforms.

Conventional scholarship has looked upon Chinese agriculture in terms of its various performance indicators. Errors in management, 'incorrect' material incentives and excessive centralisation during the Great Leap and the Cultural Revolution are invariably held responsible for past 'failures'. Confined narrowly to the sphere of economism, this approach, which coincides not only with the analysis of World Bank missions to China but also with official communist party ideology, essentially views the transformation of agriculture as an operational-managerial problem. The analysis of social classes is shoved to the background; periodisation of Chinese history, rather than being based on an understanding of the process of collectivisation, is linked up with a narrow statistical analysis of *historical trends* in agricultural output at different periods since Liberation. Declines in production are attributed to the 'excesses of collectivisation' whereas increased output is the consequence of a return to a more 'flexible' and 'liberal' economic policy. Important dislocations in production and distribution took place during the Great Leap and the Cultural Revolution. These dislocations should, however, be understood in the light of the power struggle between opposing factions in the CCP.

To reduce the present reforms, therefore, to a shift in the structure of material incentives in *sensu stricto*, inevitably avoids focusing on the changes in ownership, institutions and rural social class relations which have resulted from the implementation of the agricultural reforms.

The reforms in the 'agricultural responsibility system' implemented alongside the reforms in industry, the 'open door' policy to foreign capital, and so on, constitute a cohesive and coherent programme which undermines the very basis of socialist agriculture. The policies of decollectivisation implemented in several stages since the Third Plenary of the Eleventh Central Committee meetings in 1978 have been conducive to the fragmentation of collective landholdings, the subdivision and privatisation of the means of production and the institutional collapse of the People's Commune. The reforms have led to the reemergence of capitalist farming based on what official communist party rhetoric entitles 'the specialised household'. The transfer of collective farm machinery from the commune to the well-to-do peasantry is conducive to the re-emergence of private forms of appropriation and accumulation.

A policy of decollectivisation does not, however, signify that decollectivisation as a process is taking place in a *uniform* fashion across China. Despite the purges conducted in local CCP organisations in many rural areas the Central Committee's directives were opposed by the peasantry. Unreported peasant uprisings in poorer agricultural regions were repressed. Law enforcement agencies at the local level were instructed to protect the rich peasantry. In many rural areas, however, the household responsibility system was *initially* welcomed as a move in the direction of greater flexibility in farm management. The broader significance of the 1978 farm contract system was not initially understood by the peasantry as constituting the *first stage* in the process of decollectivisation and restoration of the rich peasant economy.

In the transition period (1979–85), there is no uniform pattern of decollectivisation: in some regions collective property and institutions were dismantled, in others the ownership and collective work process remained more or less unchanged. In some cases, the existing institutional set-up was initially maintained because commune leaders were able to negotiate with local and provincial authorities to maintain the status quo. Strong pressures, however, were exercised by the organs of the party to break up collective structures and adopt the system of individual household farming.

These organisational changes occurred concurrently with the liberalisation of agricultural prices and the development of free markets. Moreover, private forms of accumulation characterised by private purchases of farm machinery, transport equipment, and so on, including bank credit to well-to-do peasants, undermined collective ownership and encourage the concentration of land, and the ownership of farm machinery.

The Household Responsibility System

The adoption of the contract system under *bao chan dao hu* is, in this context, a transitional form towards a fully-fledged system of private household farming. Initially, under *bao chan dao hu*, the production team was formally retained as an accounting unit. Collective work, however, was abandoned, and land was allocated to each household in accordance with the active number of workers per household. The production team established an output contract with the individual household; in turn, the brigade and commune levels established output quotas for the production team. Whereas the ouput contract arrangements remained, in principle, under the 'unified management' of the production team, in practice the tendency was for the production team to disappear as a unit of collective work and ownership of farm machinery.

In 1979–80, the responsibility system took on different forms:

1) Land and production quotas were allocated to individual households (*bao chan dao hu*);
2) Tasks and land (as opposed to production quotas) were assigned to households (*bao gan dao hu*);
3) Output quotas instead of being assigned to individual households were assigned to individual labourers (*bao chan dao lao*).[2]

According to official Chinese sources, 'the household responsibility system' had been applied to nearly 90 per cent of production teams by 1982.

Dazhai production brigade in Xiyang County, Shanxi province, once considered a model of 'socialist efficiency' in the 'Learning from Dazhai' campaign, shifted to the household responsibility system in 1980. 'Learning from Dazhai' began as a campaign to promote local 'self-reliance' and putting 'politics in command'. 'Learning from Dazhai' was abandoned by Dazhai in 1980. Local party officials were purged, Dazhai's former communist party Secretary Guo Penglian was transferred and Dazhai is now said to be 'better off under the responsibility system'.[3] The purges were conducted by the threat of expulsion or punishment. At Dazhai,

> brigade members voted many times to preserve their cooperative structure, but the county party committee overrode their objections . . . and when it couldn't find a brigade member to take over leadership and carry out the reform, appointed a state cadre from outside to do the job. Dazhai Brigade now has a party secretary who is on the state payroll.[4]

In some areas the system of '*large scale responsibility for production*' was applied. Under this system the peasants signed output contracts directly with the township government (which replaced the commune); the three level collective structure collapsed, and the township appropriated the agricultural surplus directly from the individual 'tenant' households. Alternatively the production team or groups of peasants or producers' co-operatives contract directly with the state marketing board.

The Institutional Collapse of the People's Commune

According to China's 1982 Constitution, the People's Commune *formally* ceases to exist as an integrated unit of self-government. Its political and administrative functions have been transferred to the township (*cheng*) and village (*xiang*) bureaucracies, which in turn are integrated into the broader administrative hierarchy of the provincial bureaucracy. So-called 'village committees', which replace production brigades, essentially deal with community affairs and social services. Each committee administers one or several villages whereas the township administers up to a dozen villages. By 1984 more than 22 000 township governments had replaced the commune administration in more than half of China's rural counties. The establishment of township and village government was completed in most parts of the country in 1984.

Collective work broke down, land was subdivided into household tracts, farm machinery acquired collectively by the brigade or the production team was either subdivided, sold, leased or distributed by the collective to individual peasant households. Where the peasants failed to agree on *how* to divide means of production acquired collectively, farm machinery either stood idle or was simply withdrawn from agricultural production. In other, less frequent cases, collective buildings and machinery were dismantled or destroyed.

In many regions of China the three-level structure of the People's Commune was dismantled and administrative functions were transferred to the township (*cheng*) and village levels (*xiang*) as early as 1980. The disintegration of the production team as a unit of both collective property and collective work was conducive, in some regions, to the re-emergence of mutual aid teams and agricultural producers' co-operatives similar in form to those (of the less advanced type) which developed in China in the early 1950s. These new co-operative schemes enable several households to acquire farm machinery which they are not in a position to purchase individually. In other cases, as mentioned earlier, machinery is purchased individually and owned privately by rich peasants. In the rich farming areas, the formation of producers' co-operatives is dominated by the well-to-do peasantry.

The creation of producers' co-operatives does not exclude the development of hired farm labour and other mechanisms of semi-proletarianisation of the poor peasantry. The International Labour Organisation

(ILO), among other international and foreign institutions, sponsors training programmes in co-operative management in China. The communist party has stressed the importance of applying (western) 'scientific' models of agricultural producers' co-operatives as an instrument of 'socialist modernisation'. International aid and co-operation is sought, and training programmes presenting the experiences of agricultural co-operatives under capitalism are presented to Chinese cadres. As in industry, the emphasis is on the transfer of so-called 'scientific management'.

New patterns of co-operation initially emerged after 1978 in small-scale rural industries, workshops, and so on. In this context *small work groups*, involving the participation of several households, developed in activities such as carpentry, repair workshops, brickmaking, handicrafts, and so on.[5] In the workshops two or three households participated on a co-operative basis whereas in small-scale industries 10 to 15 households were involved. The smaller units were owned and managed directly by the peasants. In Henan province, for instance, households were initially shareholders in that they participated in the earnings of small-scale industry in relation to their relative contribution to the investment fund. Under this system household earnings were based partly on work performed (in terms of work-time) and partly on ownership of real capital assets.[6] These ownership structures were in many respects transitional towards fully-fledged private ownership; inasmuch as they created a situation where earnings were based on ownership of real assets they encouraged the development of private appropriation and accumulation. The underlying structure enabled individual peasant households to enrich themselves at the expense of those who 'participated' in terms of work-time rather than capital assets.

The new co-operative schemes should be distinguished from those which developed in the 1950s. While they are similar *in form*, the 1950s mutual aid teams and elementary producers' co-operatives developed *historically* within the context of the Agrarian Revolution as *transitional forms* which were subsequently conducive to the formation of more advanced forms of collective property and collective work. This restoration of elementary co-operative forms, therefore, does not constitute a repetition of the institutional set-up of the 1950s. The restoration signifies that the historical process of collectivisation and construction of socialist agriculture has been broken. Inasmuch as the new co-operative schemes may indeed be interpreted as *transitional* forms, in the economic and social process of change since 1977, they are in no way *transitional* to more advanced forms of collective work and collective property (as in the context of a transition towards socialist agriculture). As mentioned earlier, these new co-operative schemes are often characteristic of the producers' and marketing co-operatives which exist in many capitalist Third World countries and which essentially serve the interests of the farmer-entrepreneur.

The reforms have led to the private marketing of agricultural output in the form of marketing co-operatives in which peasants are shareholders.[7] In practice, the rich peasants and so-called 'specialised households' dominate the marketing co-operatives because they control a large proportion of the co-operatives' stock. The co-operative will pay dividends to shareholders. Surplus income is 'used to give financial and technical support to rural producers'.[8]

Decollectivisation and the Ownership of Land

The communist party initially stated in 1980–81 that 'the public ownership of the means of production will not change. The peasants only have the right to use, not to buy, sell or transfer the land, farm machinery, [and so on] owned by the production team'.[9] Despite government 'guidelines', however, there were numerous reports of so-called 'illegal land deals' where land was bought, sold or exchanged. These transactions took place without the existence of legal titles of ownership.

The issue is not whether private ownership of land is reinstated or not. The private farmer need not own property in the form of land; he has, however, the *private use* of agricultural land. Although public ownership of land is a *necessary* condition for the construction of socialist agriculture, it does not in itself and by itself define the basis of socialist relations of production.

Under the contract system, land allocated to peasant households 'will remain under their management for at least 15 years' with the possibility of transferring the land to their heirs.[10] These provisions (adopted by the Central Committee in 1984) are conducive in practice to the privatisation of land in that they establish *de facto* property rights. Namely, the absence of private ownership of land does not in itself preclude the development of capitalist agriculture inasmuch as communal forms of ownership allow for the private use of land. In this regard, communal forms of ownership are not limited to socialism, they have existed historically in China and in other 'semi-feudal' social formations. In this context Friedrich Engels writes:

> In reality communal ownership of the land is an institution which is to be found on a low level of development among all Indo-Germanic races from India to Ireland and even among the Malays who have developed under Indian influence, for instance, in Java.[11]

In China, communal forms of ownership were to be found in the Taiping economic system. The allocation of land to individual households under common ownership was the basis of the *Land System of the Celestial Dynasty*'.[12]

Both the Taiping Land System in China, as well as the Tsarist Russian *mir* (village community), were based on a system of private use of land, private appropriation and individual work under a system of collective ownership of land. Marx, writing in 1881, saw quite clearly that the *mir* was breaking up from within because 'labour on one's own lot was a source of private appropriation making possible accumulation of movable goods'.[13] The Russian *mir*, formally based on egalitarian structures, was in practice dominated by the rich peasantry. Whereas land was communally owned, it was cultivated individually:

> And this all the more because the communally owned land in Russia is not cultivated by the peasants collectively and only the product is divided, as still is the case in some districts in India; on the contrary, each cultivates his allotment for himself. *Consequently great differences in prosperity are possible among the members of the community, and also actually exist.* Almost everywhere, there are a few rich peasants among them – here and there millionaires who play the usurer and suck the blood of the mass of the peasants.[14]

The historical evolution of the pre-revolutionary Russian *mir* (although of a fundamentally different nature to the household responsibility system) is indeed revealing in assessing the consequences of the agricultural reforms in China after Mao. Engels further noted that the Russian *mir* was based on the complete isolation of individual village communities from one another. This isolation prevented the development of social class interests by the poor peasantry:

> Such a complete isolation of the individual communities from one another, which creates throughout the country, it is true, similar, but the very opposite of common interests is the natural basis for *oriental despotism*.[15]

Namely, in the absence of a mass movement of peasants, the development of the individual household economy contributes to a greater isolation of village communities. Moreover, it weakens collective class interests because it encourages the traditional attachment to land and the pursuit of individual profit.

The Privatisation of Farm Machinery

The ownership status of movable means of production is far more decisive than ownership over land because it defines the nature of social production relations. Whereas the communist party initially stressed, in 1978–80, collective ownership of farm machinery and draught animals, it none the less officially sanctioned the private purchase of the means of production, including the extension of bank credit to individual farmers. In other words, the agricultural system allows for private forms of appropriation which depend not only on the amount of land alloted by the 'collective' to each household, but increasingly on the existence of privately-owned means of production.

Private ownership of farm machinery developed primarily as a result of the break-down of the People's Commune with the mechanics of privatisation differing from one region to another. Generally, with the adoption of *bao chan dao hu* there was a tendency for small farm machinery and draught animals belonging to the production team to be transferred to individual households or groups of households. In some townships, collective ownership of large tractors was initially maintained alongside the privatisation of small farm machinery. The subsequent privatisation of large farm machinery is related to the development of the farmer-entrepreneur or what the CCP Central Committee entitles officially 'the specialised household'. In some cases, collectively-owned farm machinery was sold by the commune (or township), in other cases it was rented out on a concessionary basis to rich peasants who operated the tractors as private entrepreneurs by selling their services to other peasants for a fee. The concession was invariably granted to the highest bidder, that is, the household which guarantees the highest rent on the equipment to the village or township will be granted the concession. This process in effect signified the transfer of movable means of production to the more affluent peasant households (that is, those with accumulated savings).

A similar process of privatisation applied to trucks and transport equipment. The latter were transferred by the collective to a 'specialised transport service household'. Generally speaking, the township and/or village levels maintained control over the transport equipment which was required to deal with statutory deliveries to the state. Privately-owned transport and marketing companies largely developed in relation to free market sales. Thus, in Daqing Township, Yohongqu County in Liaoning Province, for instance, 'the specialised household' pays a rental fee to the township government which is equivalent to 20 per cent of its profits. In Daqing there are 40 'specialised households' in farm machinery out of a total of 2500 households'. The average annual income of the specialised household is 6000-10 000 yuan, four to five times higher than the average level of household income in Daqing. The specialised household in transportation has an annual income of 20 000 yuan. The range of income between the richest and the poorest household in Daqing Township is of the order of approximately one to twelve.[16]

By 1982 two-thirds of all farm machinery in Chinese agriculture (according to official sources) was 'owned' or managed by private households. By

1983 most of the new small farm machinery, and a significant part of large machinery, were acquired by private farmers or producers' co-operatives.

The ownership of farm machinery and the provision of agricultural credit are interdependent processes. Bank credit, through the Agricultural Bank of China and the rural credit co-operatives, previously destined solely to communes and units of the collective economy is channelled in the form of private loans for the purchase of farm machinery to private farmers.[17] The bulk of such bank credit is granted to rich peasants and 'specialised households'. Moreover, as a result of the restructuring of the banking system, the tendency is towards concentration of credit and investment money in the more prosperous farming communities. Backward farming communities and poorer peasants who no longer qualify under the new credit rules, will increasingly have to rely on their resources.

The 'specialised household'

The status of the 'specialised household' varies considerably from one township to another. This status depends on the precise relationship between the 'collective' and the 'specialised household'. In cases where the household enters into a concessionary agreement with the 'collective', the tendency is for the 'specialised household' to operate as a private entrepreneur with the ability to hire wage labour. This type of arrangement evolves towards fully-fledged private ownership of farm machinery because in this case the collective will no longer acquire new farm machinery, that is, the rental arrangement constitutes a mechanism for the *de facto* privatisation of *existing* farm machinery. New farm machinery will be acquired from the accumulated profit of the 'specialised' farmer-entrepreneur.

It should, however, be understood that the creation of 'specialised households' under the responsibility system does not constitute in itself the basis for the restoration of private ownership of farm machinery. The specialised household system has been applied widely, and it tends to evolve towards a system of private ownership under certain conditions. The question is whether the 'specialised household' operates as an 'individual entrepreneur' selling its services to other households for a fee or as a 'working unit' under the authority of the collective. In the latter case, the specialised household's income is still controlled by the collective and determined in work points. This system does not normally evolve towards private ownership unless collective structures and institutions are radically displaced, for example, collective ownership breaks down as a result of the institutional collapse of the People's Commune and the *de facto* disappearance of the brigade and production team.

The transition from collective to private ownership will also depend on the maintenance of a collective accumulation fund (controlled by the 'collective') and allocated to purchases of *new* farm machinery. As mentioned earlier, purchases of small farm machinery as of 1982–3 were private acquisitions by individual peasant households.

In Dali Commune in Nanhai County, Guangdong Province, for instance, farm machinery was owned up to 1983 by the production team. The tractor drivers, who in this case represented a 'specialised household', entered into service contracts with each peasant household. Their income, however, determined in work points, was paid by the production team.[18] In Nanhai County this contractual form of collective ownership coexisted alongside newly-acquired and privately-owned farm machinery by individual farmers. The tendency, therefore, in this case is towards the gradual displacement of the collectively-owned means of production.

In Ninguan Village (*xiang*), Yangshe Township, Yuhongqu County, Liaoning Province (1983), the farm machinery was entrusted to a 'specialised working unit' (rather than to a specialised household). There were 130 workers in the specialised working unit which was composed of 'driving units' (of four members) and 'trucking units' (of five members). Normally these are not members of the same household.[19] The village made a contract with the working unit on a profit sharing basis which in turn made a contract with the drivers. Income received was made up of a base income plus an additional payment based on year-end profit sharing. This system should clearly be distinguished from the concessionary arrangement with the 'specialised households'. Whereas the latter operate as private entrepreneurs (and in many cases hire additional wage labourers), the working unit system retained, at least initially, the structure of collective ownership. It is transitional, however, because it requires the maintenance of a collective structure at the level of the production team. It tends, therefore, to be displaced in favour of private rural enterprises operating and contracting on a commercial basis.

Privatisation and regional polarisation

Private ownership of farm machinery tends to develop more rapidly in the rich agricultural regions where the application of the household responsibility system was conducive to the rehabilitation of private forms of appropriation and accumulation.

In the rich regions, inequality in income has existed historically within the People's Commune despite the application of so-called 'equalitarian' policies during the Great Leap and the Cultural Revolution. Historical conditions of social inequality and the existence of accumulated savings by the more affluent peasants are important in explaining the transition to capitalist farming, that is, accumulated savings constitute a form of 'primitive accumulation' which enables the well-to-do peasantry to appropriate the means of production. Moreover, the communist party's policy of 'combating equalitarianism' (including measures adopted by the state security forces to protect the rich peasantry) encourages the *de facto* rehabilitation of the categories of 'rich' 'middle' and 'poor peasantry' within the same local rural community. This social polarisation interacts with the implementation of the household responsibility system. The latter, however, is not in itself instrumental to the rehabilitation of capitalist farming. In many of the poorer and backward regions where *bao chan dao hu* was applied, the tendency is precisely the opposite: poverty and backwardness, the existing social structure and the patterns of solidarity among the peasantry do not favour a process of private accumulation.

Whereas in the rich regions of commercial farming the policy of promoting individual household work evolved towards a structure of private ownership of the means of production, in the poor regions, on the other hand, *bao chan dao hu* often signified the fragmentation of land and a return to traditional agriculture with little or no farm machinery. The collapse of collective structures (and of the collective accumulation fund) in the poor regions is an obstacle to modernisation. With the breakdown of the collectives, poorer peasants are no longer in a position to privately purchase farm machinery without regrouping into producers' co-operatives.

During the so-called 'rectification period' after the Great Leap, the state favoured modernisation of the most productive agricultural regions. These policies generated economic and social disparities as well as imbalances in the productive structure between rich and poor areas as well as between communes *within* the same agricultural region. The agricultural policies adopted since 1978 favour a similar process of concentration of investment resources. Moreover, the channelling of bank credit to the more 'profitable' agricultural projects reinforces the *dual and polarised* structure of Chinese agriculture. This *economic and social duality* is increasingly characterised by the co-existence of modern commercial agriculture alongside traditional small-scale household farming.

Although the structure of economic and social dualism in 'socialist' China should be distinguished from that prevalent in the 'capitalist' Third World, the nature of the underlying policies of so-called 'modernisation', the shift in land-use patterns, the development of export cash crops and non-staple commodities at the expense of grain self-sufficiency (all of which are taking place in China) are indicative of an over-all pattern of capital accumulation in agriculture which is by no means unfamiliar in the 'capitalist' poor countries. This structure of accumulation is characteristic of the semi-colonial nature of these economies.

The underlying logic of Third World capitalist agricultural modernisation has, in this regard, been amply studied in the development literature. Stavenhagen, for instance, writing in a Latin American context evaluates this process as folllows:

> The modernisation of agriculture . . . has been occurring more or less rapidly in various [Latin American] countries, *but it has tended to benefit only a small privileged portion of farms* . . . The modernisers are consciously supporting the large estates at the expense of the small-holders and peasant economy.[20]

The less prosperous and peripheral agricultural regions in China have often little in terms of accumulative capabilities. Moreover, state equalisation payments to poor regions are discontinued, investment resources, transport and social infrastructure are increasingly concentrated in the more affluent and 'viable' regions of commercial farming.

The tendency is, therefore, towards social and regional polarisation: the development of 'modern' commercial farming coexisting alongside the fragmentation of landholdings and the rehabilitation of the individual 'poor peasant economy'.

Farm Mechanisation and Surplus Farm Labour

Historically, the mechanisation of agriculture in China was related to collectivisation. Mao Zedong viewed the transformation of social class relations and mechanisation as interdependent processes, that is, modernisation without collectivisation would be conducive to the consolidation of capitalist agriculture and the rich peasant economy. In the 1950s the debate centered on whether collectivisation should come *before* or *after* mechanisation. This debate was interwoven with the political and ideological divisions in the Communist Party leadership.

The fragmentation of individual landholdings in the early 1950s was an obstacle to the mechanisation and modernisation of agriculture. Mao considered that collectivisation *should come first* because mechanisation could not take place unless the structure of the individual economy was transformed. A factor of crucial importance, moreover, was that the modernisation of agricultural production implied a redefinition of the relationship between agriculture and industry. On the one hand, the structure of heavy industry was to be subordinated to the process of agricultural modernisation through the production of farm machinery, chemical fertiliser, and so on. On the other hand, the transformation of agriculture was to generate the agricultural surplus which would enhance the development of the industrial sector:

> We are now carrying out a revolution not only in the social system, the change from private to public ownership, but handicraft to large-scale modern machine production, and the two revolutions are interconnected. In agriculture, with conditions as they are in our country,

co-operation must precede the use of big machinery . . . Therefore, we must on no account regard industry and agriculture, socialist industrialisation and the social transformation of agriculture as disconnected or isolated things . . . Moreover, large-scale expansion of light industry requires the development of agriculture as well as of heavy industry. For it cannot be brought about on the basis of a small peasant economy; it has to await large-scale farming, which in our country means socialist co-operative agriculture.[21]

Farm mechanisation and surplus population

In most capitalist Third World countries, the surplus rural population displaced by so-called 'modernisation' and 'agrarian reform' policies drifts into the poverty belt of large urban areas where it constitutes a reserve army of cheap labour for the urban sector. In this context, the disarticulation, displacement and consequent low levels of productivity of individual subsistence farming which result from so-called 'agricultural modernisation policies' constitute the instrumental lever which replenishes – through rural-urban migration – the mass of urban unemployed and underemployed.[22]

The development of the productive forces, and the formation of a surplus population under socialism has an entirely different significance. Farm mechanisation and the development of rural industries in China have proceeded concurrently. With approximately 75 per cent of the population in agriculture, the modernisation of agricultural production was a means of channelling surplus labour into non-agricultural activities. In the 1950s and 1960s, the formation of a surplus population, rather than transforming the rural labour force into unemployed or underemployed, enabled the concurrent development of rural small-scale industries organised and run by the peasants themselves. In particular, rural industries stressed the development of a rural-based farm machinery sector which would further endorse the process of farm mechanisation. Since the Great Leap most communes had centralised food and fodder processing plants which handled the communes' agricultural production. Surplus farm labour was also used in infrastructural projects, irrigation, water conservancy, flood control and land reclamation programmes.

Decollectivisation and surplus farm labour

What are the consequences of the post-Mao agricultural reforms on farm mechanisation and the process of absorption of surplus farm labour? Inasmuch as *bao chan dao hu* initially implied the subdivision of collective land into private household tracts which were farmed individually, the agricultural responsibility system during 1979–82 discouraged the use of farm machinery because it modified the scale of the land-output unit. The reforms were therefore, *initially*, conducive to the consolidation of traditional labour intensive farming. Because land was allocated in accordance with the active number of workers per household, it not only encouraged the formation of larger household units but also constituted an obstacle to farm mechanisation and the transfer (or release) of surplus farm labour to non-agricultural activities.

Moreover, this process undermined the development of infrastructural, irrigation, water conservancy and other projects which by their very nature required *collective* rather than *individual* work. In other words, surplus farm labour, instead of being channelled into small-scale rural industries and collective work projects, was increasingly concentrated on the land in traditional labour intensive household work. This situation, however, was *transitional* because decollectivisation was also accompanied by the concentration of farm land (in the hands of the rich peasantry) beginning in 1982–3.

The Concentration of Land

The transition from collective to private and co-operative ownership of the means of production was initially conducive to the disengagement of farm machinery from production, particularly in the less affluent agricultural regions. The initial fragmentation of landholdings under a system of 'equal distribution' of land gradually evolved, however, towards the *concentration of land* in the hands of the well-to-do peasantry. This in turn increased the size of the land-output unit and encouraged the use of privately-owned (and purchased) farm machinery by the 'specialised household' farmer-entrepreneur.

The adoption of the household responsibility system by the CCP Central Committee in 1978 initially resulted in the fragmentation of collective land into household tracts. The transition from collective to private ownership of the means of production, however, created the social and material basis for private appropriation and accumulation. In turn, this process led to the transformation of the structure of land distribution. The system of 'equal distribution' of land under *bao chan daō hu* was gradually eroded. Rich peasants and owners of farm machinery (designated officially as 'specialised households') were given larger tracts of farm land under the new principle of 'contracting according to ability'. The process of land concentration proceeded alongside the proletarianisation or semi-proletarianisation of the peasantry. Hired wage labour developed with the concentration of land and farm machinery and the formation of so-called 'specialised households'. Under this system, there is no limit on the number of wage labourers which may be hired by a 'specialised household'.

As of 1983, communist party guidelines regarding land distribution encouraged the allocation of farm land to the 'specialised household' and invited less affluent households to move off the land into sidelines and rural industries. For instance, in Daqing Township in Liaoning Province, an average 10 mu (1.5 acres) of farm land was allocated to each able farm worker initially under *bao chan dao hu*. According to Li Chuanxiang, township leader, 'land is distributed according to the ability of each worker, 15 mu (2.3 acres) is the highest allocation per worker and 60 mu (9.1 acres) is the maximum per household. The minimum per household is 20 mu (3.0 acres) and 8 mu (1.2 acres) per worker'.[23] Li emphasised, however, (repeating the official CCP position) that the equal distribution of land 'is not efficient':

> We encourage small landholders to give up their land because they can move into fishing, animal husbandry, rural industries, and so on. Large holdings are encouraged so as to be able to use large farm machinery. Our target is that 20 per cent work in the fields and 80 per cent in sidelines and rural industries.[24]

In response to the question as to whether there were 'some conflicts' as a result of encouraging the 'less successful and efficient peasants' to move off the land, the township leader stated that 'this was entirely voluntary'.

In another rural township in Liaoning Province where land was initially allocated to individual workers in 1979, under *bao chan dao lao* (specific work determined for each individual worker) with approximately 5 mu of farmland per worker, village and township leaders were planning (in 1983) to transfer *all* agricultural land to a small group of households:

> We intend to allocate all the farm land to 20 to 30 households [out of a total of 901 households] which would be responsible for doing the farm work. The village would make a contract with one household which in turn may subcontract with two or three other households; the contracting family could hire its relatives.[25]

The township leader, Mr Huang, assured me:

> Voluntary selection by farming households will take place; some families, however, will have to move to other activities because we need more workers in rural factories. . .There are no problems [conflicts] because the allocation of work depends on one's own individual choice, because everybody works according to his wish'.[26]

In Dali Township in Guangdong Province, approximately 1000 households, on 5000 mu (751 acres) of farm land, were involved in agricultural production in 1983. Dali's land redistribution programme will mean that 20 to 30 households will each receive 200 to 300 (30.4 – 45.6 acres) mu of farm land (as opposed to an average 5 mu under equal distribution). These would then be broken down into tracts of approximately 100 mu and allocated to the 'subcontracting households'.[27]

In Shanxi Province the 1978 household responsibility system, based on equal distribution of land, was considered 'an obstacle to increased productivity' and the development of 'the peasants' general prosperity'. The concentration of land was officially sanctioned by the Shanxi Communist Party in 1983:

> The contract responsibility system has entered a new stage in some areas of Shanxi Province in north China: *land is no longer shared by peasant households according to their number of members; it is being concentrated into some households specialising in producing grain for sale. Others are allowed to do what they can do best . . . This year, those who are neither good nor interested in farming are encouraged to give up land*. . . Xue Shouchang. . . was allowed to contract less than 2–4 hectares of land last year. . . [this year] Xue Shouchang has contracted 15 hectares altogether, six times as much as last year . . .Given present agricultural productivity, *development of households specialising in producing commodity grain depends on further concentration of land*. The key to concentration of land is diversifying production . . .so that more households can engage in sideline occupations.[28]

Less productive households in Shanxi were 'encouraged' to move into sidelines and rural industries:

> But whether households with sidelines will be willing to give up land is another problem. Some households that want to dare not. They are not sure the collective will supply them with enough grain especially wheat. And they are afraid they will have no other choice if they fail at their new occupation. To allay their fears, the authorities in the two countries [of Shanxi Province] have decided:
>
> – Households giving up land may contract with the collective to receive their grain rations from the collective reserves at state purchased prices;
> – If they meet with unexpected difficulties and want to resume farming, the collective should provide what land they need.[29]

It was reported in 1983 that in Fenglin Township, Yangxin County, Hubei Province, a single individual contracted with the commune 5 to 6 hectares of land 'which nobody else wanted'. 'Thanks to mechanised cultivation he harvested 30 000 kilograms of grain and sold 23 500 to the state – *equal to the total quota of the production brigade*.'[30] But the work in this case is invariably performed by wage labourers who are hired by a 'specialised household':

> In Taiyuan, agricultural officials told me [W.H. Hinton] about one peasant who contracted 750 mu of land. When I said his mechanisation must be impressive and I would like to see it, they said he had no machinery at all. He farmed 750 mu with hired labour. In Low Bow the six peasants who contract the six gardens hire at least 12 full-time wage labourers to do the day-to-day work, and the man who contracted the cement mill hires 42 wage workers.[31]

Restoration of the Rich Peasant Economy

The Central Committee has officially sanctioned the unequal distribution of land as an instrument of 'socialist modernisation'. Support should be given to the rich peasant:

> The road to general prosperity was opened up by the Third Plenary Session . . . The first [objective] is to wipe out egalitarianism and the carrying out of the socialist policy of distribution according to work. . . To bring general prosperity to all peasants is our general objective. To allow some of the peasants to become well-to-do is our strategic way to reach that goal. To allow some of the peasants to become better off first, we can on the one hand encourage the poorer peasants. On the other hand it will enable the more prosperous peasants – who have experience in crop production, side-line production and various trades – to share those experiences with poor peasants.[32]

Rich peasants are now viewed as having management and scientific abilities. Their entrepreneurial skills are not seen as the basis of social division but as contributing to the promotion of *the peasants general prosperity* and to the upward social mobility of the poor peasants. According to the CCP Central Committee, the rich peasants are the agents of 'socialist construction' in China's countryside. '*They are disseminators of science and agro-techniques as well as advanced builders of socialism*'.[33] At an ideological level, the emphasis is on individual initiative rather than on collective endeavours:

> Our policy is to encourage peasants to become more prosperous, we encourage some people to be very rich and that way others can learn so

that they can become rich later, those who have skills and technology may become rich earlier.[34]

The communist party leadership admits, however, that social inequality will prevail in the short-run:

> While more peasants are leading a better life, the differences among the peasants are increasing. For some time this trend will continue. But from a long-term point of view, the gap between the better-off peasants and relatively poor ones is narrowing. Because the general income level of the peasants is rising, their scientific and cultural level is also rising and sidelines have provided poor peasants with more chances to move up.[35]

Proletarianisation of the Poor Peasantry

The impoverished peasants are being pushed off the land into sidelines or rural industries as a result of the communist party's policy of promoting the rich peasant-entrepreneur. Hired wage labour in agriculture develops concurrently with that of the so-called 'specialised household'; the displacement of the 'less affluent' peasant accompanies the process of land concentration. The latter conforms to the communist party's policy of 'distribution according to ability'. Landless peasants are 'absorbed' by rural industries or hired as day labourers by a 'specialised household'. Distribution is no longer based on work performed but on (a) ownership of the means of production, and (b) the system of unequal distribution of land.

Inasmuch as collective institutions are not entirely dismantled, township and county governments provide jobs for those who have been moved off the land. Many landless peasants, however, prefer to migrate to the cities in search of work in what the ILO World Employment Programme entitles the 'informal urban sector' made up of small-scale privately-owned and co-operative entities, petty traders and producers. This 'informal urban sector' is intended, according to the Central Committee, to absorb *urban* unemployment and provide 'jobs' for urban youth for whom jobs are not provided by the state. A private market for hired wage labour in the cities is developing both as a result of small-scale informal activities as well as the development of *larger* privately-owned undertakings (based on wage labour) in industry and services.

Rural-urban migration

As discussed above, the urban surplus population which cannot be 'absorbed' in state sector employment constitutes the basis for the development of a 'free market' for hired wage labour. Part of this urban surplus labour, however, is in fact being transformed into disguised unemployment in the 'informal urban sector'. Under these circumstances there is little room for surplus labour flowing in from the countryside. Existing social tensions in the cities and the very high rate of urban youth unemployment does not encourage the state to 'liberalise' rural-urban migration. Moreover, rural-urban migration is controlled through the system of travel and residence permits and the allocation of food rationing tickets based on approved place of residence (which means that rural migrants would have to purchase their food staples at a much higher price in the urban free market).

Despite the obstacles to rural-urban migration, the pressures and incentives for impoverished peasants to move to the cities are none the less present. The fact that rural workers are prepared to accept work in the cities for wages of the order of 20 to 30 yuan a month (US$10 to 15) constitutes a clear indication of the precarious conditions which exist in the countryside despite official figures and interpretations which suggest a *general* improvement in rural per capita income. The market for household maids, for instance, with monthly incomes ranging from 15 to 30 yuan a month (US$7.50 to 15.00) is flourishing in major cities. Maids, generally hired by cadres and intellectual households, are increasingly recruited from rural areas. In Beijing, household maids 'work in Xicheng and Haidian, two [suburban] districts dotted with government apartments and universities'.[36] Large cities have set up employment service companies which contract domestic servants directly in rural areas for employment with 'hard-worked intellectuals and cadres'.

Whereas the system of individual household farming based on (traditional) labour intensive methods tends *initially* to absorb rural surplus labour, the subsequent concentration of land and farm machinery and the 'modernisation' of the rich peasant economy, at the expense of the less affluent farming communities, increase surplus farm labour because they displace and uproot the poor peasantry. The communist party's policy consists in 'digesting' the resulting surplus rural labour:

> The collectives should be responsible for organising the development of intensive farming and other types of labour intensive production . . . With tens of millions of households fully developing their individually-managed enterprises, *tens of millions of surplus labourers will thus be 'digested'*.[37]

The factual statement that the individually-managed household economy will '*digest*' surplus labour constrains the analysis of surplus labour to the field of production engineering (that is, labour is viewed in this context as an 'input' or factor of production). The underlying changes in the rural class structure are totally disregarded. Moreover, whereas the individual household economy tends to 'digest' surplus labour, the *uneven* and *dual* character of agricultural modernisation (whereby selected regions and social categories of peasants 'modernise' alongside 'tens of millions' confined to traditional farming methods) tends on the other hand, to *increase* the surplus population concurrently with the proletarianisation of the poorer categories of peasants.

Social Inequality and the Rural Distribution of Income

Patterns of social and income inequality (between regions and within the same farming community) were to some extent maintained during the Cultural Revolution. This signified that although private forms of accumulation were constrained, the rich peasantry was not eliminated despite the emphasis on 'equalitarianism'. During the Cultural Revolution the mode of payment modelled on Dazhai was based on a combination of a guaranteed floor income in the form of 'basic rations' (*jiben kouliang*) and remuneration based on a time/rate system. The system of remuneration was, in this regard, to conform to '*distribution according to need*' and '*distribution according to work*'.

Official Chinese sources have pointed to the substantial increase in the level of living of the peasantry since the adoption of the 'household responsibility system'. The 'improvement' of living conditions in the countryside is based on a nationwide survey of 30 400 rural households in 28 provinces, regions and municipalities out of a total of close to 200 million rural households. These household surveys are not based, however, on random sample techniques.[38]

The household survey which canvasses approximately one out of 100 000 households suggests (along with the World Bank's advisory mission to China) that rural per capita income increased by more than 30 per cent in the three years after the adoption of 'the household responsibility system' by the Third Plenary of the Eleventh Central Committee of the Chinese Communist Party in December 1978. In 1983, according to the survey, rural annual average per capita income was about 309 yuan ($150),[39] but annual peasant per capita income averaged or was in excess of 300 yuan only in 29 per cent of China's counties, county level cities or districts. The 682 rich counties (out of a total of 2352) 'are mainly in Beijing, Shanghai, Tianjin, Jilin, Shandong, Jiangsu and other provinces where rural economy has developed rather rapidly'.[40] While substantial increases in rural incomes have taken place, they are largely concentrated in the rich farming communities and are accompanied by important changes in the structure of income distribution. In view of inflation in raw materials, agricultural inputs and consumer goods, the World Bank estimates a *real* increase in rural per capita income from 1978–81 of the order of 15 per cent. This change is partly attributable to an improvement in the terms of trade between the rural and urban economies characterised by a substantial increase in state procurement prices and the rapid development of free markets in major cities for fruits, vegetables and other non-staple products.

Free markets which had been closed down at the outset of the Cultural Revolution were reopened in 1979. According to the World Bank, prices of non-staple foodstuffs sold both at regulated prices by the state as well as in the free markets increased by 32 per cet in three years (1978–81). In fact, the free market prices of non-staple goods more than doubled in relation to the regulated price structure which existed prior to 1978. While the increase in state procurement prices constitutes in principle a *positive* move towards reducing income disparities between urban and rural areas, the price measures implemented in conjunction with the policies of decollectivisation, tend to benefit the well-to-do peasantry as well as a new class of merchants and of merchants and intermediaries involved in the development of free market sales.

As discussed earlier, decollectivisation in the poor agricultural regions has led to the fragmentation of landholdings and the restoration of traditional small-scale household farming. The conditions in the poor regions are, on balance less conducive to the accumulation of wealth and, indeed, income disparities are relatively less pronounced.

In the rich regions, the private appropriation of farm machinery by the rich peasant-entrepreneur, the increase in land concentration and the collapse of collective structures have been conducive to the concentration of income. In many rich agricultural regions, per capita income is more than three times the national per capita income and *twenty times higher than the per capita income in the poorest farming communities*. *Within* the rich regions income disparities between the categories of 'poor' and 'rich' peasants are on average one to seven (although often in excess of one to ten). Inter-regional social inequalities are superimposed on intra-regional disparities: the *absolute income gap* between the rich peasant-entrepreneur in the areas of commercial farming and the poor peasantry in the less affluent regions *is of the order of one to a hundred*. This absolute income disparity is the combined result of social disparities *within* rural areas (that is, between the 'poor,' 'middle' and 'rich' peasantry) and the process of regional polarisation which has substantially increased income disparities *between* regions.

Income distribution in selected rural areas

In Daqing Township, Yuhongqu County, Liaoning Province – which, in addition to rich paddy production, has a number of sideline activities – the distribution of household income (1983) was characterised by a disparity of approximately one to seven between the 'lowest' and 'highest' household income brackets.[41] Ten per cent of households in Daqing had earnings of 1700 yuan, average household income is 2400 yuan and households in the upper 20 per cent bracket have incomes in excess of 6400 yuan. This category includes the so-called '10 000 yuan households'. The richest household 'specialising' in transportation had an income of 20 000 yuan, 12 times higher than that of the poorest peasant household (1700 yuan).[42]

A similar structure of income distribution is to be found in other prosperous farming communities. In Ninguan village, Yuhongqu County, Liaoning Province, the average household income (1983) was of the order of 3000 yuan, 20 per cent of the households had average incomes of 12 000 yuan – six times that of the poorest peasant household (2000 yuan).

In a relatively affluent farming community in Heilongjiang Province (New Spring Commune, Nangang County), the poorer households earned (1983) 600 yuan as opposed to approximately 4000 for the more affluent households.[43] Disparities on a per capita basis are less pronounced because rich households are of larger size with more farm workers.

In Guangdong Province, Dali Township, with a population of approximately 23 000 households, the average household income (1983) was of the order of 2500 to 3000 yuan; 1300 households (6 per cent of the total) had incomes in excess of 5000 yuan and 120 households (0.5 per cent of the total) had incomes in excess of 10 000 yuan.[44] The richest household in Dali had earnings of 150 000 yuan (more than 50 times the average household income of 2500 to 3000 yuan).

As mentioned earlier, social polarisation is less pronounced in the less affluent farming communities. Nevertheless, income disparities have also widened in the poorer regions. In rural Jiangsu, Suqian County, for instance, with a population of approximately 200 000 households, average per capita income was 260 yuan in 1983.[45] Approximately 3400 households (that is, 1.5 per cent of the total number of households) had incomes in excess of 500 yuan and 80 households had incomes greater than 1000 yuan. Suqian County government admits that while 'the gap between the rich and the poor has widened' it is

> *mainly caused by the difference in their [the peasants] ability to work. It is not a sign of class polarisation caused by exploitation. Now that all the basic means of production are owned by the public, we'll never allow the emergence of two antagonistic classes in the countryside a second time. Our goal is prosperity for all.*[46]

Suqian County has developed 'a three point plan to narrow the income gap' which consists '*in supporting some peasants to prosper first*' by providing them with funds, technical expertise, and so on. The 'specialised households' are encouraged to open shops, run factories, buy tractors and engage in transportation. Moreover,

> all supply and marketing departments in Huaiyin Prefecture have been asked to help specialised households buy what they need and market their output. . . *Law enforcement agencies [in Huaiyin] are to provide protection for rich peasants who have prospered through their own efforts.* Propaganda teams will publicise the new economic policy and *reassure* specialised peasants that their efforts will not be denounced or impeded.[47]

Du Runsheng, director of the party's Rural Policy Research Centre, confirms that as a result of the party's new agricultural policy which grants the peasants

> greater flexibility in managing their farms and sideline industries, *some peasants are earning up to 100 000 yuan [50 000 dollars]* a year from their specialised professions. However, there is no danger of their becoming capitalists, becausse no one is allowed to get rich by exploiting other people in our society.[48]

The rich peasants should help others to prosper

The communist party, while promoting the rich peasantry, has stressed the modernising role of the 'specialised household' so that their entrepreneurial skills may 'trickle down' to the impoverished households. 'Those who prosper first must help others' is the official motto which is repeated in rural townships across China: the rich peasantry is the agent of 'socialist construction' in the countryside: 'It is no good for a single flower to bloom alone. When a man has prospered, he must help his neighbours'.[49]

The Accumulation and Public Welfare Funds

There is evidence of significant rural poverty arising from the agricultural reforms. Official surveys on rural poverty will invariably 'explain' the income differential between the affluent 'specialised household' and the poor peasantry as a consequence of 'the principle of distribution according to work' and the lack of knowledge, technology and experience in farm management of the poor peasantry.

What policies are envisaged to help the poor peasantry? The communist party's official position on this matter is to 'help impoverished peasants to prosper through labour'.[50] Inasmuch as collective institutions are still in place, impoverished peasants are often given some support from the accumulation or public welfare funds. With decollectivisation, however, the tendency is to lessen the peasants' over-all contributions to the welfare and accumulation funds. In this context, the Central Committee of the communist party issued a circular in November 1983, instructing authorities at the grassroot level to 'set a ceiling on the money a peasant will have to pay to the collective savings'. The directives also include 'requiring local authorities *not to rush into provision of public welfare undertakings* . . . setting a ceiling on voluntary labour that a peasant should spend for state construction, public welfare and water conservancy projects.' The circular was prepared by the Rural Policy Research Office under the direct authority of Central Committee Secretariat.[51]

The foregoing suggests that services from collective funds are provided in proportion to peasants' contributions. Moreover, the evidence suggests that collective work projects are increasingly entrusted to the farmer-entrepreneur ('specialised household'). The transfer of many collective work projects to 'specialised' private entrepreneurs, who establish contracts both with the collective as well as with individual peasant households for a fee, has been conducive, in many rural areas, to the neglect of water conservancy, irrigation and other collective infrastructural projects. Also, the farm contract system has serious environmental implications. With the breakdown of the collective and the liberalisation of land use, environmental conservation is neglected. The allocation of woodlands, for instance, to private households has led to deforestration. The Ministry of Forestry has urged townships to contract the planting of trees to 'specialised households'. The breakdown of collective work in infrastructure, water conservancy, irrigation, and so on has contributed to greater dangers of flooding and drought.

Towards the privatisation of social services

The disengagement of the state at the local level is particularly visible in the areas of health and primary education:

> Farmers are now gradually replacing the state in financing schools in rural Hebei . . . Many farmers have observed that it is a tradition in China for individuals to finance schools . . . At present there is a wave of school construction in many rural areas.[52]

The disengagement of the state in rural education proceeds alongside the collapse of collective institutions and the development of the rich peasant economy. The construction of eductional facilities in the countryside will increasingly be funded through individual donations by rich peasants.

'Socialised' medical care is financed from peasant contributions to the welfare fund. In the rich areas minimal fees are charged, the bulk of the costs of township clinics is financed from the welfare fund. The situation, however, is more critical in the less affluent farming regions because state subsidies have been cut or discontinued. In some regions the tendency is for health care to be financed on a fee basis per medical consultation as a result of the Ministry of Public Health's proposed 'new order' in the area of health. The latter consists *inter alia* in restoring the legitimacy of private practice alongside state and collective medical facilities. Private practice for doctors, dentists and pharmacists has been rehabilitated, and the state has also authorised the operation of private clinics. It is stated that the reform of the health care system must eliminate 'administrative disorder' as well as 'combat equalitarianism' in the distribution of medical services.[53] State expenditures in health facilities have decreased (in relative terms) largely as a result of major investment outlays in industry and foreign trade infrastructure.[54]

On the other hand, the concept of 'modernisation' applied to the health care sector signifies a shift in direction and orientation from the development of grass-roots primary health care in rural areas, based on an integration of Chinese and western medicine (emphasised during the Cultural Revolution with the development of the 'bare-foot doctors'), to the consolidation and 'upgrading' of modern urban hospital facilities based on western concepts of training and research, the incorporation of 'advanced' western therapeutic and diagnostic equipment and the development of pairing arrangements with western medical schools. Although not explicitly stated officially, medical education after Mao is geared towards a clear institutional demarcation (rather than integration) between western and traditional Chinese medicine, and the consolidation of so-called 'modern' medical practice. These developments contribute to: (a) the polarisation of health facilities in large urban areas, and (b) the downgrading of primary health care in rural areas.

The Rural Industries

With the adoption of the household responsibility system in 1978–9, the rural industries were initially transferred from commune management to that of an integrated 'holding company' made up of a professional managerial and professional team. Frequently three integrated 'holding companies' respectively in the agricultural, industrial and commercial fields were created which administered – under central management – all commune and brigade level factories.[55]

With decollectivisation, the integrated commercial enterprise previously run by the commune and responsible for supply of materials and consumer goods to the peasants, now operates as an autonomous commercial enterprise under the authority of the supply and marketing co-operative of the province.

The institutional structure of the rural industries may vary from one province to another. In Sichuan, the enterprises of the commune in the industrial, marketing and agricultural spheres were, in many cases, co-ordinated by a centralised administration in the form of a joint enterprise separate from that of the *xiang* (village) government. This joint enterprise co-ordinated the enterprises in the different economic areas.[56]

In 1981 the integrated industrial 'holding company' in Xiangyang, Sichuan province, for instance, controlled 19 commune level factories and 15 previously run by the united production teams.[57] In Anhui, on the other hand, the political functions of the commune were transferred to the *xiang* (village) level, whereas the commune, (now township), formally retained its previous identity and exercised supervisory functions over three separate companies respectively in the agricultural, industrial and marketing fields.[58]

The foregoing examples not only suggest that the democratic structures of the commune are falling apart, but also that the participation of the peasants in the running of rural industries, social services, and so on, is being replaced by a permanent managerial structure. With the collapse of democratic commune self-government, officials at the village and township levels (corresponding respectively to the commune and brigade levels) are sometimes appointed by the province, sometimes elected by commune members. With the purges carried out at the local level in 1983–4, Maoist partisans have been increasingly removed from local party and government functions.

The privatisation of rural factories

In Guangdong Province small-scale rural factories are given on a three-year concession basis by the township or village to a peasant-entrepreneur who operates the factory as a private business undertaking. These factories operate on the basis of hired day-labourers. The private entrepreneur pays an agreed percentage of the profit to the township or village government in exchange for the concession to operate the rural factory. The remaining portion of the profit may be reinvested in other industrial undertakings. The tender system is transitional, however, towards fully-fledged private ownership of small-scale rural factories. Large township level factories tend to be integrated into the state sector under township or county jurisdiction.

In Guangdong rural factories with 50 to 70 workers operate as private capitalist enterprises. In some cases rich peasants will enter into joint ventures with state factories or with a Hong Kong export-processing enterprise. In view of their special status to conduct foreign trade 'along capitalist lines', townships and counties in Guangdong and Fujian provinces have established foreign trade offices. Rural factories may thereby establish direct contractual links with a foreign company without provincial government approval. This system, which bypasses the provincial import-export corporation, contributes to the integration of rural factories into a wide variety of cheap labour export activities.

In Nanhai County, Guangdong, for instance, several export-processing factories operate at the county or township levels. In Dali Township, for instance, a garment factory with 70 workers produces Texwood jeans directly for a Hong Kong contractor. The latter pays a processing fee of HK$37 (approximately US$5) for the sewing of one dozen pieces (less than 50 US cents per pair, of which 25 cents is paid to the workers and 25 cents is allocated to the accumulation fund and social services).[59]

The break-up of the People's Commune and the privatisation of the means of production have accompanied the subordination of the rural industries to the urban industrial base. The more 'viable' rural factories concentrated in the rich rural areas and in proximity to large cities, are integrated – through subcontracting or subsidiary arrangements – into the urban state corporate structure.

Rural industries – which are no longer controlled by the collective – rather than supporting the rural economy, will now produce increasingly in accordance with the laws of the market and the requirements of the so-called 'modern sector'. These changes are not solely of an institutional and organisational nature, however, for the subordination of rural factories to the urban corporate bureaucracy contributes to the downgrading of the entire rural industrial base and the centralisation of the so-called 'modern (industrial) sector' in the cities. It also reverses the Maoist policy of reducing economic and social disparities between urban areas and the countryside.

As mentioned earlier, this process of polarisation also applies to educational, health and other services through the downgrading of the social sectors in rural areas. The rural system of education is set apart from that in the cities. The underlying structure is increasingly one of *educational apartheid* and the consolidation of a socially differentiated and hierarchised educational system.

The subordination of the rural economy to the urban industrial base is also supported by the reforms in the system of prefectures and counties under the administration of nearby cities. Those in the vicinity of urban areas will be incorporated into the city-counties. In more developed areas, prefectural governments have been merged with those of medium-sized cities.[60] Such administrative restructuring is intended so that 'production and commerce be placed under unified guidance, with the economically more developed cities acting as centres leading the surrounding rural areas'.[61]

TABLE 3.1 *The relationship between free market and state-regulated prices*

Commodity	*Free market price (yuan per catty)*	*State regulated price (yuan per catty)*
Rice	0.43 – 0.45	0.178
Sorghum	0.22 – 0.25	0.11
Millet	0.39 – 0.40	0.132
Soya Bean	0.40 – 0.43	0.17
Pork	1.20	1.26
Eggs	1.45	1.20
Green vegetables	0.20	0.12
Potatoes	0.09	0.09
Fish	2.80	0.96
Beef	1.60	0.96
Chicken	1.20	1.00
Mutton	1.50	0.92

NOTE Two cattys equals approximately one kilogram. In 1983, two yuan were equal to approximately one US dollar (at the official exchange rate).

SOURCE Shenyang Free Market, Liaoning province, September 1983.

The Liberalisation of Agricultural Markets

Free markets were re-opened a few months after the Third Plenary of the Eleventh CCP Central Committee in late 1978. Although prices of basic grain staples are regulated by the state, for non-grain commodities (for example, meat, poultry, fruits and vegetables) the tendency is towards complete price liberalisation through a gradual convergence of the regulated price to the 'free market clearing price' ('to correct market distortions').

The state has its own stands in the free markets. According to Xie Dinghao, managing director of Shenyang Free Market, 'we invite the state to stabilise the free market price. However, the state stand will never sell in large quantities so as to avoid speculation . . . To keep the price in the free market stable, we advertise the free market and state reference prices.'[62] (see Table 3.1).

Operators in the free markets are 'specialised households' which have privately-owned transport vehicles. With the development of free market outlets, there is a tendency for an urban merchant class to develop. Free market operators often purchase at official state prices and resell in the free market.

The *duality of the price structure* characterised by the co-existence of free market and state-regulated prices, has had an important effect on land-use patterns in agriculture. This duality is, however, transitional in as much as communist party policy is towards the complete liberalisation of prices in accordance with 'the law of value'. State prices are either adjusted upwards to conform with the free market price or state controls over prices are lifted altogether. In agriculture, state regulated prices increasingly apply only to staple food products which are purchased with ration coupons.

Land-Use Patterns

The over-all liberalisation of agricultural prices, particularly in non-staple foods, has favoured a shift in land-use patterns which reduces the areas allocated to staple grain production. On the other hand, industrial cash crops such as cotton, tobacco, silk, oil bearing crops, and so on, have generally been favoured at the expense of grain. Vast agricultural areas have been transformed into tobacco and cotton fields, and in the vicinity of large cities extensive fruit- and vegetable-producing areas have developed. These changes, according to Central Committee policy, should encourage 'a more efficient' utilisation of land in accordance with 'regional comparative advantage', as well as the development of export cash crops and the agro-business sectors.

In the early 1960s agricultural policy was geared *in principle* to grain self-sufficiency and 'taking grain as a key link'. During the 1960–65 period this policy was implemented essentially by using the price mechanism. Xue Muqiao describes these policies as follows:

> The state raised only the purchasing price but not its selling price. Thus the purchase price exceeded the selling price and the State had to cover the difference by spending several thousand million yuan a year. . . After the purchasing prices for grain were raised, production teams in grain-producing areas charged more for the grain allocated to their members as a matter of course. Thus peasants who produced grain paid more for it while those in cash crop areas who did not produce it paid less for commodity grain provided by the State. This was obviously unfair. To solve this contradiction, we raised the prices of foodgrain sold to rural inhabitants and placed them on a par with the purchasing prices in 1964. Peasants in cash crops didn't mind paying for their foodgrain at the same price on account of the higher purchasing prices of cash crops. But this created another problem, namely the grain sold to peasants in cash crop areas, like the grain allocated to grain producers, now became more expensive than that sold to urban workers. In other words, grain was generally cheaper in the cities than in the countryside . . . To solve this contradiction the State raised the prices of grain sold to urban residents in 1965, putting the selling prices in cities and towns at a par with those in rural areas.[63]

The distributional implications of price policies, as described by Xue, are complex and involve not only the structure of income distribution between peasants and urban wage workers, but also the rural division of income between grain and cash-crop producing collectives. At the outset of the Cultural Revolution, the procurement price structure and free market outlets were viewed as being responsible for increased social inequalities. Inasmuch as procurement prices contributed to urban-rural transfers of income, these transfers were extremely unequal and were often conducive to accentuating income and social disparities *within* the rural sector.

During the Cultural Revolution (1966–76), grain prices did not rise although the relative price structure tended to favour local grain self-sufficiency at the expense of cash crops. Although this policy promoted grain security, several writers have suggested that it prevented some of the poorest regions to increase their levels of income by specialising in cash crops. The price mechanism, therefore, was downgraded as a regulator, and agricultural policy during 1966–76 emphasised the development of irrigation and water conservancy projects based on collective work in view of increasing production potential in grain.

Decollectivisation and the Open Door Policy

The present grain policy is heavily influenced by the reintegration of Chinese agriculture into the international division of labour. The opening up of trade along capitalist lines, and the reintegration of Chinese agriculture into the world economy, conditions the structure of capital accumulation in agriculture. With the liberalisation of foreign trade, the structure of world commodity prices has a decisive impact on the internal price structure. For instance, China imports both grain and cotton: the relative world price of these two commodities will influence the *internal* relative price structure, that is, an increase in the domestic procurement price of cotton (conducive to a corresponding shift in land-use patterns) enables China to 'import substitute' cotton. Consequently, the domestic production of cotton is increased; foreign exchange is thereby saved by importing *less* cotton and *more* grain. Whereas this cost-revenue calculation is essentially sound from a strictly financial standpoint, the internal allocation of productive resources is increasingly subordinated to the laws of the capitalist world commodity market rather than to the principles of socialist planning.

Present grain policy is characterised by what might be described as 'taking the world economy as a key link'. Despite an increase in the price of grain, the structure of relative procurement prices promotes regional and crop specialisation and tends to destroy the structure of local self-sufficiency in grain. The concurrent increase in grain prices (alongside the substantial increase in the prices of non-grain products) was largely motivated so as to avoid a massive shift out of grain production.

Whereas post-1978 grain harvests have been reasonably successful, the shift in land-use patterns at a regional level, the increased use of grain for animal feed and agro-industrial use as well as the liberalisation of agricultural markets are likely to result in localised patterns of 'grain shortage'. This point was clearly brought out by veteran economist Chen Yun at the September 1985 'Special Conference' of the communist party when he criticised the agricultural reforms and warned the leadership that 'grain shortage will lead to social disorder.'[64]

The 'open door' policy and the concurrent development of agricultural export crops, industrial crops directly or indirectly for export (for example, cotton and silk for the garment export industry) and food processing for, or on behalf of, international agro-business, all influence land-use patterns as well as the underlying structure of ownership, rural income distribution and capital formation in agriculture. The shift in the structure of industrial development (that is, the emphasis on light industry) and more particularly the development of cheap labour export industries in the garment, footwear and related industries also requires the concurrent development and reinforcement of agro-industrial crops such as cotton, silk, and so on.

A policy of local self-sufficiency in grain is viewed by the Central Committee as an obstacle to the development of industrial crops:

> The growth of light industry has been hampered by the slow increase in cash crops in recent years. . . In regions suitable for growing cash crops, we must develop them in a planned way, giving top priority to the production of cotton and sugar. Simultaneously we must strive to increase the output of grain wherever conditions are suitable.[65]

Welcoming international agro-business

In 1981 Beatrice Foods, an international food-processing consortium, entered a major joint equity venture with the Guangzhou Foodstuff Corporation (a state enterprise) and China International Trust and Investment Corporation (CITIC), a state financial institution managed by Rong Yiren, a member of one of the largest Shanghai 'families' of pre-revolutionary China, and other members of the 'patriotic national bourgeoisie'.[66] The citrus juice product factory in Guangzhou is co-ordinated by a subsidiary of Beatrice, Tropicana products, the leading US producer of chilled orange juice. The same year Beatrice signed an agreement with the Chinese to form the Sino-American Food and Light Industry Coordinating and Advisory Group 'to evaluate future investments in agro-business and food processing'.[67] Moreover, the liberalisation and decentralisation of foreign trade and investment adopted in 1982–3 enables provincial authorities and state corporations to strike deals directly with international agro-business without central government approval.

In 1983, Nestlé set up a joint venture factory in the north-eastern province of Heilongjiang (see map p. xiii). Nestlé's factory will produce powdered milk both for the international and domestic markets (under Nestlé brand-name and Nestlé logus in Chinese characters).[68] The Nestlé deal was followed by a similar agreement with Bordens US, Nestlé's major international rival in the powdered milk business. 'The revenues of powdered milk exports will be used to repay Bordens for the licensing arrangement and the import of milk-processing technology.[69] Both the Nestlé and Bordens products sold in the domestic China market will complete with one another as well as with existing domestic brand names. According to Heilongjiang provincial trade officials, competition between foreign and domestic brand names 'is healthy because it forces Chinese companies to be more efficient . . . Some of these factories will close down, but under socialism this is not a problem because they can produce something else'.[70]

Hainan Island (Guangdong province) in the South China Sea (see map p. xiii) is being developed as a free trade zone specialising in tropical products by Hong Kong, American, Japanese and Australian transnationals. Jardine Matheson, the former British colonial company of Imperial China, now based in Hong Kong, has been negotiating with Hainan communist party officials since 1979 regarding the development of Hainan Island. According to Jardine Matheson officials their history as a major colonial company in pre-revolutionary China 'is an asset because for those who remember, we have more *credibility*.'

The north-eastern provinces and the Inner Mongolian region (see map p. xiii) are rapidly developing integrated projects of cattle raising, meat processing, and so on, in co-operation with foreign capital. In Heilongjiang, grain-fields are being used to produce grain for animals rather than for human consumption. Livestock ventures in co-operation with US corporate capital invariably involve integrated production from the development of grassland, processing of animal feed, meat processing for export, wool and hide. The International Fund for Agricultural Development (IFAD), the World Bank, the UNDP and other multilateral and bilateral agencies have provided funds in the areas of food-processing, animal husbandry, agricultural education, farm management, and so on.[71]

The International Development Association, the World Bank's concessionary lending affiliate, for instance, is supporting agricultural diversification and 'modernisation' primarily in livestock, fish products, agro-industry and cash crops. Guangxi has received, along with Guangdong and Fujian, increased autonomy in foreign trade and investment. The IDA loan will provide credit through the Agricultural Bank of China 'to individual farmers and collectives'.[72] In a first stage of the project, the Agricultural Bank of China's managerial and technical staff will be upgraded and its management system improved. The World Bank's Economic Development Institute is to organise and oversee courses in agricultural credit and investment appraisal.[73]

International credit channelled through the Agricultural Bank of China constitutes a powerful instrument which supports the restoration of capitalist farming as well as privately-owned rural industrial and agro-industrial enterprises.[74]

Concluding Remarks

This chapter has focused on the development of capitalist agriculture in the post-Mao period and the precise mechanics of 'transition' whereby collective structures and institutions are undone. Although these transformations were identified as the direct result of the post-Mao reforms, the collapse of the People's Commune should be understood in a broader historical context, namely in relation to the earlier process of collectivisation discussed in the previous chapter.

In this regard, the two distinct phases of *collectivisation* and *decollectivisation* belong to a single historical process in which the struggle against the established rural social order unfolds. Inasmuch as the People's Commune failed to eliminate the rich peasantry as a class, decollectivisation emerged from *within* the structure of collective agriculture, leading initially to the collapse of the collective work process and to the restoration of private production under the household responsibility system. From an initial phase based on the equal distribution of land to private households, under the so-called 'unified management' of the production team, these earlier reforms were conducive, in a subsequent phase, to the elimination of the production team and to the institutional collapse of the People's Commune. Concurrently, the fragmentation of landholdings under a system of equal distribution of land evolved towards a structure of land concentration, whereby the rich peasantry gained direct or indirect control over larger amounts of farm land. This spontaneous process, which took place in parallel with the *de facto* transfer of collective farm machinery to private entrepreneurs, was conducive to the emergence of thc so-called 'specialised household'.

The resulting unequal distribution of land and farm machinery was officially sanctioned by the CCP Central Committee as constituting the necessary avenue for the 'socialist modernisation of agriculture'. Private accumulation and appropriation by the so-called 'specialised household' is legitimised, encouraged and enforced concurrently with the development of agricultural credit to private farmers and the unfoldment of private channels of marketing and distribution initially competing with state marketing bodies.

The transition towards private commercial farming is also accompanied by a widening of income disparities in the countryside and, with the collapse of collective institutions, by: (a) the downgrading of rural social welfare programmes, and (b) the partial privatisation of health and educational programmes.

The agricultural reforms also affect in a fundamental way the relationship between the rural and urban economies. On the one hand they promote the subordination of the rural hinterland to the urban industrial base. This is particularly the case of the rural factories which are increasingly geared to the requirements of the urban economy. On the other hand the unfoldment of state capitalism in industry, and the reforms in industrial management (examined in detail in the following chapter), are conducive to:

(a) the polarisation of industry in the cities;
(b) an accentuation of urban-rural economic and social disparities;
(c) the development of a clear demarcation and division of labour between urban and rural activities.

Finally, the 'open door' to foreign capital interacts with the development of the agricultural reforms: the liberalisation of foreign trade influences the internal price structure of agricultural commodities and promotes the development of cash crops for export.

The underlying shift in land-use patterns is further accentuated by the entry of international agro-business into China's agricultural heartland, and by the concurrent development of an agricultural credit network supported by several major international banking and financial institutions.

In all their essential features those reforms constitute the basis for the rehabilitation of commercial farming and the development in China of a particular form of agrarian capitalism.

4

State Capitalism in Industry

Introduction

The Great Leap Forward and the Cultural Revolution were a struggle against the old social and managerial hierarchy inherited from bureaucratic capitalism and transposed at Liberation in the form of the Soviet model of industrial management. The various blue-prints of Soviet industrial management did not in themselves modify the social production relations which existed in Chinese industry prior to 1949. Inasmuch as they were themselves based on the practices of managerial hierarchy and centralised decision-making prevalent in the Soviet Union in the early 1950s, their formal adoption gave legitimacy to the old Confucian social order. The latter had to be broken, the democratisation of factory management could only be brought out through revolutionary struggle.

The Cultural Revolution failed, however, to radically transform the structure of factory management. In actuality, democratisation of industrial management was carried out successfully in a relatively small number of factories. It was primarily between May 1966 and the beginning of 1967 that there was a genuine attempt to establish revolutionary committees based on mass organisations and the workers' participation in the running of the factories. Had these attempts succeeded they may have led to fundamental changes in social and political relations. As of 1967, however, the political form of the Shanghai Commune was replaced by that of a revolutionary committee with limited political power. As of 1968, the revolutionary committees were increasingly under the control of the Communist party apparatus. In the aftermath of the Cultural Revolution, what remained of democratic factory management was undone, and the 'old' managerial hierarchy was rehabilitated in the context of the Central Committee's 1978 economic liberalisation policies. The development of factory management after Mao is, however, distinct from the structures proposed by the 'Rightist line' during the period of New Democracy. The 'open door' to foreign capital since 1978 will, in this regard, play an important role in the development of factory management because the international transfer of western 'managerial technology' takes place in parallel with China's reintegration into the structures of international trade, finance and investment. The liberalisation of trade and foreign investment, the establishment of joint ventures with foreign transnationals, as well as the formation in China of fully-owned subsidiaries of international corporate capital, constitute the means for the 'transfer of managerial technology', the adoption of western standards and concepts of management, and the development of educational institutions modelled on the American and Japanese business schools.

On the other hand, the 'open door' policy modifies the social class structure through the establishment of privileged links with 'expatriate' Chinese industrial, commercial and banking interests. The 'open door' policy to foreign capital and the expatriate bourgeoisie is conducive to the adoption of so-called 'western scientific management' while retaining the essential features of the old managerial hierarchy: a blend of western and oriental despotism which combines 'capitalist efficiency' with the Confucian social order.

None the less this marriage of western 'scientific management' and the old social order is not without its own contradictions. The transfer of western management methods will exert pressures on the hierarchical bureaucratic order in state enterprises which constitutes an obstacle to the 'modernisation of management along capitalist lines'. It is, however, not the old social hierarchy *per se* which is a barrier to 'modernisation', but an organisational fabric which is not tuned to the goals of 'efficiency', profit and capital accumulation.

Whether the management structure adopted at Liberation in the state sector bears formal resemblance to that prevalent in the Soviet Union is, in our opinion, of secondary importance in understanding the historical evolution of factory management in socialist China. The issue centres on an understanding of class relations within the factory characterised by the opposition, throughout the 1950s and leading up to the Great Leap Forward and the Cultural Revolution, between the 'old' managerial hierarchy of pre-Liberation and mass-line leadership based on democracy of factory management and the breaking up of the 'old' social division of labour. The organisational structure of the factory in pre-revolutionary China constitutes, in this regard, the foundations upon which despotic and hierarchical forms of management were maintained and sustained during the period of New Democracy. Whereas the old (Confucian) social order based on a strict code of discipline and authority was reformed and 'modernised' (formally along Soviet lines), several of its essential features have remained impervious to revolutionary change and the mass-line movement to democratise factory management.

In this chapter we examine first the historical origins of the factory system and the role of the national bourgeoisie in the development of modern industry. This historical background provides the basis for an understanding of:

(a) the system of state enterprises prevalent prior to 1949;
(b) the nature of the transition in the early 1950s from the 'bureaucratic capitalist' enterprises of the Kuomintang to the development of the state sector under socialism.

We then proceed to examine the managerial structures of the 1950s and 1960s in the context of the mass-movement to democratise factory management.

The industrial system after Mao is discussed with reference to the reforms adopted in several stages since 1978. Those reforms were implemented in parallel with the purges carried out at the enterprise level. Finally, the chapter discusses the new so-called 'scientific' management adopted after Mao and the concurrent development of American style business schools in support of the management reforms.

The National Bourgeoisie

What is the transition from 'bureaucratic' and 'comprador' capitalist structures during the Republican period and Japanese occupation to those which developed at Liberation under the formal impetus of the Soviet model of factory management? The structures of the pre-Liberation semi-colonial economy characterised by extraterritorial rights, the treaty ports and various spheres of foreign influence were decisive both in the growth of the so-called 'modern' factory system as well as in the establishment of 'state controlled or supervised enterprises' by the Qing and Republican governments as of the late nineteenth Century. These 'government-sponsored enterprises' which constituted the backbone of 'bureaucratic capitalism', in principle set up as a result of economic nationalism against the foreigners – in terms of the 'Movement of Recovering Economic Interests' – were at the same time an integral part of the economic structures of foreign domination: These enterprises were, in fact, primarily set up by 'the compradors who served as representatives of foreign firms . . . This was the group that was first called upon to operate the government sponsored modern enterprises and that figured prominently in the establishment of western type enterprises'.[1]

The issue is, of course, much broader in that it pertains to the historical origins of the national bourgeoisie. According to Wang Jingyu, the national bourgeoisie did not originate in feudal society in the course of the embryonic growth of capitalism in feudal society, rather it developed concurrently with the penetration of the Chinese economy by foreign capital.[2] According to Wang, the first 'modern' Chinese capitalist enterprises were established as a result of the 'Learn from the Foreigners' movement under the influence of 'the westernising bureaucrats' belonging to the landlord class. The newly-rising bureaucratic landlords who had amassed wealth by suppressing the Taiping Rebellion with the support of the foreigners, were to become, from the 1870s, a powerful force in the development of capitalism.

The bureaucratic landlords amassed considerable wealth which was invested in the formation of the first modern Chinese capitalist enterprises: The China Merchant's Steamship Navigation Company, the Kaiping Mining Bureau and the Shanghai Textile Bureau.[3] Wang Jingyu, however, suggests that whereas the bureaucratic landlords represented a force in the emergence of capitalist enterprises, 'they also bought large amounts of landed property to strengthen their position as landlords'. The main impetus in the development of industrial enterprises was provided by *comprador* investment by the money houses, that is, the profits of the *qianzhuang* (money houses) were reinvested in industry.[4]

Hou Chi-ming notes in this regard, that 'the compradors were not alone in imitating foreign firms and opening up modern enterprises. Bureaucrats, merchants, and, to a lesser degree, landlords also began to invest in varying degrees in western-type enterprises'.[5] Chinese-run enterprises were initially controlled by officials of the old social order and later on by merchants. Large Chinese enterprises in the treaty ports were either owned or backed by influential Chinese officials.[6] According to Lin Zhengping, however, it was primarily the warlord bureaucrats and compradors who invested in modern enterprises. These groups, moreover, became powerful and wealthy as a result of their association with foreign capital thereby laying the foundations for the 'westernisation enterprises'.[7]

The question is whether this movement was conducive to the formation of a 'national' capitalist class, *socially distinct* from bureaucratic and comprador capitalism. Lin Zhengping suggests that the westernisation enterprises of the late nineteenth century did not initially give rise to the growth of national capitalism but rather to the birth of early bureaucratic capitalism.[8] Other studies by Chinese economic historians confirm that comprador capital not only served imperialism in the invasion and pillage of China, but also in the setting up of industrial enterprises closely linked with foreign commercial and industrial interests in the treaty ports and leased territories. In other words, this process was not conducive to the transformation of comprador capitalism into national capital: industrial investment in 'westernisation enterprises' by compradors did not constitute the basis of the emergence of the national bourgeoisie. Zhang Guohui notes, in this regard, that 'private management under government supervision was adopted and promoted by the westernisation bureaucrats and big compradors and thus brought together the representatives of two reactionary forces: feudalism and imperialism'.[9]

Lin Zhengping and Zhang Kaiyuan, in their *History of the 1911 Revolution*, place the emergence of the national bourgeoisie as an independent and autonomous class at the turn of the century. Whereas the national bourgeoisie constituted the economic basis of the Reform Movement headed by Kang Youwei in the aftermath of the Sino-Japanese War of 1894–5 and the 1911 Revolution, it failed to become 'a strong and independent political force'.[10]

Contemporary Chinese scholars subdivide the Chinese bourgeoisie into: (1) the 'bureaucratic comprador bourgeoisie', and (2) the 'national bourgeoisie'. The process of 'distinguishing' between the two is none the less ambiguous, that is, as to 'the different interpretations of the term comprador, its range and boundaries and the different standards applied in ascertaining when a comprador became a national capitalist'.[11]

The 'National Patriotic Bourgeoisie'

The foregoing historical background is important because it enables us to identify in a correct historical perspective the role of the so-called '*national patriotic bourgeoisie*' in the development of the state sector both before and after 1949. Hence, as perceived by the 'Rightist' faction in the communist party (that is, under the influence of Liu Shaoqi), the 'national patriotic bourgeoisie' played an important role in the construction of socialism. Official CCP interpretations after Mao are, in this regard, similar to those promoted during the period of New Democracy by the 'Rightist' line, that is, the national bourgeoisie is considered 'a progressive social force' in the 'transition period'. Historically, however, the 'distinctions' and standards for ascertaining the existence of a separate and independent 'patriotic' national bourgeoisie are tenuous: communist party ideology after Mao (with the help of Chinese academic historians) has distorted the real nature of the Chinese bourgeoisie and its historical links with foreign capital. *At Liberation, historical forms of bureaucratic and comprador capitalism were maintained and embodied into the structure of the state enterprise.* The economic isolation from western capitalism (promoted by the United States foreign policy in the 1950s and 1960s), however, exerted a decisive influence on the development of the state enterprise because it deprived it of its comprador links with foreign capital. The circumstances of the state enterprise are, in this regard, radically different in the post-Mao period.

Mao on the national bourgeoisie

According to Mao, the national bourgeoisie played an important role in the development of state capitalism in the early 1950s. Mao Zedong indeed considered that state capitalism was 'the only road for the transformation of capitalis industry and commerce and for the gradual completion of the transition to socialism'.[12] The national bourgeoisie was in a sense considered a 'social instrument' of this transition process, first in the formation of joint state-private enterprises and subsequently, from the mid-1950s, in the development of state enterprises 'owned by the whole people'. The nationalisation of the joint state-private enterprises, while changing the *formal* structure of ownership did not in itself modify the underlying social relations because, despite the reforms, the state factory was still managed by representatives of the national bourgeoisie and by the mandarins, professionals and engineers of the old social order.

In this transition process, the 'national patriotic bourgeoisie' was considered a progressive social force contributing to the construction of socialism and socially distinct from the comprador and bureaucratic capitalists associated with the Kuomintang and the imperialist powers. This distinction, in many instances, was tenuous and in practice related to a *de facto* differentiation between the 'patriotic' elements of the bourgeoisie who chose to remain in China at Liberation and those who fled with the Kuomintang.

Mao Zedong's position *vis-à-vis* the national bourgeoisie, although distinct from that of his opponents in the CCP, was, none the less, one of extreme moderation. In the early period of New Democracy, Mao Zedong promoted a policy of 'class alliance' in the private sector, encouraging workers to co-operate with private capitalists.[13] The economic structures of New Democracy were (according to Mao) 'transitional', however, in that under the dictatorship of the proletariat and the leadership of the communist party, the 'patriotic bourgeoisie' – a 'progressive force' in the transition process – would gradually be taken over, leading to the formation of socialist state enterprises 'owned by the whole people'. In parallel, the national bourgeoisie would be 'remoulded'. Mao considered that this 'remoulding of the exploiters' was only possible if 'in the course of work, they should engage in labour together with the staff and workers in the enterprises.'[14]

The dictatorship of the proletariat in state industry and commerce was precarious: from the early 1950s, 'factory despotism' and the old social order and division of labour were firmly entrenched. Many members of the 'national patriotic bourgeoisie' and mandarins of bureaucratic capitalism had in fact joined the communist party at Liberation. In this context, it is understandable why the struggle against the bourgeoisie (and the so-called 'capitalist road') was also a struggle within the party against their representatives and those who under the formal disguise of Marxism-Leninism were pursuing and implementing a liberal-reformist project. It is also understandable that 'Liu Shaoqi and Company' were alternatively and equally identified (during the Cultural Revolution) as 'the Soviet Renegade Clique' and 'those who had adopted the capitalist road' because the adherents of the Soviet Model of management were essentially the adherents of bureaucratic capitalism. 'Firmly establishing the new democratic social order' proposed by the 'Rightist' faction in the CCP was tantamount to the development of liberal reformism and the consolidation of state capitalism.

Mao, in 1953, confronted liberal-reformist economic policy (which was intended to promote private capital) in his controversial attack on Bo Yibo's tax system entailing 'equality between private and public enterprises':

> That system, if allowed to develop, would have led inevitably to capitalism . . . Bo Yibo's mistake is a manifestation of bourgeois ideas. It benefits capitalism and harms socialism and semi-socialism . . . The bourgeoisie is sure to corrode people and aim its sugar-coated bullets at them. Its sugar-coated bullets are of two kinds, material and spiritual. A spiritual one hit its target Bo Yibo. He made his mistake because he succumbed to the influence of bourgeois ideas. The editorial preaching the new tax system was applauded by the bourgeoisie, and Bo Yibo was pleased. Before the new tax system was initiated, he solicited suggestions from the bourgeoisie and reached a gentleman's agreement with them.[15]

Mao's attempts to undermine the liberal-reformist line within the party failed and, as of the mid-1950s the Liu faction was in control of the Central Committee, the Politbureau and the CCP Secretariat. The 1956 Party Constitution omits reference to Mao Zedong Thought as described in the 1949 version.[16] Whereas Mao retained the chairmanship of the Central Committee, Liu Shaoqi became first Vice-Chairman and Deng Xiaoping was appointed General Secretary of the party.[17] In 1958 the Central Committee Plenum adopted a resolution

> to 'accept' Mao's request not to be the State Chairman . . . Every effort was made to convey the impression that Mao had made the move voluntarily. Mao himself commented many years later at the outset of the Cultural Revolution in October 1966: 'I was extremcly discontent with that decision but I could do nothing about it.'[18]

Bureaucratic Management under Socialism

Mao Zedong had advocated mass-line leadership prior to Liberation during the Yanan period. The mass movement in industry developed in the early 1950s, in opposition to the bureaucratisation of factory management which accompanied the formal adoption of the Soviet model of management. In 1953, under the First Five Year Plan, industrial departments adopted the system of 'one man management'. Gao Gang's Chinese version of 'one man management' was based on the granting of exclusive managerial authority to the factory director over and above that of the 'collective leadership of the party', that is, of the local party committee'.[19] 'The leadership of management was actually pitted against the leadership of the Party, denying the Party organisation a leadership role which it should play and reducing it to a subordinate status.[20]

The division of authority between the factory director and the local party committee was a contentious issue. In principle, the CCP had proposed, from 1949, a system based on the 'collective leadership of the party' involving a dual structure of authority between the party and the industrial ministries which appointed the factory director. Gao Gang's 'one man management' proposed by the 'Rightist' line reduced the influence of the local party organisation. Although the dual command structure was conducive to bureaucratisation and polarisation in decision-making, the local party committee represented an institutional channel which, in principle, enabled workers to have some input in decision-making. The extent to which this took place depended largely on the relationship between the local party organisation and the workers and the extent of genuine collective democratic leadership. In many instances the party committee monopolised all branches of administrative work, and was in fact an obstacle to carrying out the mass movement. At the Eighth CCP Congress in 1956, Gao Gang's 'one man management' was abolished, the conference system of worker and employee representatives (which in one form or another remained in existence until the present) was introduced.[21]

The workers conference system

The Workers' Conference system, superimposed on the existing managerial hierarchy, constituted the basis of a corporate industrial structure, similar for instance to that which exists today in Japan, whereby the social subordination of workers is achieved through a system of formal representation with little or no input of workers in actual decision-making. This system is based on a clear social demarcation between workers and cadres and essentially retains the authority of the managers and engineers. Li Xue-feng (Li Hsueh-feng), director of the Industrial Work Department of the Central Committee in 1957, described this system as follows:

> When it comes to the execution of the plans, these cadres also simply rely on administrative decrees rather than conduct political and ideological work among the masses. With regard to the rationalisation proposal and advanced experiences which the masses of staff and workers have made and gained in connection with production technique, they take no notice of them nor do they support them . . . The staff and workers' membership meeting and the staff and workers' congress are supposedly the best form in which to foster democracy in the enterprises. Now they

> are often turned into assemblages through which the leadership assigns tasks and the masses give pledges . . . The masses of staff and workers describe such meetings: 'The director makes the report, the party committee gives instructions, the trade union issues the call, and the masses give the pledge'.[22]

The workers' conference system was in fact an imitation of the Soviet model of 'the production conference'.[23] The dual structure of bureaucratism combining the authority of the factory director with the 'party's collective leadership' which stemmed from the Soviet model, was in contradiction with the dictatorship of the proletariat which, according to Mao, required its own system of democratic management.

The issue as to the 'correct' relationship between the factory director and the party committee was a false dilemma because it underscored the fundamental struggle against economism and the old managerial hierarchy according to which experts, professionals and managers, rather than working people, are those competent to run the factory. Yang Shiqie (Yang Shih-chieh) – then First Secretary of the Anshan Municipal Party Committee and one of the promoters of the Anshan Charter of mass-line leadership in industrial management – describes the 'two line struggle' as follows:

> One line is the correct proletarian line of running enterprises – featuring an adherence to putting politics in command, exercising the party's absolute leadership over the enterprise, and applying the work method of mass-line so that the concentrated leadership can be integrated with extensive mass movements . . . Another is the mistaken capitalist line of running enterprises – a line that insists on 'putting techniques in command', 'putting economy in command' and stresses the role of technical experts.[24]

'Putting techniques in command' coincides with a narrow economism which stresses the linear development of productive forces and which, according to its adherents, 'is based on the principles of scientific socialism'. On the other hand, it also converges with western modernisation theories which identify an emerging enterpreneurial élite with acquired professional and managerial skills as the sole social agent of modernisation. Priority is given to production, profit and a system of material incentives.

After the Great Leap, the reaction against 'mass-line leadership' gained impetus. In response to the Anshan Charter, the 'Rightists' reacted with the 'Seventy Articles on Industrial Management' drafted by Bo Yibo. This document formalised and revived the 'chief accountant system' and the 'chief engineer system', both of which were counterparts of the Soviet model of management.[25] The chief accountant system reintroduced after 1962 emphasised financial control and supervision by the chief accountant who was accountable not only to the factory director but also to higher echelons, that is, to the bureaus of the ministry.[26] The 'chief engineer system' was restored during the 1963 National Technical Conference as a result of Bo Yibo's 'Draft Regulations Concerning Production and Technical Responsibility'. The latter stated that 'technical personnel should be given authority and status; the chief engineer should serve concurrently as the first deputy director'.[27] The motto of this system was that *Non-experts should not command experts*.

Neoclassical economics has failed to understand the opposition and antagonism between these two so-called 'competing models of management' because it essentially views the problem in terms of a 'systems approach', that is, a choice between alternative abstract organisational blueprints to be evaluated in terms of their respective economic results. Ultimately, the choice between alternative models is viewed in terms of 'the trade-off between growth and justice'. According to Huntington and Nelson, the so-called 'technocratic model' stresses the role of experts and managers as an instrument of economic growth, whereas the so-called 'populist model' of management (that is, democratic management) 'emphasises distributive justice and mobilisation of industrial workers and other low income classes'.[28]

The 'choice' between models is viewed as a choice between 'competing' social and economic objectives: democratic management is incompatible with the objective of increased production, *therefore*, modernisation requires, at least in its initial stages, hierarchical, non-democratic and despotic forms of management based on the authority of managers and engineers. This is the inevitable 'social cost' of modernisation. Needless to say, the foregoing approach avoids the substantive issue of political and social struggle. The opposition between the two models is not simply a question of 'styles of management', it is a struggle of two social classes which confront one another, both within the factory and the communist party.

Apologists of 'putting technology in command' have argued that 'scientific' models of management are 'more efficient' because they encourage production and technological innovation. The presumption is that advanced technology at the factory level is solely promoted and applied by engineers, managers and experts in the context of the so-called 'specialised responsibility system' and that democratisation of management would:

> 'throw the order in production into confusion', 'destroy the equilibrium in production' and impede 'the normal progress in production'. These people describe the unfolding of extensive mass movement as 'a rural work style' . . . that once the masses are aroused, the so-called 'equilibrium in production' would be swept away. They only attach importance

to ready answers available in books, but slight the creations and inventions of the masses.[29]

The experience of 'mass-line leadership' in China, both prior and during the Cultural Revolution, suggests, on the contrary, that democratisation of factory management was not in opposition with efficiency because, rather than 'relying on a handful of experts', it mobilised the masses of workers collectively in carrying out technological improvements and increasing productivity and output.

Factory Management after Mao

In 1978, the CCP Central Committee issued its so-called '30-Point Decision on Industry' ('Decisions of the Central Committee of the Communist Party of China on Some Questions Concerning the Acceleration of Industrial Development (Draft)') to departments and localities for implementation on a 'trial basis'.[30] The document is notoriously ambiguous; it was issued at a time when Hua Guofeng was still *formally* in power and the Cultural Revolution had not yet been 'officially' repudiated. As such, it reflects the confrontation within the CCP, between 'moderate Maoists' and supporters of Deng Xiaoping.

Many of these changes, however, were being carried out in the early 1970s prior to the demise of the group of Four. In 1975 Deng Xiaoping had proposed his '20-Points on Industry' ('Some Problems in Accelerating Industrial Development') together with two other documents entitled 'On the General Programme for All Work of the Party and the Country' and 'Some Problems Concerning the Work of Science and Technology'. These documents were labelled by Deng's opponents as 'the three poisonous weeds' and were used in the course of 1976 in the mass movement against the 'Right deviationists'. Seven months after the fall of the group of Four, the 'three poisonous weeds' were praised as the 'three fragrant flowers', thus paving the way for the rehabilitation of Deng Xiaoping.[31] The '30-Point Decision on Industry', which contains those points presented in Deng's '20-Point' document, constitutes, despite its rhetorical references to 'mass-line leadership', the policy basis for restoring the authority of the factory mandarins and engineers. Whereas the '30-Point' document refers rhetorically to Mao Zedong Thought, the Anshan Charter, 'Learning from Daqing' and the reorganisation of state factories according to the principles of mass-line leadership, it also recommends reducing the authority of the party committee and strengthening that of the factory director. It also rehabilitates the role of the managers, engineers and technicians according to the system of 'specialised responsibility': 'Engineers and technicians in an enterprise shall have the power commensurate with their posts so that they shoulder real responsibility in technical matters'.[32] The document emphasises the reform of the wage system according to the 'socialist' principle 'from each according to his ability, to each according to this work' and proposes the introduction of piece-rate remuneration, bonuses and penalties.

'Democratic management' in the form of the Workers' Congress under the leadership of the party committee, will be introduced so that 'workers may hear reports on work made by the leaders of the enterprise, offer criticisms or suggestions on the work and supervise the leading cadres of the enterprise'.[33] In this corporate structure there is, however, no question of workers actually participating in the management of the factory or of managers engaging in manual labour.

It is worth noting, in this context, that both the experiences of Daqing Oil fields and Dazhai rural production brigade were given prominence in CCP pronouncements until 1982. Dazhai was first discredited on the grounds that it had reported large harvests while many peasants went hungry. Whereas Daqing's 'key experience' was strongly criticised in 1980, it was officially back in favour in early 1982 when the Central Committee called upon factory workers to emulate 'the revolutionary way workers at the Daqing oil fields had worked hard in the early 1960s'.[34] It also stated rather ambiguously that 'Daqing's key experience' was to give priority to ideological work and the creation of management systems, including personal responsibility and the role of 'experts' in running the factory. 'We must not demand that experts participate in a lot of political activities and read many Marxist-Leninist works – nor must we expect them to participate in physical labour'.[35]

This apparent duality between official CCP rhetoric (stressing Marxism-Leninism-Mao Zedong Thought), and *actual* economic and social policies, served the useful purpose of distorting the true meaning of the reforms under the formal disguise of scientific socialism, while at the same time appeasing an important pro-Mao opposition within and outside the ranks of the communist party. None the less, this duality should also be interpreted as transitional towards the development of a new communist party rhetoric and ideology first evidenced after the removal of Hua Guofeng from political power in 1980, increasingly based on the economism of modernisation.

Political purges of factory leaders

The main thrust of the '30-Points on Industry', however, does not lie in its formal provisions. Its main objective is political in that it constitutes an articulate programme for systematically conducting the purges against 'Leftists elements' and so-called 'supporters of the Gang of Four still active at the factory level':

> In the course of exposing and criticising the Gang of Four thoroughly, all localities and units must . . . devote a period of time to boldly arousing the masses to carry to success the 'double blow' struggle in a guided and systematic way under the unified leadership and plan of provincial, municipal and autonomous region party committees. The main target is the handful of class enemies engaged in disruptive activities . . . Where the power of leadership has been usurped by bad elements, it must resolutely be seized back. Work teams should be sent to enterprises where problems abound . . . [P]eople who harbour wild ambitions, who are politically deviant and have an abnoxious work-style must not be allowed to sit in leading bodies or be given important jobs.[36]

Whether an enterprise is 'effectively shaken up' is to be judged by a set of political and economic criteria pertaining to:

> whether the investigation into individuals and incidents associated with the Gang's conspiratorial activities has been successfully concluded . . . whether various rules and regulations centred around the system of job responsibility have been instituted and strictly enforced, whether the administrative structure of the enterprise has been streamlined.[37]

The 'purging' of 'Leftist elements' in state enterprises has been carried out without major upheavals since 1978, and consists essentially in rehabilitating the authority of the 'old guard' factory cadres favourable to the 'Rightist' line and demoting, reassigning and in many instances, prosecuting for 'criminal offences' those 'class enemies associated with the Gang's conspiratorial activities'.[38] There have been several 'waves' of purges and clampdowns on dissidents from the Central Committee down to grassroots' organisations. These were conducted in terms of the leadership's 'streamlining' of the state bureaucracy, communist party apparatus and People's Liberation Army discussed in chapter one. The so-called 'crack-down on corruption, economic crimes and delinquency' was in some cases used as a pretext to repress and criminally prosecute political dissidents.[39] As has been officially stated:

> We must be resolute in removing those who persist in opposing or boycotting party policies . . . Opportunists who sneaked into the party with clandestine motives and ambitious people who made trouble and engage in sabotage must be eliminated from the ranks.[40]

Maoist partisans were also eliminated as a result of the underlying institutional changes at the factory level. The reforms adopted after Mao consisted, in the first instance, in restoring or rehabilitating the old managerial hierarchy, eliminating the revolutionary committees and the workers' management groups (which had in fact already been taken over by the 'Right' prior to 1976) and rehabilitating a corporate structure of formal representation of workers, in the form of the workers' congresses, with little or no real participation in actual decision-making.

Trade union organisations are integrated into the corporate structure of the enterprise. The trade union structure at the factory level in effect overlaps with that of the workers' congress and the party committee. The grass-roots trade unions are working bodies of the workers' congress as laid down in the 1981 'Provisional Regulations for the Workers' and Staff Members' Congress', which defines the congress as the 'power organ where the masses participate in the enterprise management and decision-making'.[41] The functions of the trade union coincide, therefore, with those of the workers' congress. Inasmuch as there is 'no conflict of basic interests between the state, the enterprise and the individual', the interests of workers are 'resolved' through 'democratic management'. The trade union is also responsible for workers' education programmes, social and welfare services, and so on.

The Workers' Conference (congress), which in practice coincides with the trade union structure, is elected by factory workers, staff and cadres. The Conference in turn elects a presidium of 10 to 15 members which reports to the plenary. The latter meets once or twice a year in a formal meeting and is invariably involved in the organisation of social activities and cultural events. The presidium meets regularly with the executive committee of the factory. The presidium membership is characterised by equal one-third representation respectively of workers, white-collar staff, cadres and technicians. Technical and managerial cadres are often members of both the executive committee and the presidium. Workers, however, are not represented on the executive management committee.

In the context of corporate social relations at the factory level, the Workers' Conference and trade union system converts itself into an effective means of personnel management under the *de facto* control of senior management:

> The union's responsibility is to safeguard the welfare of the workers and help improve their living standards under the [socialist] principle 'to each according to his work'. They co-operate with government departments and factory administrations to improve the system of wages and bonuses so that *the material interests of the individual workers co-ordinate with the rate of labour efficiency and the rate of profit*.[42]

The executive management committee

The executive committee of the factory is composed of the factory director appointed by the government ministry, and six members or deputy directors who invariably are in charge of the various departments of the factory. The deputy directors and members of the executive committee are sometimes appointed by the government, sometimes by the factory director, who under the new regulations will have increased autonomy in making these appointments. According to the new rules adopted in 1983, the factory director is to be 'elected' by the workers but 'nominated and approved' by the government.

The factory is divided into a number of 'departments' or sections: for example, personnel, finance, quality control, planning and production, technology, marketing, and so on. Each of these departments is managed by a deputy director who is a member of the factory's executive management committee. The departments are in turn subdivided into workshops and/or offices. In the workshops (for example, the workshops responsible for various phases of production), the 'group leaders' or foremen are either elected by their fellow workers or appointed by the deputy director in charge of the department. The foreman is responsible for the work performed by the members of his workshop. He reports to the department director (a professional engineer or managerial cadre), who in turn reports to the factory director. The structure is hierarchical and compartmentalised: workers in the respective workshops involved in specific tasks have little contact with workers in other workshops. Orders are sent down to the department directors and then to the workshop foremen, information is communicated upwards. An apparent pseudo-democracy, characterised by the democratic election of workshop foremen, is inserted into an essentially despotic and hierarchical command structure. Democracy in the workshop thereby serves the interest of the corporate management structure because it constitutes a social mechanism which subordinates workers to the higher echelons of management.

The leaders of China's 'modernisation' are a new generation of managers and engineers. An entrepreneurial élite class of mandarins and decision-makers has replaced the masses of workers and peasants as the 'agents of China's socialist construction'. '"We must rely on the working class", not because of that class's spirit of initiative but because "*it is strictest in observing discipline and obeying orders*"'.[43] Workers are *socially* removed from the processes of deciding how the factory is run. With the development of *socially* stratified categories of factory employees, *cadres* are not only 'divorced from the masses'; the new system requires a network of authority and supervision which enforces discipline and the workers' social subordination to the material process of production.

Although the party still performs important functions within the factory, the party committee 'no longer intervenes in management'. In some factories, one or two members of the party committee are on the executive management committee; increasingly the tendency is for the executive committee to be composed only of managerial and technical cadres.

Selected cases of factory management (see Table 4.1)

In Shenyang Small Tractor Factory, Liaoning province, the executive committee is composed of the director, four deputy directors, the party secretary and one other member from the party. Party officials do not intervene in production management, they are responsible for education, ideology, social welfare and cultural events:

> Before the Cultural Revolution we had the Soviet management responsibility system which implied centralised management. During the Cultural Revolution, party leadership was integrated into management and the party intervened in the running of the factory. Now we have divided the functions. The party only works in party affairs. During the Cultural Revolution there were workers' management committees of 30-40 members responsible for quality control, production, technology, etc. The members of these committees were in principle elected but in fact they were appointed by the party. There were workers, cadres and technicians on each of these committees. The committees reported to the Revolutionary Committee. During the Cultural Revolution there were three committees: *production and planning, political*, and *social services*. Now we have 16 committees which correspond to the different departments – e.g. they are specialised in various activities such as quality control, production, marketing, etc. The cadres and technicians dominate these departments. *The workers, however, are the masters of the factory*.[44]

In municipal factories and enterprises the structures tend to be more democratic than in state factories. In Chang Zheng Municipal Garment Factory in Shenyang, for instance, there is no executive management committee. The factory director and the deputy director, although appointed by the municipal government, were nominated by their fellow workers. There are ten sections (departments) under the authority of the factory director. The standing committee (presidium) of the workers' conference with representation from workers, cadres and staff meets once a month:

> Before the Cultural Revolution we adopted the Soviet system of centralised management. The Cultural Revolution was a reaction to this structure. During the Cultural Revolution, the party secretary decided everything: both political and production decisions. Now we have management by managers and the workers congress for democratic management. The director and the deputy director are responsible to the workers' congress. Although the party secretary is mainly involved in

political activities, important decisions will have to be approved by the party committee.[45]

Guangzhou Shipyard Container Factory was set up in 1978 as a co-operative joint venture based on compensation trade with ICT (International Container Transport) – a US-owned container rental company – to produce containers for ICT. Before 1978 the factory was a branch of Guangzhou Shipyard involved in shipbuilding:

> In 1978, we combined foreign management with domestic management and we adopted the specialised responsibility system according to which each working position is assigned predetermined tasks. There is a director and a deputy director, there is no [executive] management committee, there is no workers' congress in this factory although there is representation of this factory at the level of the Guangzhou Shipyard. There is no standing committee of workers in the factory.[46]

In Parker Hubei – an equity joint venture between Parker Seals (US) and Hubei Auto Works – the factory is run by an executive director who is appointed by Hubei Auto Works. (For further details on the nature of the Parker Hubei joint venture see chapter 8.)

The board of directors of five members includes the factory director, two members appointed by Hubei Auto Works and two members representing the US Company. There is no workers' congress:

> We will use modern management methods. We co-operate in management with Parker; some management methods are American, some are based on our domestic experience because it is quite different in China. The engineers are responsible for the departments and direct the specific tasks of workers in particular areas. The engineers report to the factory director. The factory does not have departments (sections) and workshops as in a regular state factory. The engineers administer both technical and managerial functions. In other state factories, managerial and technical functions are divided.[47]

The Transfer of Scientific Management

The process of 'combination' of state enterprises with foreign capital exerts a decisive influence on the structure of enterprise management and factory organisation. The issue does not pertain to the adoption of western methods of cost accounting, quality and production control, inventory management, and so on, *per se*. Indeed, many of these techniques can be

TABLE 4.1 *Management structure, selected factories*

Factory	*Management structure*	*Composition of work force*	*Workers' congress and trade union*
HUNAN AUTOMOTIVE PARTS FACTORY, CHANGSHA, HUNAN (1982)	Executive management committee of 6 members who are deputy directors of various departments (technology, sales, production) headed by factory director appointed by provincial government.	300 workers, 251 engineers and technicians	Workers' congress of 300 with a presidium of 11 members composed of one-third workers, one-third engineers and technicians, one-third cadres. Presidium and trade union coincide.
HUNAN JIAN XIANG PORCELAIN FACTORY, CHANGSHA, HUNAN (1982)	Factory director is appointed by the government and the department directors by the Light Industry Bureau, Hunan. No real consultations with workers regarding these appointments.		The presidium is composed of 15 members. Presidium reports to the plenary, the presidium meets in joint sessions with committee.
GUANGZHOU MACHINE TOOLS FACTORY (1982)	Factory director appointed by the government, factory run by enterprise management committee composed of department directors. Six members and director.	9 workshops, 2400 workers, 192 staff and supervisory, 120 technical and engineering	No representative council of workers since 1978.
HARBIN WOOL WEAVER FACTORY, HARBIN, HEILONGJIANG (1983)	Executive management committee of six members plus director. Factory director appointed by factory members.		Workers' congress with elected presidium.

SHENYANG SMALL TRACTOR FACTORY, LIAONING (1983)	2 party members, 5 cadres of which factory director. The party does not intervene in management. In the workshops, group leaders are elected.		Workers' congress with elected presidium. During the Cultural Revolution the revolutionary committees were formed of cadres and workers responsible for management. They were in principle elected, in practice nominated by party (15 members). The revolutionary committee had subcommittees of 30–40 members in each section. Now each section is under control of cadres and engineers.
SHENYANG MUNICIPAL GARMENT FACTORY, LIAONING (1983)	No management committee. The director and deputy director are responsible directly to workers' presidium, 10 sections under management of director. Party secretary does not intervene in management. Factory director elected by workers.		Workers' congress and presidium. The presidium is composed of workers, managers and staff, meets once a month.

SOURCE Factory interviews conducted in China in 1982 and 1983.

usefully adapted and applied in a socialist economy. Mao 'On the Ten Major Relationships' stated that while

> we must firmly reject and criticise all the decadent bourgeois systems . . . this should not prevent us from learning the advanced sciences and technologies of capitalist countries and whatever is scientific in the management of their enterprises. In the industrially developed countries they run their enterprises with fewer people and greater efficiency and they know how to do business.[48]

The issue pertains not to the adoption of managerial techniques *per se* but to the embodiment of the social relations, structure of authority and division of labour prevalent in the advanced capitalist countries.

Management education after Mao

Chinese managers are to be trained at American style business schools set up in China since 1979. Many of these are established through pairing arrangements with an American, Canadian or Japanese university. USAID and its Canadian counterpart CIDA are funding agreements between major US and Canadian business schools and the large 'key' Chinese universities. These agreements involve scholarships to the US and Canada at the Master of Business Administration (MBA) and PhD levels; visiting professors in the fields of business, finance, marketing, and so on, visit China to advise on the setting up of equivalent 'fully-owned and operated' MBA programmes in China. Visiting professors will help train and upgrade the Chinese teaching staff and act as consultants in curriculum planning.

The establishment of these agreements, and the transfer of managerial technology, seems to accompany the entry of western capital into China, and the establishment of joint ventures. The major joint ventures have provisions for the training of managerial and technical staff. In 1981, when Coca Cola established its bottling plant in Beijing, the company set up a scholarship programme (financed by Coca Cola) sponsoring Harvard University Master of Business Administration (MBA) scholarships for Chinese students.[49] Xerox Foundation (in the context of Xerox's operations in China) and Unison International are sponsoring jointly with the China Enterprise Management Association (CEMA) a lecture series 'on business strategy, business policy and decision-making methods used by US businesses'.[50] The three-year lecture series funded by Xerox will visit several major industrial centres, and be conducted by faculty members from US graduate schools of business administration.

Concurrently, the study of western 'scientific management' is promoted by the translation of western texts on management and the publication of several academic and technical periodicals in the areas of western business administration and management science.[51]

At the Dalian Centre for Industrial Science and Technology Management Development, a fully-fledged American Master of Business Administration (MBA) programme was set up in 1979 in co-operation with New York State University (NYSU). (Since then similar MBA programmes have been set up in many of China's key universities). *It is NYSU and not Dalian which is the degree-granting institution – that is, a US university grants an American MBA degree at a Chinese state-supported academic institution.*[52] The Dalian programme is jointly sponsored by the US Department of Commerce under an American government science exchange programme.

Richard Lee of the US Department of Commerce stated in an interview that: 'The Americans [at Dalian] were at first worried about the ideological differences. But the Chinese told us, "Don't worry about that. Just tell us how you work and we'll adapt to our society".'[53]

The response of the 700 graduates of Dalian's six-month trainee programme for senior managers and factory directors was reported as 'enthusiastic':

> 'Of course I didn't learn how to be a capitalist', said Zhang Shu'en, a graduate of the course who works for the Ministry of Urban and Rural Construction. 'But I did learn many useful things about management' . . . Yu Fuxiang, deputy director of the Shanghai Electrical Appliance Corporation, explained that his company was importing some foreign equipment and technology. What he'd learned in the course about depreciation, predictions of service lifecycles and management accounting had proved very useful in deciding what to buy. Ji Guocai talked enthusiastically about financial control mechanisms.[54]

The policy of the Dalian Institute is that graduates share what they have learnt as widely as possible thereby contributing to the training of junior and mid-career managerial cadres: *[o]ne group of centre alumni from the Shanghai Economic Planning Committee have already set up a research and teaching unit on American Management techniques.*[55]

The agreement with NYSU and the US Department of Commerce is geared towards a major American input in the first years of operation of the 'joint venture'. Thereafter, Dalian should become 'self-reliant', and capable of developing its programme on the basis of its own resources and academic staff:

> American experts from the University of California at Berkeley, the City University of New York, Columbia, Massachusetts Institute of Technology and New York State University have been invited to teach. . . In

> the first few years, the Americans carried the major share of the teaching load but this year [1983] the Chinese faculty taught seven of the seventeen courses. Both the Chinese and American staff are heavily involved in curriculum planning. *Much of the original teaching material was also American*, but it is now rapidly being supplemented by specially developed Chinese materials.[56]

At Dalian the motto is 'Adapt, Not Copy' because 'whereas market knowledge is important . . . market forces will always be subordinate to the planned economy':

> Profits, which American texts talk of as the sole goal and reason for being of an enterprise, will never play the same role in Chinese enterprises . . . Chinese manaagers also have a lot to learn about cutting costs and raising productivity, but the common western method of firing workers will never be an option in socialist China.[57]

The Dalian Institute is to develop China's management theory and practice, 'using beneficial portions of American experiences as input': 'We are not here to tell the Chinese how to run their enterprises, but to introduce our practices from which the Chinese can pick and choose'.[58]

None the less, although many of 'the techniques' of management could indeed be usefully applied, the underlying framework, including the American case study teaching method and the computer simulation game of rivalry between competing firms in the market, is by no means an 'ideologically neutral' device for 'scientific management' under socialism:

> Another intriguing pre-graduation exercise adopted from American practice is a computer simulation game. The trainees are divided into five member groups, each in charge of an imaginary competing company. . . By the end of the exercise some of the managers have gained a big profit, some have just about broken even, while others have gone bankrupt.[59]

In the words of Mo Zhongyu, a Dalian graduate whose 'company' went bankrupt in the simulation game, the exercise 'had taught him that failure was due to poor market surveys, . . . and loose financial controls . . . "[I]t gave me a taste of the ruthless capitalist style competition between enterprises. I feel lucky I'm not the manager of such a company in real life"'.[60]

At the Management Training Programme of the Shanghai Institute of Mechanical Engineering (SIME), a Master's level degree is offered in a co-operative venture with the Sloan School of Management, Massachusetts Institute of Technology and the School of Engineering, Stanford

University. The Shanghai Master's programme trains a select number of 'would-be lecturers' in management. The programme is modelled on those of 'the best' US business schools. *Instruction is (with the exception of one course on the Chinese industrial enterprise) conducted entirely in English by US professors.* The programme at SIME consists of 'core subjects' in micro- and macro-economics, behavioural science, financial management, decision analysis, marketing, and so on, with a 'major area of concentration' in operations management and a 'minor' in information systems. The major purpose of this SIME programme is to train Chinese professors to teach in independent (and 'autonomous') Chinese business schools.

Whereas the setting up of American style business schools is consistent with the general direction of the reforms in the system of enterprise management, there is also evidence of considerable resistance by factory cadres to the adoption of western management tecniques. This opposition, however, is only partly ideological in nature (that is, based on an 'anticapitalist bias'), that is, the main thrust of resistance to so-called 'scientific management' takes its roots in the 'old' bureaucratic social order and hierarchy of central planning. None the less, the state is exercising strong pressures on factory directors to 'modernise' and graduation from the new western style management training programmes is generally a means to both advancement and promotion.

The transfer of intellectual technology

It is worth noting that these reforms in management education have not been carried out in isolation but in the context of a major restructuring of China's system of higher education. In universities, 'Rightist' intellectuals, many of whom had been unjustly persecuted during the Cultural Revolution, have been rehabilitated. Senior positions in departments and institutes were handed over to returning 'Overseas Chinese' and to academics trained in the West. According to official sources, more than one-third of the heads of research institutions in 1984 were Overseas Chinese.

An élitist system of education based on key universities has been reinstated. Ninety-eight universities and institutions of higher learning are singled out as intellectual growth poles. Twenty-six out of these will have their research facilities upgraded with the support of a major loan from the World Bank.[61]

In this regard, the educational system is on the one hand the reflection of the class structure. On the other hand, it is a reflection of the material and social requirements of production. Education is no longer viewed as a social objective in itself but as an instrumental means for the training of skilled, specialised and professional manpower. The 'output' of the educational system constitutes an objective 'input' of so-called *human capital* into production. Education is subordinated to the process of capital accumulation:

universities, colleges and technical schools are geared towards the formation of an élite army of engineers, managers and technicians for China's 'modernised' state enterprises. In many respects the American college model which shaped the development of the Chinese university system during Chiang Kaishek's Kuomintang rule is being restored. The educational reforms promulgated in 1922 had been modelled on the US educational system. The US had 16 American missionary colleges and controlled the larger Chinese universities through direct funding and the leadership of American trained academics and intellectuals. The US had also an important influence in the primary and secondary education established under the Kuomintang. This American influence on the development of the Chinese educational system has now re-emerged in a new form; training and research programmes in China are being developed in collaboration with foreign academic and research institutions.

With the opening up of educational exchanges and scholarship programmes with overseas universities, high level cadres are increasingly anxious to send their children to academic institutions in the United States, Western Europe and Japan. In 1893, 17 000 Chinese students were studying abroad of which more than 10 000 were in the United States.[62] This includes an important contingent in American business schools as well as a group of Chinese students and scholars learning the economics of Milton Friedman at Chicago University.

Public fee-paying as well as private institutions intended for an affluent élite are reinstated. The new universities such as the new Shanghai University, are modelled on the US college structure with colleges of arts, sciences and business administration.

All these developments are significant because they constitute a means for 'the transfer of intellectual technology' from the academic growth poles in the West to the 'Chinese academic subsidiaries'. The new educational system seems to be geared towards the economic requirements of capitalist development, not only by supplying the necessary specialised manpower and managerial cadres but also by producing 'correct' and 'suitable' intellectual interpretations of China's 'modernisation process'. The transfer of intellectual technology, therefore, is part and parcel of the 'open door' to foreign capital and the global process of reintegration of China's economy into the structures of world capitalism. Western concepts of modernisation based on the role of the individual entrepreneur gradually permeate economics, social sciences, and management curricula in the universities. Marketing, international business and management studies gradually replace the traditional political economy courses. These developments in university and college education in turn, interact with the reforms in enterprise management.

Concluding Remarks

The post-Mao reforms rehabilitate many features of 'bureaucratic capitalism' characteristic of the Republican period. Whereas the state sector remains the dynamic and predominant force in modern industry, the tendency is towards the development of state capitalism under various forms of joint-ownership with foreign and overseas Chinese capital. In this process, private and state ownership are not mutually exclusive. On the contrary, the development of state capitalism endorses the parallel development of private corporate capital by the national patriotic bourgeoisie, the expatriate bourgeoisie and foreign capital. Private ownership is, therefore, not the cause but the consequence of more fundamental changes in the structure of state ownership.

The system of state enterprises which is unfolding in the post-Mao period is closely tied in to the interests of foreign capital. The nature of this relationship under the 'open door' policy is in some respects similar to that of the 'government sponsored' enterprises of the Republican period. The enterprise reforms, the development of management education, and the open door policy are interconnected processes. The setting up of American style business schools and the transfer of managerial technology accompanies the entry of foreign capital. Our analysis of the 'Open Door Policy' in Chapters 8 and 9 will identify the nature of this relationship and the precise mechanics whereby foreign capital penetrates key sectors of Chinese industry.

The following chapter discusses the changes in the wage system which accompany the reforms in enterprise management.

5

Wages and the Labour Process

Introduction

The reforms in enterprise management discussed in the previous chapter profoundly modify social production relations at the factory level and the position of workers in the social and organisational hierarchy. The subordination of working people to the material requirements of production for maximum profit modifies the social and economic basis of wage determination. Hierarchy in the structure of wages and the classification of wage-earners into differentiated social compartments of *manual* and *mental* labour proceed alongside this reorganisation of state factories.The revolutionary committees are abolished and replaced by a factory management committee composed of the directors and top technical and supervisory personnel. Workers' participation is constrained to *formal* workers' councils without decision-making power.

Inasmuch as enterprises are geared towards profit maximisation, production decisions are increasingly expressed in terms of a narrow cost accounting economism, where workers alongside raw materials, equipment, and so on, are considered as 'inputs' or 'factors of production'. Wages, and the increase in wages, are no longer 'a benefit' accruing to workers (in a socialist enterprise in which workers 'democratically decide') but wages are an input price, that is, the price of a particular factor of production, the price of the services of labour.

The enterprise becomes a unit of cost accounting in which the structure of authority, the labour process and the social division of labour are geared towards the maximisation of the internal rate of return.

The economic reforms after Mao constitute a coherent and consistent structure. To what extent are they conducive to the parallel restoration of wage labour as a commodity? To what extent is wage labour, in commodity form, an essential component or ingredient of this over-all structure? Whereas a free market for labour has developed in the sector of small-scale privately-owned enterprises as well as in agriculture, the statutory wage scale in the state sector has so far been maintained. The issue, however, is much broader, in that it also pertains to the changes in the structure of hiring and firing, and personnel management in state enterprises and the policy regarding redundant workers. Historically, the system of state-assigned jobs has been excessively bureaucratic and inflexible in that it limits the freedom of workers to choose their jobs, and prevents them from moving from one enterprise to another. Whereas the reforms adopted after Mao are likely to promote greater freedom of choice in employment, they tend at the same time to undermine the security of employment characteristic of the system of state-assigned jobs.

This chapter focuses on the historical evolution of the wage structure, and examines the direction towards which the structure of wages and the contract system are developing as a result of the reforms.

The Structure of Wages Prior to Liberation

Historically the structure of industrial wages has evolved in close relation to the division of labour and the structure of factory management. Prior to Liberation, extreme wage differentials between blue-collar, technical and managerial cadres were characteristic of the 'modern' factory system both in Japanese-occupied Manchuria and the treaty ports.

Whereas wage differentials between skilled and unskilled blue-collar workers prior to Liberation were of the order of 1 to 2.5, the over-all *absolute* span of incomes in the factory between blue-collar, technical and managerial categories was often in excess of one to forty.[1] In Manchuria, in the 1930s, the wage differential between Chinese and Japanese workers in the same occupational category was of the order of one to three.

Wages Under New Democracy

In the 1950s the wage differential between skilled, technical and unskilled categories remained more or less of the same order of magnitude as in pre-revolutionary China. Disparities between blue-collar workers and professional and managerial personnel were substantially reduced. The wages of senior managerial and professional cadres were brought down in enterprises in the state sector. The reforms in the wage structure during the period of New Democracy were often ambiguous and indeed a reflection of the power struggle within the communist party. Whereas spontaneous reforms led by the workers were conducive in some factories to reducing the income span down to between 2 and 3.5 fold, the official guideline in the mid-1950s (with Liu Shaoqi in control of the party organisation was to maintain a six- to seven- fold structure between the lowest and highest wage in the factory. Spans of five- to seven- fold were common, whereas in

Manchuria wage differentials were substantially greater (up to ten-fold) and in excess of official guidelines.[2]

The early wage reforms implemented by the north-east communist government in Manchuria in 1948 were in principle modelled on the Soviet system. In effect, following the Sixth National Labour Congress in Shenyang, workers in Manchuria were to retain pre-Liberation wages so that in effect, with the exception of managerial incomes, the anomalies of the Republican and Japanese colonial wage structures were often maintained intact.[3]

Moreover, there were also important wage differentials between state enterprises, and between economic sectors and regions. Wages in the collective sector and in neighbourhood co-operatives were not subject to the official wage scale. Wages in these sectors were often 50 (or more) per cent lower than in the state sector.

From 1949 to 1953 wage reforms were implemented on a regional basis. Under the impetus of 'Rightist' policies, and in parallel with the changes in factory management, the major object of these reforms was to 'combat equalitarianism' and support increased differentiation based on levels of skill and educational or technical achievement.

The first unified national wage system was established in 1956 under the influence of Liu Shaoqi.[4] These reforms *unified* and gave legitimacy to the prevailing structure of inequality by:

1. Granting greater wage differentiation to managerial, technical and professional staff in relation to skilled (blue-collar) workers.
2. Managers were to receive higher wages than technical and professional staff.
3. Wage differentiation within the category of (skilled and unskilled) blue-collar workers was to increase.

These modifications occurred concurrently with other major changes in the management of the labour force. The social subordination of workers to management was tightened alongside a clear *social* demarcation between blue-collar workers on the one hand and technical and supervisory personnel on the other. The labour process was intensified with measures intended to reinforce labour discipline. The 1956 reforms divided workers and staff in economic enterprises of the state sector into the following categories: (a) production workers; (b) apprentices; (c) skilled and managerial staff; (d) ordinary staff; (e) miscellaneous personnel and (f) guards.[5] Within the production workers' category there was a distinction between skilled and unskilled workers as well as between permanent and temporary workers. The 'skilled and managerial staff' category pertains to engineers, technical, professional and managerial cadres. In 1956, industrial workers were classified in an eight-point wage scale system. The classification of engineering and technical personnel is more complex and involves a 17-grade hierarchy ranging from the category of 'Assistant Skilled Worker' to 'First Class Engineer'. The wage scale of (blue-collar) workers in government institutions is characterised by a ten-point scale; that pertaining to administrative staff by a 30-grade scale governing wages of senior government cadres of the State Council and Standing Committee of the NPC down to county and district officers and administrative cadres, clerical and low-level office workers.[6]

The unified wage scale gave formal legitimacy to the unequal distribution of income based on a hierarchical and socially stratified occupational structure within the factory. The policy of granting above-average wage increases to managerial and technical cadres allowed many cadres to double their own salaries.[7] The policy also contributed to widening disparities between the state and collective sectors of the economy, as well as accentuating rural-urban income disparities.

The 1956 wage structure remained virtually intact until the onset of the Cultural Revolution. During the Great Leap Forward, however, piece-wages were significantly curtailed.[8]

Economic liberalisation and 'rectification' carried out by Liu Shaoqi in the aftermath of the Great Leap were conducive to further accentuation of income and wage disparities. By 1963 top salaries of government officials (of 600 yuan a month) were 12 times the average industrial wage. The urban income span was of the order of 1 to 20.[9]

In 1963, however, top government salaries were brought down from 600 to 400 yuan, higher and middle salaries of many technical and managerial cadres were frozen.

The 1956 wage reforms while,in principle, modelled on the wage structure in the Soviet Union, were conducive to the *de facto* maintenance of a structure of income inequality similar to that prevalent prior to Liberation. The wage structure was, in this regard, a reflection of a Confucian social and managerial hierarchy in the factory, based on a clear social demarcation between workers on the one hand and managerial and technical cadres on the other.

Wages During the Cultural Revolution

The reforms in the wage structure during the Cultural Revolution were invariably interpreted by the western China-expert as a move 'against material incentives' and against the use of wage differentials 'as an instrument for the efficient allocation of human resources'. The main thrust of the Cultural Revolution was not the repudiation of material incentives *per se* but the struggle against an economism based on social differentiation in the work-place and personal rewards based on individualised work and performance. The wage and bonus structure was said to embody the 'sugar-coated bullets of economic benefits' which were used to

> lure a part of the masses . . . What kind of stuff is economism? It is a form of bribery that caters to the psychology of the masses, corrupts the masses revolutionary will and leads their political struggle on to the wrong road of economism, luring them to seek only personal and short-term interests in disregard of the interests of the state and the collective and the long-term interests.[10]

Wage differentiation *within* the blue collar workers' category was viewed by the 'Left' as a source of division which weakened workers' solidarity by linking personal gain to individual rather than collective endeavours. On the other hand, the movement against material incentives was often carried too far with serious consequences for production.

The reforms in factory management during the Cultural Revolution, however, only partially modified the eight-grade wage hierarchy. Wages in urban factories were in principle based on three criteria: technical skill, length of service and attitude towards work and fellow workers.[11] The highest wages went invariably to veteran workers for their skills and accumulated experience which they passed on to younger workers. The wage span between the highest and lowest wage was of that order of one to three during the Cultural Revolution. Namely, veteran factory workers earned approximately three times more than a worker in his first year of apprenticeship:

> At Chien Shih Machine Building Plant in Shanghai, for instance, the highest paid worker was a veteran getting 137 yuan a month; the lowest – in his first year of apprenticeship – earned 42 yuan. The average for the whole plant was 65 yuan. If one excluded apprentices and workers in their first post-apprentice year, the average wage taken home was 70 to 80 yuan.[12]

Disparities between the managerial and professional categories on the one hand and blue-collar workers on the other were reduced in factories where democratic management was applied:

> The criteria for my salary is the same as for any other worker . . . We are promoted to management by the workers, so it is natural that we get the same wages. [In the Chien Shih Machine Building Plant] management cadres also did their ordinary factory work two days a week.[13]

Material incentives

During the Cultural Revolution the issue of material incentives was at the centre of the political struggle in the factories. The movement against material incentives was a struggle against an economism which weakened collective work by promoting 'a money-grubbing attitude' based on individual gain. Material incentives in the form of piece-rate wages had been used in China as a despotic means of intensifying the labour process. In this context, the base wage is substantially reduced, thereby linking a large portion of the monthly salary to the 'individualised' performance of the worker. These procedures loosened workers' solidarity, reinforced management's control over the labour process and significantly weakened collective endeavours.

The 'old' social and managerial structure meant production for production's sake, accumulation and profit maximisation. The responsibility of factory managers and 'specialists' was to efficiently manage both the 'material' and 'human' 'factors of production'. The supervision of workers and the monitoring of labour productivity were implemented in much the same way as the maintenance, repair and overview of the plant, machinery and equipment. Material incentives viewed in this perspective were an integral part of economism and were used by the management hierarchy to subordinate workers to production. Through the creation of the Revolutionary. Committees and workers' management groups, the Cultural Revolution brought about both a fundamental reversal in this process as well as in the role and significance of material incentives. 'Putting politics in command' signified that productive activity was subordinated to the workers rather than the other way round. Material incentives, however, were not scrapped during the Cultural Revolution, their meaning and significance were changed in parallel with the social changes brought about in factory management:

> [E]very enterprise which practices democracy in production can turn to better account the zeal and creative character of its workers, improve the relations between cadres and the masses, advance technical innovation and revolution of management.[14]

The Cultural Revolution's struggle to abolish bureaucratic management and implement factory democracy was followed by the backlash of the CCP establishment 'against the evil tide of anarchism'. By 1972, 'the tide' was reversed: whereas the revolutionary committees were formally maintained, the old bureaucratic management hierarchy was gradually rehabilitated together with the restoration of the social division of labour and the social differentiation of workers, professionals and managers in the factory.

The Structure of Wages after Mao

The wage structure as of 1972–3 was much the same as that prevalent in 1956 subsequent to the implementation of the unified wage scale.[15] The legitimacy of the eight-grade wage scale (which in fact was never officially abandoned during the Cultural Revolution) was restored.

The present structure is characterised by an intricate grade-scale system for different categories of workers. Workers are identified according to unskilled, skilled and technical and professional categories respectively. Within each category there are between five and eight grades in the wage scale. Thus, the income differential between a senior professional (for example, 'first class engineer') and an unskilled worker (for example, 'apprentice' or 'assistant skilled worker') is characterised by a ratio of one to eight. Skilled workers, on average, earn between two and three times more than unskilled workers.[16]

Wage levels in 1972–74 varied from a low of 24 to 40 yuan a month for a worker in his first post-apprenticeship year to a high of 130 yuan for blue-collar workers at the top of the wage scale. In July 1978 the Central Committee, in its 30-point document entitled 'On Some Questions concerning the Acceleration of Industrial Development', proposed a reform in the structure of wages according to the principle of 'to each according to his work, more pay for more work and less pay for less work'. 'While opposing a wide wage spread, we recognise necessary differences and oppose equalitarianism'.

Inflation and the structure of wages

Wage adjustments and up-grading of certain categories of workers and employees have been carried out since 1977. Over-all adjustments in wages were implemented, largely in response to the increase in the cost of living which resulted from the government's policy of price deregulation and liberalisation. This policy, which consisted in increasing agricultural procurement prices and restoring free markets for non-staple food products, was conducive to a substantial increase in the urban price of food. Moreover, from early 1979, the prices of a wide range of essential non-food consumer goods and services were increased – including the price of services, transportation, hospital fees, and so on. Although many of the price increases were not officially 'authorised', they were the logical consequence of the government's policy of price liberalisation and the emphasis on profit maximisation and 'market socialism' as instruments of resource allocation.

In 1979 the 'authorised' increase in the price of eight basic food commodities was of the order of 33 per cent. It is estimated, however, that the actual price increases were substantially higher.[17] With the restoration of free markets, a dual price system came into existence, often characterised by a discrepancy of 50 to 100 per cent (or more) between the state-regulated and free market price. Under these circumstances it is, of course, difficult to correctly assess the actual increase in the urban cost of living, since a calculation based on official prices would seriously underestimate the *actual* rate of inflation.

Grade promotions were carried out in 1977. Cash rewards, allowances, piece wages and bonuses, which had been cancelled during the Cultural Revolution, were restored in the form of a so-called 'extra-wage' to workers and office employees.[18] With the reforms in enterprise management, the authorities would only authorise wage increases inasmuch as they were compatible with the principle of profit maximisation, that is, enterprises which are unable to cover their losses would not be authorised to increase wages. Needless to say, this policy tended to further encourage enterprises to put up their prices. Despite periodic increases in nominal wages since 1977, the material and social conditions of the lower wage categories of urban workers has deteriorated. Chen Po-wen estimates that, in 1979, the average urban standard of living was lowered by 16.6 per cent.[19]

The tendency is towards greater social hierarchy in the wage structure, with readjustments essentially favouring the managerial, technical and professional categories, whose salaries in the early 1980s were not out of proportion with those of senior blue-collar workers. A process of upgrading of managerial and engineering cadres was initiated in 1983.

Outside the state sector, that is, in neighbourhood collectives, individual small-scale enterprises, as well as in privately-owned factories, wages are governed by the laws of the market and are substantially below those in the state sector. The tendency is towards wage liberalisation both in the private and collective sectors.

The system of state-assigned jobs

In state enterprises, the system of state-assigned jobs is to be gradually replaced by a more flexible contract system. The latter will enable management increasingly to:

1. hire temporary contract workers, who would, in principle, 'not belong to the factory' and could be dismissed at short notice;
2. 'bid' directly for wage labour in the labour market outside the system of state-assigned jobs;
3. independently decide on the factory's wage structure and use part of the accumulation fund to substantially increase the salaries of managers and engineers.

TABLE 5.1 *The structure of industrial wages, selected factories (yuan)*

FACTORY	*Minimum*	*Average*	*Maximum blue-collar*	*Maximum engineer & cadres*	*Average engineer & cadres*	*Bonus (in yuan)*	*Bonus and wage structure*
Harbin wool weaver factory, Heilongjiang (1983)	40	66	80–90	200	100	6	
Shenyang water pump factory, Liaoning (1983)	40	57	100+	160+	—	10	Piece-rate system adopted. Monthly earnings = Basic wage + bonus + piece-rate
Shenyang small tractor factory, Liaoning (1983)	n.a.	50-60	n.a.	100	70–100	n.a.	
Shenyang municipal Chang Zheng garment factory, Liaoning (1983)	40	48	100	n.a.	n.a.	12	60 yuan on average including base wage, piece-wage and bonus. According to the factory director, 'the average is lower than other factories because of the large number of young female workers'.
Container factory, Guangzhou shipyard, Guangdong (1983)	n.a.	70	n.a.	n.a.	80	30	Average blue-collar earnings with bonus are 100 yuan.
Parker Hubei Seals Co. Ltd. Joint venture factory, Wuhan, Hubei (1983)	n.a.	50	n.a.	n.a.	85	—	The average wage is 50 yuan because most of the workers are new. Because the factory is not yet operative the 'old' wage structure is applied. Managerial and engineering staff will get substantial increases.

Wuhow iron and steel complex, Wuhan, Hubei (1983)	n.a.	65	n.a.	n.a.	n.a.	10	
No. 2 automobile factory, Beijing (1983)	n.a.	53	n.a.	n.a.	70	12–13	Average wage is low because there are many young workers.
Beijing air food catering, joint venture factory (1983)	n.a.	70	n.a.	n.a.	n.a.	—	Earnings are made up of base wage plus monthly bonus (for fulfilling quota) according to point system. Another award applies to overfulfilling assigned tasks according to point system. The first bonus is an average of 17 yuan or 25 per cent of base wage, the second amounts to 20–30 yuan.
Guangzhou machine tool factory (1982)	40	90*	150*	n.a.	n.a.	n.a.	
Hunan porcelain factory, Changsha (1982)	40	80*	180*	n.a.	n.a.	n.a.	
Changsha motor works, Hunan (1982)	37–45	45–50	100	140–168	100	n.a.	

* Including bonuses
n.a. Not available
SOURCE Factory interviews conducted in China in 1982 and 1983.

It is worth noting that whereas salaries of managers and engineers remain relatively low, the levels of non-wage benefits, allowances and privileges (for example, automobile, housing, expense accounts) financed from the accumulation fund have substantially increased since 1977.

Towards a flexible wage scale

With the adoption of the profit retention scheme in 1984, which essentially gears the enterprise towards the objective of profit maximisation, the managers of state enterprises were granted increased 'flexibility' in personnel management and the hiring (and firing) of workers. The elimination of the lower and upper limits on bonuses in 1984 will result in increased inequality in urban industrial wages because it essentially transfers the decision regarding wage determination to the factory director.[20]

The new bonus scheme constitutes the first step towards the liberalisation of wages in the state sector. It tightly links monetary rewards to 'labour productivity' and subordinates individual workers to the labour process:

> This bonus scheme, based on the contracted responsibility system, closely links the workers' incomes to their personal contributions and over-all business performance. It ensures that those who have done excellent jobs get higher bonuses, those who have done poor work get little or no bonuses, and those who have done shoddy jobs have their basic wages deducted.[21]

The emphasis is on 'individual' rather than 'collective' endeavours: invidualised work and performance is paid according to 'individualised' rewards. The policy is intended to stop employees, from 'eating out of the same big pot'.

Under the 'flexible wage system', which combines a fixed statutory wage with a flexible bonus system, the eight-point wage system will essentially convert itself into a set of minimum wage levels for different grades and categories of workers:

> After delivering taxes to the state as required, the enterprises have the authority to decide on the amount of wages and bonuses . . . [E]nterprises may adopt various forms of remuneration such as bonuses based on work points, piece-rate wages, floating wages . . . Where conditions permit, enterprises may initiate wage reforms financed by themselves . . . So far as bonuses . . . are concerned we will introduce the practice of imposing 'no ceiling or lower limit'.[22]

The emphasis on profit maximisation as an index of enterprise performance, alongside the liberalisation of the hiring of workers, while not necessarily conducive to dismissals of workers, will by no means encourage factory directors to increase their permanent work-force. These reforms, while encouraging labour saving, and labour saving technology, in individual enterprises, will not be conducive to the increase of urban industrial employment in the state sector.

According to the Shanghai Labour Bureau, 'one worker out of every eight in China's state-owned industries is not needed . . . and this is too much by ten million or more'. With the system of state-assigned jobs, however, the surplus workers 'cannot be dismissed because their employment is guaranteed by the "iron rice bowl"'.[23]

Although there is considerable resistance to changes in the system of state-assigned jobs, the leadership's position is to replace this system by a more 'flexible' contract one in which workers may 'be dismissed in cases of redundancy or having been proved unfit for the work assigned'. The unemployed are urged by the authorities to 'find their own jobs' or to become self-employed. According to a *People's Daily* editorial, factory managers should be given:

> The right to sack workers . . . Factory managers now do not have the right to discipline or dismiss workers . . . *Giving managers the right to sack would allow them to retaliate against workers who opposed their policies . . . sackings could be governed by regulations that socialism too* [in comparison to capitalism] *required labour discipline and that while society had institutions to deal with troublemakers, factories were now being forced to act as reform schools, detracting from their real work.*[24]

Concluding Remarks

The reforms in the wage system are consistent with those in the structure of factory management: the rehabilitation of a market for wage labour whereby workers can be hired and fired is characteristic of the unfoldment of state capitalism in industry and the restoration of a narrow framework of enterprise cost accounting. In this system, labour costs are kept down so as to maximise the enterprise's rate of profit.

The development of a wage labour market proceeds alongside the rehabilitation of social status and hierarchy at the factory level and social hierarchisation in the structure of earnings. The tendency is, in this regard, towards increased differentiation between various categories of workers in the factory. This means that, whereas the earnings and status of professionals, cadres and engineers are upgraded, those of unskilled blue-collar workers are increasingly determined by the market for wage labour. Moreover, the process of employment creation in the urban economy has been modified largely as a result of the 'modernisation' of the state sector at the expense of the collective sector of neighbourhood factories. The latter, which are relatively more labour intensive, have historically played an important role in the promotion of urban employment. The relative downgrading of the collective sector, as well as the spontaneous process of privatisation of neighbourhood factories, are conducive to increased urban unemployment and a consequent decline in the level of urban wages for 'temporary' and contract labour. These tendencies are further endorsed through official encouragement to various forms of what is best described as 'self-unemployment' in a growing and sprawling 'informal urban sector'.

The next chapter focuses on the reintegration of the profit-maximising industrial enterprise into a market system, and the concurrent partial collapse of the system of centralised economic planning.

6

'Market Socialism' or 'Market Capitalism'?

Introduction

It is not 'market socialism' and the application of economic calculus by individual state enterprises which is at issue, but the particular economic, social and institutional conditions under which so-called 'market socialism' is applied: It is indeed essential under socialism that state enterprises maximise *some measure of profitability* and respond to the structure of market demand. But this does not mean that socialist enterprises should apply economic calculus and cost accounting in the same way as under capitalism: In a capitalist enterprise wages are a cost of production which is to be minimised or *kept down* so as to increase the enterprise's rate of return. The cost concepts and the social process of 'keeping costs down', therefore, are an expression of capitalist production relations which evidently are contradictory with the operation of an industrial enterprise under socialism.

Whereas some aspects of the post-Mao enterprise reforms imply less bureaucracy and greater efficiency at the enterprise level – and in this regard constitute positive achievements – the restoration of profit maximisation and the market process are also accompanied by major changes in social and organisational relations. The latter in turn define the precise role of the market process and the way in which the market mechanism – under China's particular conditions – undermines the system of central economic planning based on the allocation of resources in accordance with clearly stated social and economic objectives. The shift towards the market as an instrument of resource allocation, alongside the adoption of 'socialist competition', modifies in a fundamental way the structure of the economic system as well as its social priorities in terms of 'what is actually produced' and 'for whom'.

Profit Maximisation

A profit retention scheme initially established on an experimental basis in 1979 was subsequently adopted in 1984 for all industrial enterprises of the state sector. The latter were encouraged to finance their operations and investments out of profits, after having paid the state's withholding taxes. Enterprises 'should be allowed to maximise profits' and 'apply economic calculus' according to 'the law of value under socialism':

> Practice has proved that in state-owned enterprises, it is more advantageous to replace profit delivery with tax payments . . . enterprises will retain more earnings from their newly increased profits, thereby increasing the incentive for better economic performance . . . [T]hrough the regulatory function of the taxation lever, contradictions arising from the current irrational price system will be alleviated and enterprises will thus be able to compete with one another after the wide gap in their profits is narrowed. This will encourage enterprises that are advanced and spur those that are backward . . . After the switch from profit delivery to tax payments, the relationship between the state and the enterprises in financial distribution will be in the main resolved, thus providing a prerequisite for smashing the 'big pot' practice within the enterprises.[1]

Grant finance to state enterprises under the state plan will be curtailed and partially replaced by a system of state loans channelled through the various credit and banking institutions. Capital construction projects and heavy industry will be financed by bank loans, foreign capital and state funds. In the reforms of the banking system, loans granted to industrial enterprises will be based strictly on financial calculus and conventional rate of return – essentially to the detriment of the weaker and less-advanced units of the industrial system. Under these conditions, state funds and bank loans will increasingly be channelled to 'modern industry' and to those state enterprises which are linked up in one way or another with foreign capital.

Inasmuch as the allocation of funds is based on 'market criteria', these measures will be conducive to the gradual phasing out of the 'less competitive' entities of the industrial sector, increased industrial concentration and polarisation of economic activity.

The gradual phasing out of state funding will eliminate the structure of equalisation payments which enabled less-advanced industrial enterprises to up-grade their facilities. Similarly, the reforms are conducive to increased regional disparities because they contribute to the consolidation of the 'modern sector' located in the coastal industrial cities.

Decentralisation

The granting of economic autonomy to grass-roots enterprises is in itself positive, because it weakens the bureaucratic state hierarchy in which the individual state enterprise is inserted. But it is not enterprise autonomy which is at issue, because this form of decentralisation essentially grants authority to the factory director who is a state-appointed official. Ironically, those within the CCP who now favour greater enterprise autonomy were precisely those who were against it during the Cultural Revolution because enterprise autonomy (under unified planning) was an essential feature of the mass movement to democratise factory management. Mao Zedong, 'On the Ten Major Relationships', opposed the bureaucratic authority of the state over the enterprise: Centralisation and enterprise independence constitute the unity of opposites, 'there must be both centralisation and independence . . . Every unit of production must enjoy independence as a correlative of centralisation'.[2]

So-called 'decentralisation' after Mao grants independence to the enterprise by destroying the 'correlative of centralisation' namely the relationship of the enterprise with state planning, that is, the delegation of authority to the factory director is carried out *against* the workers through the centralisation of authority *within* the enterprise. It is, therefore, incorrect to view these reforms as a move in the direction of workers' self-management.

'Socialist Competition'

According to the communist party leadership, 'socialist competition' is to be distinguished from 'capitalist competition' in that the former is developed on the basis of the public ownership of the means of production under the guidance of the state plan:

> To develop competition, an enterprise must be granted greater power to make its own decisions and its status as a relatively independent commodity producer must be respected. No local authority or department is allowed to interfere with the rights which an enterprise is entitled to enjoy under government policies, laws and regulations, rights with regard to production, supply and marketing, personnel, finance and materials.[3]

'The protection of socialist competition' is conducive to what might be described as 'socialist combination':

> It [socialist competition] plays an important role . . . in promoting the combination of enterprises and further activating our economy . . . It is illegal to adopt administrative means to protect the backward and restrict the advanced, obstructing the normal circulation of commodities.[4]

With regard to the future of the so-called 'backward enterprises', 'some shall be reorganised, some should be consolidated . . . change their line of production or merge with other enterprises. They shall be encouraged to take the path of combination'.[5]

China versus Eastern Europe

At first glance, the reforms resemble some of those carried out in Eastern Europe and the Soviet Union in the 1960s and 1970s which stressed investment through retained profits and bank credit and liberalisation of the price system.[6] In Hungary, these reforms were conducive to the development of conglomerates or 'trusts' through the competitive displacement of 'less efficient' enterprises. In 1971, the Hungarian government decided to split up the 'trusts' because they were considered incompatible with the system of 'socialist competition'.[7]

Similar monopolistic tendencies have existed in China since 1979. The Chinese government has encouraged the formation of industrial conglomerates with the ability of establishing subcontracting links with other (weaker) state enterprises, as well as with surbordinate enterprises in the rural and collective sectors.

According to Ma Hong, President of the Chinese Academy of Social Sciences, and an influential economic advisor to the Central Committee, 'the socialisation of production' is to be carried out through 'socialist combinations' of production, marketing and transportation enterprises, and the formation of holding companies (entitled in Chinese terminology 'mother and son companies') through the combination of several factories and communes. Ma also proposes the formation of joint agro-industrial-commercial complexes.[8]

The displacement of neighbourhood factories

'Socialist competition' displaces or subordinates the collective industrial sector characterised by small-scale neighbourhood factories. Although 'less efficient', and invariably labour intensive, neighbourhood factories constitute an important sector of employment creation in urban areas. The government has adopted a *laissez faire* attitude regarding the 'self-reliant' units of the collective economy, that is, state funds will not be provided, in many instances, and the state has encouraged the *de facto* privatisation of small-scale factories of the collective sector.

The asymmetry in technological endowment between 'modern' and 'less modern' enterprises within the state sector, as well as between the state sector on the one hand and the collective and rural sectors on the other hand, is conducive to the competitive displacement, closing-down, reorganisation or subordination of so-called 'backward' enterprises. This process contrasts with the 'Maoist strategy' of industrialisation adopted in the 1950s and 1960s characterised by the 'economic coexistence' of 'modern' and 'less modern' productive units. Intermediate technology and labour-intensive methods were promoted alongside the development of modern industry. The industrial base was decentralised in an effort to reduce economic and social disparities between the city and the countryside as well as between the coastal regions and the interior. The concentration of 'modern' industry in the coastal regions was the product of China's colonial history. Mao Zedong, 'On the Ten Major Relationships', stressed that 'the greater part of the new industry should be located in the interior so that industry may gradually become evenly distributed'.[9]

Although 'the intermediate technology enterprises (the five small industries) (established in the 1950s and 1960s) were 'inefficient' and often wasteful in terms of their use of energy and raw materials, they contributed to the absorption of surplus labour into productive employment (in a country of more than one billion population), and the fullest utilisation of China's industrial capacity. The reversal of this strategy (after Mao), and the channelling of most of the country's resources into a short-sighted process of 'modernisation', will accentuate the unemployment situation and exacerbate existing social tensions created as a result of the growth of various forms of petty commodity production trading and disguised unemployment in China's major cities.

Social inequality under 'market socialism'

The reforms signify that enterprises will decide 'what to produce' in accordance with the principle of profit maximisation, thereby initially favouring the production of highly-priced goods which are in short supply. From 1979, a large number of enterprises switched their production lines both as a result of market demand as well as of the government's 'economic readjustment' policy. This resulted in temporary surpluses of specific consumer goods. These were subsequently eliminated as a result of price declines and 'socialist competition'.

The process of 'socialist competition' was conducive to the revision, and in some cases de-regulation, of state prices:

> To develop competition, irrational prices must be readjusted gradually. The prices of certain commodities selected by the state are allowed to fluctuate within a prescribed range. In accordance with state policies and the changes in the condition of supply and demand on the market, the enterprises have the power to lower the prices of the capital goods they have turned out . . . If an enterprise wants to increase the prices of its goods, it must obtain the approval of the relevant authorities.[10]

Inasmuch as important inequalities in income prevail as a result of the Central Committee's policy of 'combating equalitarianism', the structure of market demand will reflect the structure of social inequality. The market mechanism will thereby favour production for the upper income groups, that is, the allocation of resources and the underlying structure of accumulation which results from the market process will undermine the production of necessary mass consumer goods. This, however, is not the consequence of the market mechanism *per se*, because in the absence of social inequality, market prices would indeed transmit correct 'signals' to the units of production.

In view of the prevailing social inequalities (including those which result from the decollectivisation of agriculture, the reforms in urban wages, and so on), 'socialist competition' will therefore be conducive to a decline in the (relative) prices of 'luxury goods' and consumer durables and a rise in the price of necessary consumer goods for mass consumption. This process – as discussed later in this chapter – is conducive to a major restructuring of the process of economic growth through the lop-sided and rapid development of consumer durables and semi-luxury goods at the expense of necessary consumer goods (that is, basic human needs) for mass consumption.

'Market Socialism' and the Open Door to Foreign Capital

The liberalisation of foreign trade interacts with the development of 'market socialism'. The internal price mechanism responds to the structure of world market prices, both as a result of external demand for Chinese exports as well as through the penetration of the Chinese market by foreign capital, and the absence of an effective structure of protective tariffs. Under the Central Committee's 'open door' policy, joint ventures, as well as fully-owned subsidiaries of transnational corporations (located in the designated coastal city ports and 'trading areas') may sell part of their output in the domestic market thereby competing with Chinese enterprises of the state sector.[11] This process is not only characterised by the competitive interaction of foreign and domestic enterprises in the national market, it profoundly modifies the form and nature of the 'socialist competitive struggle' *between* domestic enterprises. Inasmuch as foreign subsidiaries and joint venture enterprises are more advanced technologically, they will gradually displace their 'less modern' national competitors of the state sector.[12]

The liberalisation of foreign trade and investment, which grants increased autonomy to individual state enterprises to undertake joint venture deals with foreign capital, interacts with the competitive struggle and encourages the combination of national enterprises with foreign capital.

Starting in 1983 with the automobile industry, entire branches of industry – which hitherto had operated according to the principle of 'economic self-reliance' – are 'combined' and transformed into joint venture operations with foreign capital.

The technological endowment of individual enterprises will determine their fate in the 'socialist competitive struggle'. The fabric of Chinese industry is, in this context, hierarchical, characterised by different levels of technological endowment. The 'backward self-reliant enterprise', the rural factory and the neighbourhood collective are at the bottom of the ladder whereas the 'modern' joint venture assembly line using the most advanced (foreign) technology is on top.

The competitive displacement of the 'less modern' self-reliant enterprise is part of the process of penetration of the Chinese economy by foreign capital. It is not, however, the adoption of advanced foreign technology *per se* which is at issue, but the process whereby foreign trade and investment is carried out at the institutional and economic levels. The *unregulated entry* of foreign capital, and the development of foreign trade 'along capitalist lines', subordinates the national economy to the world market, and the capitalist international division of labour in the context of an increasingly dependent process of capital accumulation.

Market Socialism and the Law of Value

The disruptive effects of 'socialist competition', the tendency towards industrial combination and centralisation could, in principle, be dealt with – in a genuine structure of market socialism – both through fiscal instruments as well as administrative controls. As initially formulated by Oskar Lange and Fred Taylor in the 1930s, 'market socialism' did not imply price determination via the competitive interaction of state-owned enterprises as in a capitalist economy. Under 'market socialism', the Central Planning Bureau would establish a set of prices which would, in turn, govern the socialist enterprises' output decisions. The planning bureau would thereby 'perform the functions of the market' through the determination of prices, the latter in turn would determine industrial outputs and the allocation of resources.[13] Lange and Taylor, however, considered that 'the decisions of managers [of state enterprises] are no longer guided by the aim of maximising profit. Instead, certain rules are imposed upon them by the Central Planning Bureau which aim at satisfying consumer preferences in the best way possible'.[14] The setting of prices (which equalise supply and demand for individual commodities), and the structure of income distribution, however, are interdependent processes, that is, the structure of consumer demand is determined as a result of the inequalities in the distribution of income. Relative income equality is required to avoid a lop-sided development of consumption geared towards the needs of the upper income groups.

In China, the Central Committee's policy of 'combating equalitarianism' is, in fact, embodied in the structure of economic planning: the relative prices of many consumer durables are lowered, price controls over basic food staples and necessary consumer goods are loosened and government subsidies are phased out.

Economic liberalisation and the restoration of the 'market mechanism' are justified by the Central Committee in terms of the so-called 'objective laws of the socialist economy' including 'the law of value' which 'had been neglected' as a result of 'Left errors' and the 'pernicious influence of the Gang of Four' during the Cultural Revolution.

The law of value in Marx

Marx, in *Capital*, defines the magnitude of value of a commodity as determined by the socially-necessary labour time required to produce it. Marx's analysis identifies the relationship between prices and value in terms of the transformation of value into prices and the problem of 'prices of production'.[15] Marx's analysis of value and price applied to the workings of a capitalist economy focused on the process of price formation under particular historical circumstances (namely the transformation of competitive capitalism into monopoly capitalism in the nineteenth century). Marx examines, in this regard, the departure of prices from value and the formation of the average rate of profit under capitalism. Whereas the basic value relationship which expresses the value of a commodity in terms of the labour time expended in its production is valid in different modes of production, Marx's analysis of price formation and the particular relationship between price and value under capitalism cannot be mechanically transposed to that of a socialist economy.

'Market Socialism' or 'Market Capitalism'?

Does the evolution of economic planning after Mao conform to the regulatory principles of 'the law of value' under socialism? The reforms seem to imply that the 'law of value' not only applies to commodities for personal consumption, but also to exchanges between enterprises, namely to the buying and selling of the means of production. In the words of economist Liao Jili of the Chinese Academy of Social Sciences:

> *Both the means of production and the means of subsistence should be treated as commodities* except for a few commodities that are vital to the

> national economy and the people's livelihood . . ., *all other commodities should be allowed to be sold or bought freely* . . . General product prices should be fixed on the basis of product cost and average profit rate, and readjusted periodically to keep up with the changes in product cost and in accordance with supply and demand.[16]

This policy signifies, in concrete terms, the establishment of a system of so-called 'floating prices' under state jurisdiction for some goods and the extension of free market prices to all other commodities. Fixed prices would be maintained for 'major agricultural products', fuels, for some raw materials and for 'major consumer goods'. The banking system would be responsible for 'issuing both circulating funds and capital construction loans', in accordance with market criteria.

The means of production as a commodity

Preservation of *institutional plurality*, (that is, the state, collective and rural sectors) and *technological hetereogeneity* as characterised by the coexistence of 'advanced' and 'intermediate' technologies would require the allocation of the means of production by the state (to the various units of production) in non-commodity form. Abandoning the policy of funding investment through state grants will be conducive to the gradual phasing out of the 'less modern' productive units.

The Chinese government's policy consists in: (a) reducing the importance of state grants; (b) liberalising the sales and purchases of raw materials and equipment between enterprises; (c) encouraging the 'financing' of an important part of the means of production by foreign capital.

The 'proportions' between light and heavy industry will be readjusted. Enterprises in heavy industry which are 'non-profitable' are to be closed down or merged with more profitable enterprises. Heavy industry should gradually produce according to the law of value and sell its output directly in the market place. This process of liberalisation was in operation as early as 1980 when iron and steel enterprises sold 2.91 million tons of steel in the free market (11 per cent of national steel output). State enterprises under the First Ministry of Machine Building sold (in 1980) nearly 50 per cent of its total output on the open market.[17]

Exchange centres to handle the markets for capital goods were established in most large industrial centres. Capital goods, which were normally produced and allocated according to the state plan, were also available on the open market. The immediate result of this phenomenon was the development of a dual price structure.

Economic Growth and the Market Process

The partial restoration of the means of production as a commodity is carried out in parallel with the government's policy of 'economic readjustment, consolidation and improvement' adopted initially in 1979. This policy redefines the broad relationship between light and heavy industry.

'Economic readjustment', together with market liberalisation and the enterprise reforms, has been conducive to the decline and stagnation of heavy industry: the light industrial sector has grown at the expense of heavy industry production.

In 1981, heavy industry experienced (according to official statistics) a decline in output of 4.5 per cent. Production was 'suspended' in many industrial enterprises 'whose manufacture entails high energy costs'; the production of heavy industrial enterprises engaged in capital construction declined as a result of the reduction in investment in capital construction and the corresponding decrease in orders for equipment.[18] The over-all structure of capital accumulation thus responds to the reforms in factory management, wage scales, foreign trade, and so on. The *composition of social production* both *between* and *within* broad sectors of the economy is modified, the structure of capital accumulation in terms of *what is actually produced* interacts with new patterns of consumption and income distribution. In turn, the new structure of 'effective demand', which results from the market process, contributes to changing the composition of social output:

1. The light industrial sector is geared towards the production of consumer durables for the upper end of the income scale;
2. the reinsertion of the Chinese economy into the world market subordinates the relationship between light and heavy industry to the capitalist international division of labour;
3. stagnation in heavy industry has direct repercussions on the development and growth of agricultural infrastructure and the production of farm machinery.

The 'modernisation' of consumption patterns

Socially differentiated patterns of consumption have developed as a result of the market process. The changes have occurred as a result of: (a) greater hierarchisation in the structure of urban wages; (b) the restoration of the rich peasant economy. Access to 'more sophisticated' and 'stylish' levels of consumption is, however, reserved for certain categories of people. Small pockets of 'western' consumption are to be found in major Chinese cities. This tendency has been reinforced as a result of the 'opening up' of trade and the entry of western consumer goods (on a limited scale) into the

Chinese market. Reynolds tobacco company is producing 'Made in China' 'Winston' and 'Camel' cigarettes and Philipp Morris produces 'Marlboro' in a joint co-operative venture. China-produced Coca-Cola can now be purchased for the equivalent of 25 per cent of a day's wage per bottle so that only the more affluent will have the privilege of drinking 'The Real Thing'. Pierre Cardin, the French multi-national fashion designer goes to China; prices of Cardin's China produced *haute couture* will be much the same as in western countries *mais avec une difference*: 'some adjustments will be made for local market conditions'.[19]

In a similar fashion, patterns of urbanisation have been affected by the influx of foreign investment into property development and real estate Joint ventures in residential property with Hong Kong and overseas capital – in the construction of large apartment complexes and hotels – are likely to modify both the spatial as well as social configuration of urban areas. Numerous 'Hong Kong style' apartment high-rises (luxurious by Chinese standards) with swimming pools and shopping centres are sprouting up in Guangdong province. These apartments, however, seem to be intended for a privileged market, that is for certain categories of people (such as party and managerial cadres, intellectuals, 'former capitalists' and relatives of Overseas Chinese who purchase the apartments in hard currency.

Joint ventures with foreign property developers are modifying the norms and standards of China's residential construction industry. Under present conditions of housing shortage, the transfer of 'western' standards of housing accomodation is conducive to the development of a socially privileged housing market characterised by *socially* differentiated and compartmentalised residential areas within the city.

The international advertising business has entered the Chinese consumer goods market. The pink neon signs of SANYO and HITACHI light up a hitherto sedate and muted Canton skyline; urban life becomes 'more exciting', the display of fashionable imports in Beijing department stores, the numerous billboards advertising 'Seiko' watches and 'National' colour television sets not to mention Beijing's advertising break on the national TV network are, according to conventional western yardsticks, definite symptoms of 'progress' and 'modernisation' of a society which 'wants to improve the standard of living of its people'. Patterns of consumption and leisure including Beijing's somewhat subdued night-life will become more 'colourful' but, at the same time, these 'excitements' will be reserved for those who can afford 'the pleasures of modern life styles'.

Holiday Inn, Sheraton and Intercontinental go to China. Luxury hotels are being built in major cities, modern summer resort areas fully equipped with American-style golf, tennis courts and swimming pools are being developed in Guangdong province. The French *Club Méditerranée* has built a sea-side resort centre in the Shenzhen Special Economic Zone in Guangdong.

Whereas this tourist infrastructure is ear-marked for the foreign visitor and Overseas Chinese compatriot there is reason to believe that foreign investment in the tourist, leisure and related industries will gradually acquire access to a small privileged 'local market' made up of high-ranking party and managerial cadres.

The private ownership of automobiles is restored, the emphasis is on the development of the sector of consumer durables and semi-luxury consumption at the expense of necessary mass consumption. Whereas the availability of both imported or more stylish 'Made in China' consumer goods is insufficient to modify the over-all pattern of consumption, the tendency is towards the development of a dual and divided structure of social consumption where a relatively small minority will have access to higher levels of consumption. This process together with the Central Committee's policy of 'combating equalitarianism' coincides, however, with an accentuation of income and social inequalities.

The growth of light industry is characterised by the rapid development of the sector of consumer durables (for example, television sets, stereo cassette-recorders, washing machines, and so on) at the expense of *necessary consumer goods*. As mentioned earlier, this reorientation in the structure of production is consistent with the reforms in the system of wages and the restoration of the rich peasant economy: industry is increasingly geared towards meeting 'effective demand', that is, hierarchy in the structure of earnings changes the patterns of consumer demand, the *composition of social production* in terms of what is actually produced is modified in accordance with the widening of social inequalities. In turn, the new composition of social production characterised by a *relative* scarcity of consumer essentials, contributes, on the supply side, to the further accentuation of social inequalities. Insofar as market forces are allowed to operate, the new patterns of consumer demand will modify the structure of relative prices.

Foreign trade and the relationship between light and heavy industry

The development of trade 'along capitalist lines' integrates Chinese light industry into the structure of peripheral capitalism. The export of light manufactured goods diverts resources away from the domestic economy in general and heavy industry in particular. Investment is channelled towards the consolidation of a light industrial sector which stands increasingly aloof of the domestic market for consumer essentials. In the textile, garment and footware industries, for instance, the rapid development of exports (in these sectors) generates *relative* scarcities in the availability of a large range of necessary consumer goods. In turn, the development of heavy industry is subordinated to new patterns of technology imports. The latter are geared towards the requirements of foreign capital in industrial export processing, raw materials and energy exports (minerals, nonferrous metals, coal and petroleum), as well as cash crops, food processing and agro-business.

Whereas official foreign trade policy is, in theory, geared towards the so-called 'modernisation' of the material means of production through the adoption of 'the most advanced western science and technology available', the *actual* patterns of technology imports rather than promoting economic self-sufficiency, contribute to *technological subordination* and dependency on foreign capital. Chinese industry is increasingly incorporated into an international network of patents, licencing agreements and brand names which clearly demarcates the division of labour between *software* (that is, activities of mental labour) and *hardware* activities (that is, of manual labour). (For further details see our analysis in chapters 7 and 8).

Towards a new structure of capital accumulation

The rate of economic growth (in terms of real gross national product (GNP)) during the so-called 'disastrous years' of the Cultural Revolution was (according to 'friendly' CIA sources) on average 9.6 per cent per annum, industrial production over the same period increased by more than 15 per cent per annum and the production of machinery increased fourfold over a ten-year period (1965–75). Official figures (after Mao) give recognition to the high rate of economic growth. According to post-Mao official statistics, national income increased 2.3-fold from 1965 to 1978 (an average annual increase of 7.7 per cent per annum over a 13-year period.) In the same period the index of gross indusrial output increased 3.5-fold (an average annual increase of 27.2 per cent). The output of heavy industry increased by an average 11.8 per cent (per annum) over the period 1966–78 as opposed to 1.3 per cent over the period 1979–81. The average annual growth of light industry was 10.2 per cent (over 1966–78) and that of agricultural production was 4.0 per cent. Agricultural output increased (from 1965 to 1978) by 42.3 per cent and grain production (measured in metric tons) by 46.4 per cent.[20]

The balance sheet of economic performance from 1977 to 1981 exhibits the major changes in the structure of capital accumulation which resulted from the readjustment policy. Between mid-1977 and mid-1979, the average annual rate of growth of Chinese industry according to official statistics, fell below five per cent. This pattern of economic growth was a direct consequence of the phasing out of an important sector of heavy industry. In 1979 and 1980, the rate of growth of (total) industrial production increased by 8.5 and 8.4 per cent respectively.[21] In 1980, heavy industry stagnated with a rate of growth of 1.6 per cent, whereas light industry output increased by 17 per cent. In 1981, heavy industry production declined by 4.5 per cent.[22] Based on the same sources, the United Nations Economic and Social Council for Asia and the Pacific (ESCAP) estimates that China's real rate of growth in 1981 was 1.7 per cent.[23] The ratio of light to heavy industry had, however, been modified drastically: in 1981, light industry accounted for 51.3 per cent of industrial output as opposed to 43.4 in 1978. Light industry production in 1981 increased by 10.5 per cent.[24]

After 1981, the rate of economic growth (according to official figures) increased substantially in relation to the 1979–81 'economic recession'. From 1980 to 1984, the real annual (average) rate of growth was (according to official statistics of the order of 6.6 per cent. The 1979–81 period, therefore, should be viewed as a *structural recession* characterised by a process of programmed stagnation in certain areas of the economy, that is, programmed stagnation (which resulted from official government policy) consists in the phasing out of designated areas of economic activity (for example, in heavy industry) while actively promoting others (for example, consumer durables).

It would be tempting to make *graphical* comparisons between the post-Mao period and that of the Cultural Revolution. Comparisons of this nature are significant although self-evident. Patterns of economic growth since 1977 should be viewed in the context of the major upheavals in the organisation of the economy, that is, programmed economic recession in heavy industry (during 1979–81) is a transitional strategy towards the consolidation of a new pattern of capital accumulation which substantially modifies the relationships and ratios between agriculture, heavy industry, light industry and foreign trade.

The changes in the pattern of capital accumulation exhibit a coherent shift in the composition of social output:

1. the rate of growth of consumer essentials in agriculture and in light industry declines in relation to that of non-essentials,
2. the programmed stagnation of heavy industry endorses the changes in the composition of social consumption through the reorientation of its productive structure. In the words of Zhao Ziyang, 'This is inevitable, in the course of *readjusting the service orientation and production mix of heavy industry*',
3. the structure of capital accumulation reinforces the foreign trade sector both in light and heavy industry.

The general picture in the transition period (1977–82) was one of *extreme economic imbalance*: stagnation in some sectors against very rapid economic growth in other sectors of economic activity. These imbalances are the concrete expression at the macroeconomic level of the contradictory nature of the economic and social reforms.

Marx's analysis of social consumption

Marx's analysis of social consumption in *Capital* exhibits the dual and divided structure of social consumption discussed in previous sections in the Chinese context. Marx draws, in this regard, a clear distinction between *necessities of life* (department IIa), namely 'articles of consumption which enter into the consumption of the working class' and *articles of luxury* (department IIb) 'which enter into the consumption of the capitalist class'.[25]

Whereas our proposed abstract *subdivision* of social consumption follows Marx's analysis, the relevant concepts of necessary and luxury consumption (that is, in contemporary China) depart from Marx's consumption categories in *Capital*, which were developed in relation to the social class structure prevalent in the nineteenth century in the advanced capitalist countries. In the Chinese context, *necessary* consumption coincides in our analysis with what conventional economics identifies as 'basic human needs', that is, necessary consumption may be broken down into its various components (for example, nutrition, shelter, health and educational services, and so on). Luxury and semi-luxury consumption, on the other hand, is defined in relation to the existence of what M. C. Tavares identifies in a Third World context as the privileged 'middle stratum'.[26] In other words, the consolidation of a small urban-based consuming class endorses a high demand for consumer durables and semi-luxury goods.

The proposed consumption categories (and abstract subdivisions of department II) correspond to the dual, divided and socially hierarchised structure of social consumption prevalent in contemporary 'socialist' China and other 'capitalist' Third World social formations, that is, luxury and semi-luxury goods consumed by a social minority as opposed to necessary consumer goods consumed by the large masses of workers and peasants.[27]

Our analysis has centered on the relationship between capital accumulation on the one hand, and the structure of social consumption and income distribution on the other hand. The supply and availability of necessary consumer goods in the Chinese case will depend on the division of productive capacity between *necessary* and *luxury* goods, that is, between subdepartment IIa and subdepartment IIb. In turn, the articulation of department I (means of production) and heavy industry in particular, in relation to the consumer goods sectors, will infuence the relative growth potential of the two subdivisions of department II, that is, does heavy industry production endorse the development of the consumer durables sector or the production of necessary consumer goods?

Under the 'open door' policy, it is also necessary to identify the division of productive capacity between production for the domestic market and production for export. To what extent does the development of cheap labour exports undermine the growth of the sectors of necessary consumption?

In other words, the availability of articles of necessity for mass consumption, as they are defined in relation to China's particular conditions, depends on the prevailing conditions of supply in department II. Human and material resources are reallocated between IIa and IIb as well as within department I: built in scarcities in the availability of necessary consumer goods coexist alongside the dynamic development of designated sectors of semi-luxury consumption.

Concluding Remarks

The analysis of this chapter suggests that the restoration of the market mechanism under China's particular conditions has contributed to important dislocations in the structure of economic growth. It is not the market mechanism *per se* and its operation under socialism which are at issue, however, but the social and institutional relations which underlie the integration of China's economy into a market process.

Prior to 1976, the Chinese economy was largely geared towards the development of: (a) heavy industry, (b) the sector of necessary consumer goods, and (c) the provision of essential social services. Whereas serious misallocations occurred as a result of bureaucracy and inefficiency in the system of centralised economic planning, largely in the area of heavy industry, the 'Maoist economic system' was largely successful in alleviating the situation of rural and urban poverty prevalent before 1949 and radically changing the material and social conditions of livelihood of millions of people. This objective was achieved by subordinating the allocation of productive resources to politically defined and chosen objectives, that is, geared towards the provision of basic human needs. In other words, the pre-1976 economic system was not conducive to the lop-sided development of the consumer goods sector, that is the emphasis on 'equalitarianism' did not, on balance, favour the development of consumer durables and semi-luxury goods at the expense of basic human needs. This is important, because in a country with a population of one billion, with a per capita annual income of less than 300 dollars, the balance between poverty and subsistence is, of necessity, extremely precarious.

The pre-1976 economic structure has been modified in a fundamental way by the post-Mao reforms, and the adoption of the market as an instrument of resource allocation: chosen objectives are replaced by those of the market, the allocation of resources subordinated to the structure of market demand interacts with the underlying patterns of social and income inequality favouring the development of small pockets of consumerism, largely at the expense of the basic human needs objective. Under present conditions in China, the dynamic development of consumer durables and semi-luxury goods will necessarily benefit a small social minority rather than contribute to an improvement of the material conditions of life of the broad masses. It is in this context that the market process favours the transition towards a new structure of capital accumulation. The latter unfolds alongside the development of a relatively privileged (Third World) urban 'middle' stratum. In turn, the development of this 'middle class' endorses the CCP's ideology of 'modernisation', thereby granting the party leadership the required element of social cohesiveness and support for its policies.

The adoption of the market mechanism also interacts in a decisive way with the 'open door' to foreign capital – examined in detail in the following chapters. Not only is China's market system subordinated to the laws of the world market, foreign capital displaces and subordinates – via the market process and in the absence of protective measures – important areas of Chinese industry. Our analysis in this chapter confirms that the restoration of the market mechanism under China's particular conditions – and in the context of the 'open door' to foreign capital – is conducive to economic and social polarisation, industrial concentration and a tendency towards the technological subordination of Chinese industry to foreign capital.

7

The Open Door to Foreign Capital

Introduction

The issue does not pertain to 'the opening up' of trade *per se*, but rather to the precise nature and framework whereby trade and foreign investment take place. Trade with foreign capital is established in the context of particular social relations and class interests. Technology transfer and licencing agreements, joint equity ventures, compensation trade and the formation of extra-territorial 'development zones' proceed alongside the reforms in factory management,wage scales and labour discipline. In turn, these reforms in the structure of the labour process reinforce the development of trade and foreign investment 'along capitalist lines' by creating the appropriate social and organisational conditions at the level of the individual factory.

In 1979–80 regulations were adopted to promote joint ventures with foreign capital, 'capitalist' free trade zones were set up in Guangdong and Fujian provinces essentially geared towards the development of cheap labour manufacturing and assembly industries for export. These initial overtures to foreign capital were to be followed by the establishment in 1984 of fully-fledged extraterritorial '*development zones*' in 14 coastal city-ports – many of which were foreign colonial concessions during the Qing and Republican periods – in which transnational capital would set up corporate subsidiaries and invest entirely 'along capitalist lines'. Hong Kong 'compatriots' and foreign businessmen were invited to invest in industrial ventures as well as in real estate, property development, residential construction and tourism.

Whereas the particular conception of the 'open door' adopted by the CCP Central Committee is not formally comparable to its historical antecedents, and the structure of extraterritoriality and colonial trade which developed in China from the middle of last century, it rehabilitates many features of China's foreign trade relations which existed prior to 1949. Our historical analysis suggests that against a long historical background of commercial and bureaucratic practices, new *comprador* relations are now emerging as a result of the integration of Chinese state enterprises, trading corporations and financial institutions, into the structure of the world capitalist economy. Moreover, the regional configuration of China's foreign trade – which developed historically in the former treaty ports and coastal provinces – conditions the modalities and precise nature whereby foreign capital penetrates the Chinese economy.

Towards new forms of extraterritoriality

Whereas the 'special economic zones' in Guangdong and Fujian are closely modelled on the Taiwan-South Korea cheap labour export processing zone (that is, with generous tax holidays, government controls over wages, and so on), 'the development zones' and 'trading areas' in the 14 coastal city-ports rehabilitate a new form of extraterritoriality (*zhewai faquan*) on Chinese soil. The leadership claims that the extraterritorial development zones do not imply the surrender of political sovereignty as in the case of the *shang pu* (treaty ports) and foreign establishments which flourished in Shanghai, Guangzhou, Tianjin and elsewhere as a result of China's defeat in the Opium Wars. None the less, the history of China's colonial trade structure prior to Liberation influences the scope and direction of the 'open door' policy, as well as the precise nature of the Central Committee's decision to establish fully-fledged 'capitalist enclaves' in several of China's most advanced industrial cities.

Economic self-reliance is undermined in favour of an *extraverted* economic structure which promotes the dynamic development of those sectors of the economy which are linked up with foreign trade. The reorientation of China's transportation network (since 1980) in favour of the coastal regions and the former treaty ports proceeds alongside the development of the 'open door' to foreign capital. This reorientation serves the interests of the export economy at the expense of internal self-reliance and the economic integration of the coastal regions with the interior.[1]

Industrial development based on the so-called 'modernisation' of state enterprises is concentrated in the coastal provinces and city-ports. Moreover, foreign capital, technology and the transfer of 'scientific' management are closely tied into the communist party's 'guidelines' for the reform of industrial management.

The class basis of the open door policy

The open door policy characterised by new forms of extraterrioriality in China's coastal cities and provinces, and the development of trade and foreign investment 'along capitalist lines', interacts in a consistent and coherent fashion with the decollectivisation of agriculture, the liberalisation of commodity markets and the restructuring of state industry.

Whereas the latter constitute in themselves a major upheaval in the foundations of Chinese socialism, the development of trade and investment 'along capitalist lines', together with China's reintegration into the capitalist international division of labour, further contribute to undermining the economic and social basis of socialism. The mandarins, managers and professionals of China after Mao, operating in the state and party apparatus as well as in industrial, banking and commercial undertakings, are the new compradors of international capital. Their interests and outlook are coincident with those of their 'foreign partners', their training and education, particularly in the field of management studies, are increasingly dominated by western techniques, standards and concepts.

The Open Door in Historical Perspective

The class basis of the 'open door' policy is none the less complex in that it involves an understanding of the historical evolution of class relations from the late Qing and Republican periods. The term 'open door' was first used by the imperialist powers in the nineteenth century in the aftermath of China's defeat in the Opium Wars.

The 'opening up' of trade leading to the development of foreign establishments and treaty ports was imposed by the imperialist powers through the force of arms. Britain's representative Lord Napier had attempted, in 1834, to negotiate with the Qing imperial court a policy of 'trade liberalisation' which would break-up the monopolistic-bureaucratic control exercised by the official Qing merchant guild, the Co Hong, which regulated foreign trade through the port of Canton (Guangzhou). Britain's attempts were not only intended to 'open up' China to foreign trade but to legalise the opium contraband.[2]

When opium shipments were destroyed in the port of Canton in 1839, Britain claimed that the destruction of the opium was 'an infringement of the property rights of British merchants' based on China's refusal to 'treat on terms of equality with the foreigners'.[3] 'Treating on terms of equality' would constitute the rhetorical cornerstone of colonial policy from the Opium Wars to the Second World War.

'Open door' policies of one form or another will be used by the imperialist powers as a pretext or motive for aggression and warfare. In a note to Cheng Yucai, Viceroy of Guangdong in 1844, the U.S. Cushing mission to China had declared that 'refusal to grant American demands might be regarded as an invitation to war'. The Cushing mission resulted in the treaty of Wanghsia which provided (as in the case of the Treaty of Nanjing with Britain) the 'opening up' of five ports to American traders. In the same year, France concluded a similar treaty.[4]

Rivalries between imperialist powers towards the end of the nineteenth century threatened the partition of the Chinese empire. Although the imperialist powers were anxious to secure special spheres of influence in the form of extraterritorial rights, railway concessions, and so on, they were also anxious (Britain in particular) to secure, in addition to these specific rights and concessions, 'an open door for trade'. Britain had approached Washington in 1898 to 'suggest joint sponsorship of a movement for equal commercial opportunity in China'.[5]

In 1900, in the settlement arising from the Yihetuan Uprising (Boxer Rebellion), the United States again reiterated the development of an 'open door' policy which would consist in the liberalisation of trade and foreign investment according to the principle of 'equal opportunity'. The Anglo-Japanese agreement stipulated in somewhat different terms 'the preservation of the common interests of all the powers in China by insuring the independence and integrity of the Chinese empire and the principle of equal opportunities for the commerce and industry of all nations in China'.[6] In this context, 'equal opportunity' (*between* the imperialist powers) signified equal right and opportunity to plunder the Chinese economy.

By 1907, foreign capital dominated 84 per cent of shipping, 34 per cent of cotton yarn spinning and 100 per cent of iron-ore production; by 1911, 93 per cent of railways in China were foreign dominated.[7]

In the aftermath of the First World War, Japan and the United States emerged as the most dynamic imperialist powers in China. This is important because their economic and geopolitical rivalry, leading up to armed confrontation in the Second World War, remains an important element of Japanese-American relations today in China and the Far East.

From 1907, as a result of the Russo-Japanese convention and the Sino-Japanese treaty of 1905, Japan gained virtual political control in southern Manchuria, including railway concessions and mining rights. The government-general of Kwantung (in Manchuria) was established in 1906 to administer the *lease territory* including the railway zones.[8] Whereas, 'the Kwantung leased territory became an island of Japanese society and culture on the mainland', the remaining part of south Manchuria was opened to the Japanese for residence, commerce and manufacture.[9] With the decline of Britain's commercial and financial hegemony after the First World War, the weakening of French and German spheres of influence in Shanghai, and the October Revolution (which signified the *de facto* withdrawal of Russian interest from China), Japan consolidated its position in Manchuria and extended its spheres of influence in the 'treaty ports' of Shanghai, Tianjin, Xiamen (Amoy), Hankou and Guangzhou (Canton). In 1931 Japan, taking advantage of Chiang Kaishek's counterrevolutionary war and Encirclement Campaigns against the Communists, occupied China's north-eastern provinces. Japanese expansion in railways was characterised by the development of state capitalist enterprises, controlled and supported by the Japanese government. The railway corporations in turn had investments in mining, public utilities and real estate. During the First World War Japan also consolidated its position in the banking sector as well as its control over China's state finances.

U.S. interests in China (contrary to those of Japan and the other imperialist powers) were concentrated in trade, commerce, banking and state finance, rather than industry, mining and the railways. In other words, American interests were concentrated in commodity trade and in the extension of loan capital to the Qing and warlord governments. The value of American holdings of securities and obligations to the Chinese government was estimated by Remer, in 1931, to be of the order of 42 billion dollars.[10] The US increased its economic position in China after the First Word War in the foreign establishments mainly at the expense of Germany, Russia and (to a lesser extent) Great Britain.

Although U.S. direct colonial involvement was weak in relation to Japan and Britain, the U.S. was, in the 1930s, the second largest trading nation in terms of trade volume (16.5 per cent of total trade) after Japan (24.7 per cent and before Britain (7.8 per cent).[11] *It is significant that in the post-Mao period, Japan and the United States occupy much the same relative trading positions as in the 1930s*.

The history of extraterritoriality

Foreigners could reside, own property and engage in industry and commerce under the extraterritorial jurisdiction of the foreign power's consular office. In the so-called 'foreign concession' 'entire areas of the city were expropriated or purchased by the Chinese government and leased in perpetuity to particular powers.'[12] The International and French 'Settlements' in Shanghai consisted of areas for residence by foreigners. In this case, the Chinese authorities issued title deeds to the foreigners which were registered in the foreign consulates.[13]

The extraterritorial concessions ensured the imperial powers *de facto* control of trade and industry in the coastal provinces. Inland trade was controlled through the railway concessions and the inland river treaty ports. Foreigners were also established in several inland cities.

Maritime Customs in Shanghai were handed over to Britain as a result of the Treaty of Tianjin of 1858. The treaty stipulated in this regard that:

> The high officer appointed by the Chinese government to superintend foreign trade will be at liberty to select any (British) subject he may see fit to aid him in the administration of the Customs Revenue.[14]

The inspector-general of Maritime Customs, although formally appointed by the Qing government, was *ex officio* British, thereby ensuring British trade hegemony in the treaty ports.

The Structure of Foreign Trade After Liberation

The structure of foreign trade which developed in China in the 1950s was partly a consequence of the United States' policy of containing and isolating China. The U.S. trade embargo and the development of economic ties with the Soviet Union were conducive to China's *de facto* isolation from the world capitalist market. In the 1950s foreign trade was subordinated to the principle of '*economic self-reliance*' and regulated centrally by the state.

'Economic self-reliance' was to some extent a *de facto* rather than a deliberate policy. China's economic isolation from western capitalism in the 1950s and 1960s affected class relations in that it undermined the comprador links with foreign capital. This, to some extent, constrained and conditioned the scope and direction of the reformist policies put forth by Liu Shaoqi and the 'Rightist' line.

Japanese–US rivalries

The relationship between Japan and the United States has evolved from the U.S. occupation of Japan in the early post-war period, Washington's drive towards geopolitical control of the region, and its attempt to isolate Japan from South-east Asia and China in the 1950s, to the present 'US – Japanese Trade War'.[15] China is, in this regard, a crucial pawn in the struggle for economic and geopolitical hegemony in South–east Asia and the Far East.

China's economic isolation from the world capitalist economy largely prevailed until the signing of the first Sino-Japanese trade agreement in 1963 (the Liao-Tagasaki agreement). During the 1960s relations with Japan and western Europe were fostered in the face of withdrawal of Soviet economic and technical aid. During the US policy of isolation and 'containment' of China, Sino-Japanese trade provided China (particularly in view of the cancellation of Soviet aid programmes) with a window to the outside capitalist world, while at the same time surbordinating the inflow of imported Japanese technology to specific policy guidelines on the conduct of foreign trade under socialism. Prior to 1977, imports of technology were regulated by a policy which relied heavily on the import of whole plants rather than foreign investment in the traditional sense of the word.

In 1972, the signing of the Shanghai Communiqué, while opening the road for the 'normalisation' of Sino-American trade relations, at the same time exacerbated geopolitical and economic frictions between the U.S. and Japan. Shortly after the signing of the Shanghai Communiqué, Japan's Prime Minister, Kakuei Tanaka's, New China Policy established the basis for diplomatic relations between the two countries and solid grounds for the development of trade and foreign investment relations. Purchases of Japanese and German technology in the early 1970s were channelled towards the reinforcement of China's heavy industrial base. During the 1960s and early 1970s, transfers of western science and technology were monitored and controlled by the Central government industrial ministries. The tendency was towards the import of whole plants in areas where China lacked technological expertise.

This importing of foreign technology and equipment was geared towards the consolidation of China's heavy industrial base. The setting up of large-scale iron and steel complexes using German and Japanese equipment, for instance, enabled China to transform its iron ore industry and become more or less self-sufficient in steel production.

Although the institutional set-up was often bureaucratic and cumbersome, foreign trade and investment policies prior to 1977 contributed to the *selective* transfer of advanced western technology without undermining the structure of self-reliance. It is, therefore, not the opening up of trade *per se* which is at issue, but the precise nature and framework whereby foreign trade is established, that is, the importance under socialism of maintaining a state monopoly over foreign trade rather than establishing trade and investment relations in accordance with the laws of the world market.

The Open Door After Mao

'*China has opened its door and will never close it again . . . China always keeps its door open to friends*'. These were Premier Zhao Ziyang's words to Ronald Reagan during his 1984 Washington visit.[16] The liberalisation of trade, the development of joint ventures, the setting-up of special economic zones, development zones and trading areas under a new system of extraterritorial rights, and the development of cheap labour export processing industries constitute the essential features of what the CCP Central Committee describes as 'China's Open Door Policy'.

The liberalisation of foreign trade was initiated in 1978. The following year the National People's Congress gave special rights in foreign trade to the two southern provinces of Guangdong and Fujian, thereby approving the formation of China's 'special economic zones', a modern blend of extraterritoriality combining China's colonial tradition with South-East Asia's export platform or free trade export processing zone. Also in 1979, the National People's Congress adopted China's law on joint ventures which enables foreign corporations 'to incorporate in China in ventures with Chinese companies, enterprises and other economic entities'.[17] Provisions for 'Labour Management in Chinese-Foreign Ventures' were adopted in 1980 to regulate 'the employment, dismissal and resignation of the staff and workers of joint ventures and their production and work tasks, wages and awards and punishments.'[18]

In 1984, the Central Committee approved the formation of 'trading areas' and 'development zones' in 14 coastal city-ports. At the institutional level, the authority to conduct foreign trade was transferred from the central government level to the provincial and local levels.[19] The foreign trade procedures increasingly enable individual Chinese state enterprises to enter *directly* without government approval into trade, joint ventures and other 'co-operative' arrangements with foreign capital. Prior to the establishment of provincial and other state trust and investment companies in the early 1980s, China International Trust and Investment Corporation (CITIC) was one of the key financial institutions for the negotiation and setting up of major industrial and financial joint ventures, credit, banking, commercial and other arrangements with international capital. In the words of its chairman Rong Yiren:

> The Corporation should make itself an excellent socialist state-owned enterprise, strive for efficiency and prevent the practice of bureaucracy. It has 50 working personnel. *Some are former industrialist and businessmen* . . . I think there are bright prospects ahead. *The international trust and investment business is a long-term undertaking that can play a considerable role in the new 'Long March' towards China's socialist modernisation*.[20]

In 1979, Deng Xiaoping's visit to the United States led to the signing of a comprehensive Sino-US trade agreement which incorporated granting of 'most favoured nation treatment' to China, and provided among other things the possibility for American banks to operate in China. The first National Bank of Chicago was the first US bank to estalish its representative office in Beijing in 1978. The other major US banks followed suit shortly thereafter. In 1979, First National of Chicago signed an agreement with the Fujian Investment and Enterprises Corporation, thereby becoming the first US bank lending money to a Chinese province and thereby establishing the institutional and financial structure which enables international banking to influence investment decisions of national and provincial state entities.[21]

Also in 1979, First of Chicago entered an agreement with CITIC to promote joint ventures and US investment in China. In 1980, First National of Chicago, together with the Industrial Bank of Japan, joined hands with the Bank of China and China Resources (a Chinese state investment corporation) to form a joint venture finance company and merchant bank in Hong Kong, CCIC Finance Ltd, which was subsequently involved in several important syndicated loans including a US $100 million loan to the Philippines (along with 24 other major international banks).[22]

The 1979 visit of Deng Xiaoping to the US was followed in June 1980 by the equally significant encounter in Wall Street of Rong Yiren, chairman of

CITIC, and David Rockefeller. The meeting, which was held in the penthouse of the Chase Manhattan Bank Complex, was attended by senior executives of close to 300 major US corporations. Chases's president, Willard Butcher, said on that occasion 'they are very conservative bankers – I like doing business with them'.[23]

A major agreement was reached between Chase, CITIC, and the Bank of China, involving the exchange of specialists and technical personnel 'to identify and define those areas of the Chinese economy most susceptible to American technology and capital infusion . . . Certain industrial sectors will be singled out and Chase will be charged with trying to recruit specific American firms to provide both the know-how and the money'. At that occasion the Chinese delegation stated that the communist party's policy was 'to pump as much money and technical aid into those areas with greatest export earnings potential: coal, minerals, metals and . . . petroleum resources'.[24]

The adoption of a 'socialist version' of the 'open door' should be understood in the over-all context of the economic and social reforms implemented since the downfall of the so-called 'Gang of Four' in 1976. The 'open door' to foreign capital proceeds alongside the reforms in factory management, the decollectivisation of agriculture, the deregulation of internal prices, and so on. The 'liberalisation' and 'modernisation' policies are concurrently conducive to the parallel development of entirely new patterns of trade and foreign investment with the capitalist world economy.

The 'opening up' of China to western capitalism takes place in accordance with precise class interests and should therefore be understood in relation to the role both of the 'national' and 'expatriate' Chinese bourgeoisie. New comprador relations are developing in China as a result of the Open Door Policy. The social class base of this policy is complex. It involves an understanding of the internal struggle within the communist party which was conducive to the displacement of Maoist partisans from political power, and of the political purges carried out after the fall of the so-called 'Gang of Four'. The consolidation of a corporate bureaucratic and managerial élite firmly committed to the 'Rightist' line in the party and state apparatus as well as in state industry, financial institutions and trading corporations interacts with the development and implementation of the 'open door' policy.

The Expatriate Bourgeoisie

The *expatriate bourgeoisie* plays an important role in the process of class formation in China in the post-Mao period. Whereas the national bourgeoisie formally ceased to exist as a property-owning class within

China as of the mid-1950s, the expatriate Chinese merchant and industrial class constitutes a powerful base of capital accumulation in Hong Kong and South-East Asia. The patterns of class formation of the Hong Kong bourgeoisie are intimately related to the flight of national Chinese capital and the settlement of members of the national bourgeoisie in Hong Kong after the Second World War and since 1949.

The expatriate Chinese bourgeoisie constitutes a vital link in the establishment of trade, joint ventures and international credit operations. These relations are not solely commercial and economic links *sensu stricto*, they are characterised by family and class ties *within* the Chinese bourgeoisie, between members of the so-called 'national patriotic bourgeoisie' who remained in China after Liberation and expatriate bourgeois families in Hong Kong, Taiwan, Singapore and elsewhere. Moreover, it is worth noting that a Chinese merchant bourgeoisie constitutes the dominant economic élite in Thailand, Indonesia, Malaysia, Burma and (to a lesser extent) the Philippines. These 'national' groups of Chinese extraction are not isolated from one another: the Chinese (expatriate) bourgeoisies in the various countries in South-East Asia are integrated both in commercial, banking and financial undertakings, as well as through family and class ties.

The Hong Kong-based Chinese bourgeoisie plays, in this regard, an important role as a contractual intermediary in major financial and commercial undertakings and joint ventures between the People's Republic of China and western capital. Hong Kong capitalists are directly involved in developing cheap labour export processing industries on the Chinese mainland, similar to those which already exist in Hong Kong, Taiwan, South Korea and elsewhere in the 'capitalist Third World'.

Former 'national capitalists' in Shanghai are involved in commercial and business undertakings with relatives from Hong Kong, and senior members of the Chinese Communist Party have privileged links with members of the Hong Kong bourgeoisie, and so on. Li Kar Shing, managing director of Cheung Kong holdings (a major Hong Kong property consortium) and Fok Ying Lung (also a Hong Kong-based property developer), for instance, are *ex officio* members of the board of directors of CITIC.

Moreover, there is evidence that Hong Kong 'compatriot' capitalists are not only consulted but are involved in the *actual* formulation of foreign investment regulations, tax laws, and so on. In the special economic zones (SEZ) they constitute a powerful lobby which dominates the process of decision-making at a local level. Labour hiring and dismissal procedures in the SEZs, for instance, were negotiated with the 'overseas compatriot lobby'.

In the banking sector, the expatriate bourgeoisie controls over 100 commercial banks in South-East Asia. The Hong Kong '(Compatriot) Chinese Banking Group' of 24 private banks is interlocked with a powerful regional and international financial network. The orientation of economic policy in China under Deng Xiaoping seems to favour increased interaction and financial integration between the Bank of China banking group and the group of 24 Hong Kong commercial banks controlled by expatriate Chinese financial interests (for example, Bank of Canton, Wing on Bank, and so on).

Prior to 1979, the Bank of China was directly under the control of the People's Bank of China. Since 1979 it operates in a far more independent fashion. Together with its 13 Hong Kong subsidiary banks, the Bank of China has been active in the establishment of joint financial ventures with Overseas Chinese and foreign banking interests.[25] It has also joined syndicated loans with American, European, Canadian and Japanese banks and is active in real estate and property development in Hong Kong. All these developments seem to suggest a *tendency* towards *specific* forms of economic and financial integration between expatriate Chinese capital and the People's Republic of China state capitalism. The mechanics of integration are reinforced by the existence of class and family ties with 'former' national capitalists.

These developments are related to the special status of Hong Kong after 1997 agreed between the British and Chinese governments. The communist party's position is to maintain Hong Kong as a capitalist autonomous region for another 50 years, which means effectively that it will be controlled by the Hong Kong-based Chinese bourgeoisie. Hong kong would thereby *de facto* become China's major international financial centre. In turn, the latter is expected to play an important role in China's 'modernisation' programme. It is thus unlikely that Hong Kong, under formal Chinese jurisdiction, would remain separate from the mainland economy. The tendency will be for the economic and social fabric prevalent in Hong Kong to gradually penetrate Guangdong Province, thereby undermining further the very social and economic basis of Chinese socialism.

The Central Committee's policy towards the so called 'Overseas Chinese' as expressed in China's 1982 Constitution is not merely a 'new departure' but the expression of class ties with the expatriate bourgeoisie. In this context, the regime is encouraging the return of expatriate capitalists to the motherland:

> Some of these Hong Kong men, who a few years ago escaped from the mainland, and made money in Hong Kong are now coming back with money to invest. There are even former landlords who escaped and made money in Hong Kong.[26]

Both the central and provincial authorities have issued regulations ordering that houses of Overseas Chinese seized both during, as well as before, the Cultural Revolution be returned to their 'rightful' owners:

> Seized houses must be returned . . . the pace of returning these houses is too slow . . . All units and individuals who occupy houses of Overseas Chinese must return these houses within a prescribed period in compliance with regulations of the central government.[27]

Inheritance rights are restored on confiscated assets and property. The inheritance of property is extended to members of the expatriate bourgeoisie and Overseas Chinese living abroad, including Taiwan. In the words of Guo Di-huo, a member of the Kwok family which founded the Wing On business empire in pre-revolutionary China:

> Many of us will have assets returned to us. And the investment law will include guidelines so that Overseas Chinese can contribute to the Four Modernisations.[28]

With regard to the 'regain of confiscated homes and property', the State Council's Office of Overseas Chinese Affairs confirms that 'the Government intends to return all homes confiscated since 1949 even where property was 'voluntarily handed over'' by owners classed as landlords'.[29]

The Office of Overseas Chinese Affairs has also sent representatives to tour the United States and Canada's Overseas Chinese communities in an effort to encourage the return of expatriate capitalists with 'money to invest in the motherland'.[30] In all cases confiscated property is returned or, compensation is paid. The expatriate bourgeoisie is invited to develop privately-owned business enterprises in industry, services, construction and the tourist industry. The Chinese 1982 Constitution states that the basis of the socialist economic system is 'ownership by the whole people and collective ownership by the working people' (Article 4).[31] With regard to foreign ownership, however, it allows foreign enterprises 'to enter into various forms of economic co-operation with Chinese enterprises' (Article 18).[32] Whereas there are no legal provisions for the reinstatement of private ownership, private corporate capital based on wage labour has been in operation since 1979, gaining impetus in 1982–3 in contravention of state guidelines which limit private ownership to individual commodity producers with no more than six wage labourers.

An article published in Shanghai's *Wen Hui Bao* (in 1979) confirms that 'former capitalists' in Shanghai, in collaboration with overseas Chinese capital, had already set up a multimillion yuan construction company, in 1979, to build apartments using the interest payments on property nationalised by the state in the mid–1950s, which had been confiscated during the Cultural Revolution and reinstated after 1976. The new apartments will be sold to overseas Chinese or to their Shanghai relatives through a Hong Kong property developer, as well as to the city's former capitalists 'who have housing problems'.[33]

In Guangzhou (Canton), a section of the service industry, hotels, taxis, restaurants, construction and transport companies are controlled by Hong Kong capital. Hong Kong's Hopewell group, together with other Hong Kong property developers, are investing in the development of industrial, construction and tourist complexes in southern Guangdong Province. Hong Kong capital is also financing a super-highway integrating Canton with Hong Kong and Macao. Increasingly, the tendency is towards the *regional* integration of Hong Kong, Macao and Guangzhou and the creation of a powerful pole of capital accumulation in southern Guangdong Province largely controlled by Hong Kong financial and industrial interests.

This process interacts with the development of the off-shore oil industry in the South China Sea and the Pearl River basin and the establishment of joint ventures between the South China Sea Oil Company (Nanhai Oil Company) and international oil consortia (for further details see our analysis of off-shore oil in chapter 8).

The Transfer of 'Western' Consumption Patterns

Whereas socially differentiated patterns of consumption develop in parallel with a greater hierarchisation in the structure of wages and the underlying changes in the urban and rural distribution of income, the development of 'more sophisticated' and 'stylish' levels of consumption reserved for certain categories of people, is reinforced as a result of the 'open door' policy. Whereas the latter opens a 'half-closed door' to imported western consumer goods, 'the demonstration effect' encourages national state enterprises and/or joint ventures to emulate their foreign competitors in the domestic consumer goods market and to gear production decisions accordingly. In other words, the entry of western consumption patterns takes place through the important changes in the composition of social output, that is, in terms of what is actually produced by Chinese industry.

The open door to Madison Avenue

Alongside the entry of foreign capital and the restructuring and 'modernisation' of consumer preferences, China has opened its doors to the multibillion transnational advertising business.[34]

Commercial advertising had been denounced during the Cultural Revolution. By 1979 it was not only back in favour but China was to 'learn from foreign advertising, make things foreign serve China and draw on the strong points of certain countries' advertisements to help develop socialist advertising'.[35]

In early 1979, domestic product advertising developed in Chinese newspapers. Shortly thereafter advertisements for foreign made products appeared in newspapers in Shanghai. The Shanghai Advertising Corporation (SAC), a government sponsored agency initially established in 1962 to promote Chinese exports, has been revitalised as a means of promoting foreign advertising business in China.

In March 1979, commercials on Chinese Television were introduced:

> The first ad appeared during a live broadcast on Shanghai television of a woman's basketball game. It featured a popular Chinese basketball star and several team mates drinking a local softdrink Xinfu Cola (Lucky Cola) Lucky Cola's Shape and logo resemble those of Coca Cola.[36]

The advertising business is controlled through Hong Kong intermediaries. The Chinese authorities named *Wen Wei Po*, a pro-Beijing newspaper in Hong Kong, 'their sole agent in the co-ordination of ad placement in virtually all Chinese media including publications, broadcasting and billboards'.[37] Space was then sold to foreign corporations wishing to advertise their products in China (even prior to these products being actually available in the Chinese market).

Robert Chua publications of Hong Kong was hired to handle the production of TV commercials for China in partnership with *Wen Wei Po*. Chua productions served as a buying agent and film producer for Guangdong Television. Robert Chua was the sales agent of at least eight Chinese TV stations.[38]

In 1979 about 100 companies were formed in Hong Kong to 'jump on the Chinese advertising bandwagon'. China Advertising Company is a Chinese state enterprise under the jurisdiction of the Foreign Trade Ministry with offices in Hong Kong. The Company represents about 30 newspapers and a dozen TV stations in China.[39]

In 1981, the China Foreign Trade Advertising Association, made up of provincial advertising agencies, was formed to co-ordinate the influx of foreign advertising. Also in 1981, the government established the China United Advertising Corporation to handle advertising by domestic companies.[40]

Japan is by far the largest advertiser in China. In 1979, the Shanghai Advertising Corporation and the largest Japanese Advertising transnational signed an agreement for the promotion of Japanese products in China.

The entry of western consumption patterns into China does not take place in the abstract. The development of social status and privilege together with a socially-hierarchised wage structure, the restoration of the rich peasant economy, and so on, are affected and conditioned by the opening up of trade (and vice-versa). Whereas the availability of either imported or 'more stylish Made in China' consumer goods is insufficient to modify the over-all pattern of consumption; there is a clear *tendency* towards *the development of a dual and divided pattern of social consumption* where a small minority has access to the 'better and more enjoyable things of capitalist society'.

Rather than contributing to improving the standards of material life, our analysis in chapter 6 suggests that these changes in consumption patterns, which are partially the product of the 'open door' policy, have serious repercussions on patterns of production, by distorting the allocation of resources and increasing the availability of durable and more stylish consumer goods at the expense of necessary mass consumption. In other words, the underlying pattern of capital accumulation interacts with the changes in social consumption; the latter conditions the former, and in turn, the changes in the allocation of productive resources in the economy are conducive (on the supply side) to the creation of (*relative*) built-in scarcities in the availability of necessary consumer goods for ordinary workers and peasants.

The Transition to Socialism

The 'Open Door Policy' is viewed by the leadership as a necessary stage 'in the transition to socialism' and in the 'modernisation' of the means of production. Since 'according to Marx' capitalism must necessarily precede socialism, the development of foreign trade 'along capitalist lines' strengthens socialism and upholds Marxism: socialism requires the adoption of the 'best capitalist technologies available'. '*China's pursuit of the policy of co-operation with foreign capital is a restoration and preservation of the traditional viewpoint of Marxism*'.[41] The 'open door' is viewed by the leadership as 'a policy of redemption' towards the foreign capitalist and expatriate bourgeoisie:

> Some exploitation [of workers] does exist [as a result of the open door] but allowing foreign or overseas capital to gain profits, is in a sense a policy of redemption . . . [After the founding of the People's Republic in 1949] the leadership adopted a redemption policy towards the national bourgeoisie . . . Now we are employing a redemption policy to win the co-operation of foreign and overseas capital . . . the special economic zones do not represent the revival of the former concessions because authority over them is entirely in Chinese hands.[42]

In the coastal free ports and special economic zones 'it is not only the law of value that is operating but the law of surplus value'.[43] This, according to economist Xu Dixin, constitutes 'capitalist exploitation' but which is necessary to modernise the means of production. The joint ventures (in the special economic zones and coastal free ports) are perceived as characteristic of state capitalism: 'They constitute a link and a form of co-operation between China's state administration and capitalism'.[44]

The 'national patriotic bourgeoisie', the expatriate bourgeoisie and foreign capitalists, rather than working people in agriculture and industry, are the agents of socialist construction, the 'modernising élites' of the transition to socialism. The next chapter analyses in greater detail the structure and institutions of foreign trade and investment, that is, the setting-up of *de facto* corporate affiliates of transnationals in the form of 'joint ventures', licencing and technology agreements, as well as the underlying framework of 'extraterritoriality under socialism'.

8

Transnational Capital in Socialist China

Joint Ventures

The legal and institutional provisions of the 'open door' policy determine the contractual forms of foreign trade and investment transactions. In turn, these provisions establish the legal and institutional mechanics whereby foreign capital gains access to Chinese resources and labour power. Moreover, they invariably delineate 'the division of labour' in production between the foreign and Chinese 'partners' in a joint venture. These provisions are an expression at the legal and institutional levels of the 'law of unequal exchange'.

The law on Joint Ventures adopted by the Second Session of the Fifth National People's Congress in 1979 enables multinational enterprises to establish *de facto* corporate subsidiaries in China under a *formal* structure of joint ownership. The text of the law is significantly ambiguous. There are no precise stipulations regarding levels of Chinese ownership, formulae concerning profit sharing and profit repatriation. Neither is there any indication as to what types of industries China wishes to attract.[1]

Ironically, the contribution to registered equity capital of the so-called 'foreign partner' shall not be *less* than 25 per cent. On the other hand, no maximum percentage of foreign equity control is stipulated. In this regard, Chinese government authorities had indeed emphasised, shortly after their adoption in 1979, that the joint venture regulations do not exclude the establishment of fully-owned subsidiaries of transnational capital, and that the absence of a ceiling on the percentage of foreign ownership was intended precisely for that purpose. In practice, however, fully-owned subsidiaries are primarily set up in the 14 designated coastal city-ports.

The joint venture regulations provide considerable latitude to foreign capital to 'strike deals' directly with individual Chinese state enterprises in areas which are essentially profitable to the 'foreign partner'. Since no priorities concerning the transfer of specific advanced technologies are stipulated, technology agreements tend to be governed by the laws of the capitalist world market. Transnationals will, therefore, enter joint venture agreements which enable them to:

1 penetrate the Chinese market, thereby in many cases competing and/or displacing existing Chinese state enterprises;
2 produce, process or assemble goods for the export market using China's abundant reserves of cheap labour. At the official exchange rate, *the cost of labour in the state sector is less than one dollar a day*, that is 30 times lower than the average wage in comparable industries in the advanced capitalist countries and several times lower than in alternative 'capitalist' cheap labour locations in South-East Asia (for example, South Korea, Taiwan, Hong Kong, Singapore).

Other important areas of foreign capitalist penetration are in off-shore oil, coal, ship-building, primary and strategic raw materials, agro-business, nuclear and hydroelectric power.

Compared to foreign investment legislation in many capitalist Third World countries, China's law on joint ventures is a blueprint of economic liberalism. China 'has opted for an apparently generous form of tax holiday. The exemption from income tax covers the first two or three profit-making years of the joint venture'.[2]

Labour management in joint ventures

Personnel management and labour relations of joint ventures are regulated by a separate set of provisions. Former Vice-Premier Yu Qiuli reassured Japanese businessmen in a press conference in 1980 that, 'joint ventures have the right to hire or fire their workers in accordance with the needs of management. Punishment including dismissal may be meted out to those who seriously violate the [sic] labour discipline'.[3]

Article 4 of the 'Provision for Labour Management in Chinese Foreign Joint Ventures' stipulates that 'a joint venture may dismiss staff and workers who become superfluous as a result of changes in production and technical conditions.' Article 5 states that 'a joint venture may impose necessary sanctions against staff and workers who violate the rules and regulations of the venture and *thereby cause certain bad consequences*'.[4] Article 6, however, provides for some safeguards: 'If the trade union considers the joint venture's dismissal of, or imposition of, sanctions against staff and workers to be unreasonable, it has the right to raise an objection.'[5]

The transfer of 'scientific' management

The management reforms in China's state enterprises have proceeded alongside the establishment of joint ventures with foreign transnationals. The transfer of 'capitalist managerial technology' and western and Japanese methods of personnel management are not only an essential ingredient of the joint venture, they constitute, according to Central Committee guidelines, a 'model of scientific management' which is to be adopted by state enterprises across China. As was discussed in chapter 4, the entry of foreign capital has, in this regard, been accompanied by the development of numerous agreements involving the setting up in China of business schools modelled on the American MBA, and numerous management training programmes and scholarships for Chinese students to study the art of capitalist 'scientific management' in American and Japanese business schools.

The management structure of joint ventures

> Equality is the basis on which China signs any agreement . . . with a foreign company. Joint ventures are run by the Chinese and foreign parties under a system in which the board of directors is the highest organ of authority.[6]

The relationship *in practice* is very much one of *inequality* and *subordination* of the 'Chinese partner' (a state enterprise). The corporate head-office of the 'foreign partner' sells technology, licences and production rights to the joint venture (which is a separate legal entity). The latter in turn 'sells back' finished output to the mother-company. The equity sharing arrangement means 'equality' in the sharing of profits and losses. The tendency in China's joint ventures is for the 'foreign partner' to make most of its money through the sale of technology, know-how, production licences, and so on, in 'exchange' for finished output. Moreover, the foreign partner retains a monopoly in the international marketing of the product. The corporate head-office of the transnational will purchase the finished output from its Chinese joint-venture subsidiary at an agreed price. This and other procedures enable the 'foreign partner' to appropriate excess profits through transfer pricing.

In the first years of operation, the joint venture will often make losses which in principle are shared *equally* under the formal system of joint ownership. In actuality, the burden of these losses falls on the 'Chinese partner' who bears most of the real costs (for example, labour, factory space, and so on).

Once the joint venture starts to make profits, the foreign partner is exempted from income tax through the tax holiday provisions of the 'Rules for the Implementation of the Income Tax Law concerning Chinese Foreign Joint Ventures'.[7] Not only is the tax on repatriation of profits extremely low (10 per cent), the regulations also have provisions which enable authorities at the provincial and municipal levels to reduce or exempt foreign companies from income tax. Provisions of this nature not only encourage provinces and municipalities to compete with one another by offering the 'best' possible terms to foreign capital, they also constitute the basis upon which new *comprador* relations develop at the provincial and municipal government levels.

Foreign enterprises will invariably negotiate with government authorities in several provinces prior to establishing a trade or joint venture agreement. Although in principle the contractual terms are set by the central ministries, provincial trading corporations and state enterprises have considerable latitude to negotiate directly with foreign capital.

The various provisions are indeed 'flexible' and often ambiguous. The *actual* practice of trade and foreign investment transactions, therefore, often transcends the boundaries of the regulatory provisions, that is, the actual form and nature of the 'joint venture' depends largely on the individual deals reached between a Chinese state enterprise and a foreign counterpart.

Co-operative joint ventures

In contrast to *equity* joint ventures, *sensu stricto*, characterised by formal joint ownership, foreign capital favours in many areas what the Chinese call 'a co-operative joint venture'. The latter may be characterised by an export processing contract with a state enterprise, a licencing agreement, compensation trade with buy-back provisions, and so on. In many cases the contractual terms of the agreement are not spelled out, and invariably they involve an 'exchange' of foreign technology, materials, parts and equipment for a finished product which is sold by the 'foreign partner' on the world market. In most of the (co-operative or equity) joint ventures, the Chinese side supplies all the labour, the factory space and part of the industrial hard-ware.

Compensation Trade and Export Processing

The contractual nature of joint ventures, compensation trade agreements, and so on, are the institutional expression of unequal exchange and China's reinsertion into the capitalist international division of labour in a wide range of cheap labour industries.

Compensation trade is the most prevalent contractual form in light industry and export processing. In compensation trade transactions the foreign contractor will provide a Chinese factory with equipment or technology. In turn, the Chinese factory will supply through a (provincial) government import-export corporation, a finished commodity at a so-called 'friendship price' over the period of repayment of the equipment. The official export price is regulated by the provincial import-export corporation. The 'friendship price', however, is below the regulated price, that is, the differential between the two prices constitutes 'repayment' (over *x* years) of the machinery supplied by the foreign contractor. In many compensation trade transactions, however, the agreement is not clearly specified in value terms. In the garment industry 'highly-priced' second-hand equipment is often exchanged for finished output.

In many cases, the 'foreign partner' will establish a long-term agreement with a Chinese manufacturer through the provincial import-export corporation. Whereas the cost of machinery (often overvalued in relation to its world market price) is repaid over a period of say three years, the Chinese State enterprise agrees to supply its foreign partner at 'the friendship price' over a period of seven to eight years. This means that the machinery is paid for several times over.

Joint Ventures, Selected Case Studies

The following case study illustrations are useful in identifying the institutional and organic structure of joint equity and co-operative ventures, compensation trade arrangements, and so on, in that they enable us to pinpoint the exchange relationship at the microeconomic level. The illustrations envisage both cases of traditional labour intensive manufacturing, as well as examples in the shipbuilding, automobile, aircraft and auto-parts industries. Examples in agro-business and food processing were discussed in chapter 3.

Changzheng municipal garment factory, Shenyang

Changzheng Municipal Garment Factory is typical of China's cheap labour export clothing industry. There are 700 workers (85 per cent of whom are women). The average wage (1983) was 48 yuan a month (17 US dollars). With the adoption of the piece-rate system, workers can earn 60 yuan a month (21 US dollars). This includes a flat basewage plus a bonus based on piece-rate productivity. The working week, excluding over-time, is 48 hours involving a six-day work week of eight hours a day.

Designs are provided by the foreign contractor. More than 80 per cent of the factory's output is sold to a single US company: The Lemar Apparel Group. The factory produces middle and high quality garments for the US, Hong Kong and Japanese markets:

> We produce a man's suit for the Lemar Apparel Group in the US [*Jordache*], we have a contract with them to produce 100 000 trousers and we hope to increase that to 300 000 trousers. Our factory is very competitive.[8]

Changzheng factory also sells to a Hong Kong company which in turn sells under a western brand name, 'Made in Hong Kong' to US and Canadian distributors. This is a standard procedure in many Chinese export factories. *It is none the less significant because it means that an important part of Hong Kong's cheap labour exports to the international market are in fact produced in the People's Republic of China.*

It is worth noting, in this context, that Chinese import-export corporations do not require state factories to put the 'Made in China' label on their export products: 'Sometimes we put our label, sometimes the foreign company changes it and puts their own'.

Changzheng factory sells their finished output to the provincial import-export corporation which in turn establishes contracts with the foreign garment companies: 'We did some compensation trade to buy foreign sewing-machines, we also are involved in straight sales through the import-export corporation.'[9]

Ironically, the imported sewing machines were second-hand used models which were old fashioned in relation to the domestic Chinese model. So much for the transfer of science and technology.

Changzheng factory will sell its finished output to the Liaoning provincial import-export corporation at an agreed price (100 yuan for a middle quality man's suit bearing the *'Jordache'* brand name). The dollar sale price is negotiated between the foreign company and the import-export corporation. This price is regulated by an internal settlement exchange rate of 2.80 yuan to the dollar (1983). This represents a 40 per cent premium over the official exchange rate of approximately 2 yuan to the US dollar (1983). It, therefore, signifies that *the effective cost of wage labour (1983) in the case of Changzheng and other similar factories is of the order of 21 dollars a month* (that is, in the case of an average monthly wage including bonuses of 60 yuan).

American Export Corporation of California's factory in Qingbu County, Shanghai municipality

The White Crane Garment Factory in Qingbu County is a modern export factory set up in 1979 to supply finished garments to the American Export Corporation of California (Amerex), a multinational garment conglomerate which purchases and produces garments in several South-East Asian countries.[10] The White Crane Factory is, in fact, a co-operative joint venture between the Shanghai Garment Import-Export Corporation and White Crane People's Commune (White Crane Township since 1982). Although, in theory, the factory is a rural industry under the jurisdiction of the commune, its management largely depends on the Shanghai Import-Export Corporation and the County government. The only link with the

White Crane Commune is that 'they supply the female labour to the factory'. The five factory leaders were appointed by the import-export corporation and the County government. The managing director, previously a senior cadre of the Shanghai Import-Export Corporation reports directly to Shanghai and has no formal links with the County or Commune (township) level *cadres*.

The factory was built from scratch in 1979 under a compensation trade agreement with Amerex. Amerex co-ordinates its activities in the factory – 'our Chinese factory', in the words of its Hong Kong representative, – through its Hong Kong branch office. Under the terms of the agreement, Amerex supplies the factory with *all* the necessary equipment (including a Toyota mini-bus and two colour TV sets for the *cadres* as 'free gifts'). The Chinese side provides the labour and the factory. Finished high quality garments bearing Amerex 'Mulberry Street' brand name are sold at a 'friendship price' to compensate for the imported equipment provided by Amerex.

As in the case of Changzheng Factory in Shenyang, the average monthly wage (1983) is 60 yuan a month (21 US dollars). The minimum guaranteed wage (1983) is 40 yuan (14 US dollars) and the maximum is 70 to 80 yuan (26 US dollars). A piece-rate system is applied although a minimum base wage of 40 yuan is guaranteed. The factory has 900 workers of whom 90 per cent are women, all senior factory leaders are men.

The Amerex representative from Hong Kong will supply the factory with specific designs. A Hong Kong designer paid by Amerex resides at the plant and the factory will produce samples which are approved by the Hong Kong branch. Sales are transacted through the import-export corporation. The imported equipment (some of it second-hand) supplied by Amerex is repaid in finished output over a period of five years.

Guangzhou shipyard – International Container Transport co-operative joint venture

In late 1978 Guangzhou Shipyard and China Machinery Import and Export Corporation began negotiations with International Container Transport (ICT), a US multinational container rental firm, for the setting up of a container factory in Guangzhou under a 'joint co-operative venture':

> The foreign company gives us the equipment, we produce the containers. The contract is between a Hong Kong investment firm CIVET Investment Ltd, China Machinery Import and Export Corporation (Guangdong branch) and Guangzhou Shipyard. The Hong Kong company will invest in China, we provide the factory and the workers at the Guangzhou Shipyard. CIVET makes the contract with International Container Transport which purchases the containers from us.[11]

Under the terms of this triangular agreement, CIVET provides money to buy the technology from ICT which in turn purchases back the finished output:

> We build 50 000 containers in five years for the repayment of the equipment to the Hong Kong company. After five years we can sell the containers to whom we please. The raw materials are imported from Japan, Britain and the US because the domestic steel plates do not meet international requirements . . . In 1981 the Hong Kong company asked ICT to buy the raw materials in the international market . . . our factory buys them, they pay for it.[12]

Under the terms of the compensation trade agreement, the container factory will only start making profits after five years: 'China needs containers to support its foreign trade . . . The containers are sold to ICT's terminal in the port of Huangpu [on the Pearl River]'.[13]

International Container Transport then rents back the containers in Huangpu to Chinese State export and shipping companies. Not only are the containers produced free of charge for five years in a Chinese factory by Chinese workers but the container transnational rents them back to China for a fee in the true Chinese spirit of 'equality and mutual benefit'. These 'drawbacks' are presumably compensated by the transfer of advanced technology and equipment involved in welding six plates of metal into a finished container in China's national shipbuilding industry.

The foregoing example is typical of a form of export processing which destroys the internal forward and backward sectoral linkages because all the equipment and raw materials (including the paint) are imported.

Joint ventures in the automobile industry

Prior to Liberation, motor vehicles were either imported or assembled in China from imported parts. China's auto-industry developed in the 1950s with the first designs imported from the Soviet Union. In 1983 there were nine major plants producing automobiles, jeeps, and heavy and light trucks.

In 1980 the government liberalised the import of automobiles, thereby enabling Nissan and Toyota to flood the domestic Chinese market. With large-scale imports from Japan, the domestic production of motor vehicles declined by 22.3 per cent in 1981. In 1982 the National Automotive Industry Corporation was set up to 'centralise and integrate the various automobile plants' as well as to 'promote the import of technology' and the export of finished vehicles. In 1983 the production of the domestic '*Shanghai*' automobile model was discontinued indefinitely. The national automobile industry (production of cars) has been 'taken over' by Volkswagen.

The Shanghai-Volkswagen joint venture factory

The Shanghai-Volkswagen plant established under joint venture agreement with the Shanghai Associated Motor Vehicle Company signifies that the *entire* national production of automobiles (previously producing the Chinese '*Shanghai*' model) is subordinated to foreign technology. The Shanghai plant becomes a mere VW assembly line similar to those which exist, for instance, in Mexico or Brazil. Volkswagen not only takes over the domestic market, but also uses the Chinese plant and Chinese workers (paid at one dollar a day) as an export base to sell 'China Made VWs' to the Far Eastern markets. The export of finished VWs are to pay for the import of technology and equipment from Germany.[14]

As in other (capitalist) Third World countries, the Shanghai-VW plant will, in the first stage, assemble motor vehicles using a large percentage of imported parts and equipment. The Chinese joint venture will subsequently produce the automobile parts domestically in the Shanghai plant according to VW designs and technology.

Rather than encouraging the selective transfer of technology so as to upgrade China's automobile industry, the Shanghai-VW joint venture means that China has entirely foregone the possibility of developing an automobile industry of its own.

The Beijing Jeep-American Motor Company joint venture

In a similar fashion, American Motor Company (AMC) entered a joint venture with Beijing Jeep Factory in 1983. This joint venture displaced the domestic Chinese model jeep, the factory was transformed into an assembly line of AMC/Renault. As in the case of VW, AMC 'China Made' jeeps are exported to reimburse AMC for the transfer of equipment and advanced technology. Initially, 40 per cent of the finished AMC jeeps will be sold in the international market.[15]

Beijing no. 2 automobile factory, an example of economic self-reliance

Beijing no. 2 automobile factory was founded in 1956 and is one of the major Chinese producers of light trucks:

> We produce light trucks according to our design and technology. We have had talks with foreign auto-producers, but they ask us to reorganise our workshops and undertake assembly using foreign parts. But we feel that this type of arrangement is not suitable for us so we just have technological exchanges with them. We had talks with Citroën, Toyota and Mitsubishi but we are not interested in designs or licensing agreements.[16]

None the less, the pressures to enter these agreements are very strong because the Central Committee's policy is to promote 'socialist competition' within the automobile industry. Under these circumstances, factories which rely on their own efforts are at a disadvantage in relation to their Chinese competitors who enter into production assembly contracts with a foreign auto-producer. Agreements in the production of light and heavy trucks with Japanese and Western auto producers will eventually displace the self-reliant factory ('which does not want to modernise') through 'socialist competition'.

Joint ventures in auto parts: the example of Parker-Hubei (China) Ltd

China is rapidly becoming a cheap labour producer of automobile parts, components, machine tools, and so on. Western auto producers, as well as producers of auto parts, will *subcontract* the production of designated auto parts with a Chinese state enterprise in compensation trade or joint venture agreements.[17] Parker Seals (US) a multinational producer of auto gaskets and rubber seals, entered a joint equity venture with Hubei Auto Industry in 1980 in which Hubei has 51 per cent of the equity.

Lu Fengming is Chairman of the Board of Directors of Parker-Hubei Seals Co. Ltd:

> Hubei province has friendship relations with its twin Ohio State in America. It is in this context that we established contact with our US partner in late 1979. We co-operate with a subsidiary of the Parker group located in Lexington Kentucky. Last year (1982) we were in the US for the board of directors' meeting of the joint venture. Next year the President of the US Company Mr Parker himself accompanied by his First Vice-President will come here for the board meeting.[18]

The Chinese side supplies the labour, factory space and part of the equipment produced in China under Parker license. The plant is intended to produce both for export and the domestic markets. Parker decided on the Chinese location (after having examined an alternative cheap labour location in the Philippines) so as to supply the South-East Asian market:

> At the beginning, the US company will provide the raw materials because 65 per cent of total output is for export. According to state policy, imported raw materials to be processed for export are not subject to customs duty. All equipment imported by joint ventures are exempted from import duties.[19]

The liberalisation of import tariffs signifies, in this context, that joint ventures and/or firms undertaking compensation trade are in effect submitted to the same duty-free structure as enterprises located in the coastal cities 'development zones', 'trading areas' and 'special economic zones'.

Parker (US) provides 50 per cent of the machinery, much of which is rebuilt machinery previously in use in the American plant. The Chinese side provides the remaining machinery produced in China according to Parker designs. Parker (US) has full control over international sales and marketing through its agent in Hong Kong; the Hubei Province import-export corporation is in no way involved in the joint venture's exports as in the case of compensation trade transactions. The factory export price is in principle negotiated by both sides, in practice Parker (US) is 'buying' from the joint venture subsidiary at a substantial discount and is, therefore, making the bulk of its profit through transfer pricing.

Average monthly wages in the joint venture were (in 1983) 50 yuan a month (18 US$). This is *lower* than the average in the state sector: 'this is because the workers in this factory are new and younger workers'. According to state regulations, wages in a joint venture must be 20-50 per cent higher than the average wage of the state sector in the province, 'but this is flexible, we intend to apply this system when the factory becomes operative'.

Lu Fengming expressed his desire to apply the 'scientific methods of management' applied by Parker in the United States: 'US engineers help us here and we send managerial staff for training to the US but we will attempt to combine American management with our domestic experience'.[20]

'We are also interested in applying American methods of hiring and personnel management' because the Chinese system gives too much security to workers. 'It is the iron rice bowl'.

Workers at Parker-Hubei are selected after an examination and a period of training. They are not 'contract workers' as in other state factories:

> They can be dismissed and transferred to another factory if they are no longer needed, they can also be fired for disciplinary reasons including shortcomings in their technical skills, health or *ideological problems*.[21]

Joint ventures in aircraft parts and assembly

Subcontracting and compensation trade are the predominant forms of trade in traditional cheap labour export processing (for example, garment, footwear, electronics) as well as in more sophisticated and 'heavier' industrial products, that is, machines, machine tools, engineering products, shipbuilding, and so on. For instance, China Trade Corporation of New York has signed an agreement with China on behalf of US firms producing aircraft parts, railway undercarriages, engine parts, and so on. The agreement for the production of railway undercarriages is with Seattle-based Paton Corporation, which sells the technology to China.[22] Production prototypes are then purchased back by the US firm for testing. While the Chinese are interested in railway technology for the internal market, exports of China-made railway equipment (under a US brand name) is envisaged in the second stage of the joint co-operative venture. A similar agreement has been reached between a US manufacturer and a Chinese aircraft corporation for the manufacture of parts and airframes for small passenger jet aircrafts, both for the internal and export markets.[23]

McDonnell Douglas had established links with China's Aerospace Technology Import-Export Corporation as early as 1979, regarding a 3 billion dollar project for the production of DC9s in Shanghai. This project was turned down by the Chinese authorities. McDonnell Douglas has now entered a somewhat smaller and different project which involves the production of 100 to 200 sets of landing-gear doors which would be produced in China under McDonnell designs and specifications and exported back to McDonnell Douglas plants in the US.

The foregoing illustrations exhibit various forms of export processing, in heavier and more sophisticated sectors of economic activity. The mechanics of subcontracting, however, are substantially the same as in the 'traditional' sectors of cheap labour manufacturing and light industry. The design is submitted to the Chinese party who produces the commodity according to the specifications of the foreign contractor.

The transfer of technology

The underlying division of labour which characterises the joint venture relationship exhibits a consistent and coherent pattern: the design and know-how are developed by the foreign corporation whereas the hardware industrial process is produced and managed by the Chinese partner. There is a clear demarcation between intellectual and manual labour (that is, between the software and hardware stages of production).

The integration of the capital goods and technology-producing sectors into an international network of licensing agreements, patents and brand names, while formally contributing to the incorporation of advanced western technology, is at the same time conducive to the technological subordination of Chinese industry to foreign capital. The issue, however, is not the import of technology *per se*, but the precise framework and conditions which characterise the transfer of technology and which constitute an obstacle to the development and consolidation of a self-reliant national technology producing sector.

Self-reliance is undermined in favour of an economically 'extraverted' structure characterised by the implicit integration of China's manufacturing industry into the prevailing structure and logic of the world capitalist economy.

'Extraterritoriality under Socialism'

The special economic zones

The 'special economic zones' first established in 1979 in Guangdong and Fujian provinces combine China's tradition of extraterritoriality with the South-East Asian version of the free trade export processing zone. The special economic zones are essentially geared towards the development of cheap labour export processing industries in electronics assembly, garments, light industry, and so on. Four SEZs were established in 1979–80: Shenzhen across the border from Hong Kong, including the Shekou industrial zone administered by China Merchants Steamship Navigation Company, Zhuhai in the area of Macao, Shantou in southern Guangdong, and Xiamen on the Fujian coast directly opposite Taiwan. Similar 'open door' procedures were applied to the development of Hainan Island in south-western Guangdong as a free trade zone specialising in tropical cash crops.

Shenzhen, the largest of the SEZs, is to some extent an extension of the Hong Kong industrial base in the New Territories, providing cheaper sources of labour inside the territory of the People's Republic of China. Her Majesty's Hong Kong dollar banknotes are legal tender along with the Bank of China's Foreign Exchange Certificates, a convertible hard-currency Renminbi (People's Currency). This situation is reminiscent of the treaty ports of pre-Liberation days where the imperialist powers issued the concessions' banknotes.

In 1980 the National Peoples' Congress adopted 'Regulations on Special Economic Zones in Guangdong Province' which enables 'foreign citizens, overseas Chinese, compatriots in Hong Kong and Macao to open factories or set up enterprises with their own investment or undertake joint ventures with Chinese investment and their assets, due profits and other legitimate rights and interests are legally protected' (Chapter I, Article 1).[24]

The CCP Politbureau has ensured foreign business interests that 'government offices [in the SEZs] should by no means interfere in the management of the enterprises but give them a free hand to develop their potentials and run their own business'.[25]

A regime of apparent *laissez-faire* is promoted in the SEZs.

> 'The zones' business management should be separated from government departments and local government should not interfere . . . All enterprises in the special zones whether affiliated to the central, provincial or zone government and whether they are run co-operatively by Chinese and foreign businessmen or are solely foreign investments, should be managed independently so long as they pay taxes as stipulated.[26]

The income tax rate levied on foreign enterprises in the SEZs is 15 per cent, machinery, parts, raw materials brought into the SEZs are exempt of import duty, a tax holiday applies to the first two years of operation of the enterprise and after-tax profits can be remitted out of China. Investors who reinvest profits in the SEZs are eligible for tax exemption.

At the official exchange rate, the dollar cost of labour in China's SEZs is less than one-third that of Hong Kong. Foreign enterprises do not, however, purchase the services of labour directly in the market place. Labour is hired in a contractual arrangement with 'Chinese Labour Service Companies' set up by the Administration of the SEZ. The Labour Service Company recruits and screens workers on behalf of the foreign contractor:

> Chinese staff members and workers to be employed by enterprises in the special economic zones are to be recommended by the local labour service companies . . . the employees of the enterprise in the special zones are managed by the enterprises according to their business requirements and if necessary, can be dismissed in line with the provisions of the labour contracts.[27]

Hiring will increasingly be formalised in terms of employment contracts which contain provisions pertaining to dismissal, reassignment, retirement, disciplinary actions, working hours, holidays, and so on: 'Workers can be dismissed in cases of redundancy or having been proved unfit for the work assigned'.

The price of labour in the SEZs is substantially higher than that in state export factories elsewhere in China. The 'recommended' price of labour power to a foreign enterprise and/or joint venture was set (in 1982) at 180 yuan (US $64) a month for a 48 to 60 hour week in Guangdong province (and 150 yuan in Fujian province). Of this amount, 50 per cent (80 yuan) is paid to the workers in the form of a basic monthly wage, 20 per cent (on average 36 yuan) is to be used as incentives in the form of floating wage payments. Twenty-five per cent (45 yuan) is turned over to the SEZ authorities who administer the 'welfare fund' and the remaining 5 per cent is allocated to the factories' medical and recreational fund.

In practice, there seems to be considerable variation in wages, bonuses and fringe benefits paid in the SEZs. Basic wages (excluding bonuses) in the SEZs vary from a low of 30 yuan (US $11) to 100 yuan (US $36) a month (in 1982) depending on the level of skill and the type of enterprise. With the influx of foreign capital, a piece-rate system is increasingly being adopted. In the words of Premier Zhao Ziyang:

> [T]he salary system in the special economic zones should be reformed and the thought that income is guaranteed for everybody regardless of their work should be cast away. He said that besides basic salary, floating wages are also preferable.[28]

Under the provisions of the SEZs, land is leased to foreign enterprises in a contractual agreement with the SEZ or provincial authorities. The annual rental rate in Shenzhen is US $3 to 10 per square metre per year and US $2 to 5 in Xiamen under (extendable) lease terms which average 25 years. The land utility cost is more than ten times lower in Shenzhen than across the border in Hong Kong. As mentioned earlier, the control over industrial land leases tends to be concentrated in the hands of Hong Kong real estate and property developers. A similar situation exists in residential and tourist land development projects.

The Hong Kong connection

The SEZs are earmarked for investment by Hong Kong 'compatriots' and Overseas Chinese essentially in light manufacturing and export processing. The relative importance of the special economic zones in the over-all structure of China trade and foreign investment should by no means be overrated. Not only is the development and expansion of the SEZs limited in scale, it is largely circumscribed to the 'overflow' of small-scale manufacturing from Hong Kong. In fact, the production process between Hong Kong and the SEZs may be entirely integrated, that is, industrial components and materials are shipped into the SEZ for assembly, the product is then returned to Hong Kong in finished or semi-finished form and exported to the international market. In many cases the product assembled in the SEZ will bear the Hong Kong or foreign brand name and label and will be identified as 'Made in Hong Kong':

> With Hong Kong wage rates three or four times higher than in China, the advantages of using mainland workers for assembly, packaging and other manual tasks are obvious. Such co-operative deals need not entail even an investment in plant or construction by the Hong Kong investor, goods can be sent in, processed and returned to Hong Kong for export or local sale.[29]

The coastal free ports and development zones

In 1984 the Central Committee approved the establishment of 'development zones' or 'special trading areas' in 14 designated coastal cities several of which were, prior to Liberation, treaty ports under extraterritorial colonial jurisdiction (for example, Dalian, Tianjin, Qingdao, Shanghai, Ningbo, Fuzhou, Guangzhou).

In these designated coastal ports, foreign capital may establish fully-owned subsidiaries or joint ventures with Chinese participation. 'Development zones' with industrial, commercial and banking infrastructure are set up, other areas of the city are earmarked for the development of foreign residential concessions in which overseas business executives and their families will live. No customs duty nor taxes will be levied on machinery or materials imported into the development zones until 1990. Moreover, foreign capitalists have been reassured that not only will they be offered long-term, low interest loans for the import of means of production but also 'the state will not expect a share of the profits for five years'.[30]

Former inland river treaty ports were excluded from the Central Committee's 1984 decision. Wuhan, capital of Hubei Province, however, and its river port of Hankou was granted the status of 'pilot area for the reform of the economy'. In addition to a target of one billion dollars in foreign investment in Wuhan and in other parts of Hubei Province over a period of 15 years, the provisions will grant Wuhan the status of a foreign trading port with the right to conduct trade directly with foreign businessmen.

The most important 'special trading area' is in Shanghai where entire sectors of the city will be developed as industrial development zones and 'foreign residence concessions'. The Minhang development zone, which covers an area of 230 hectares was designated by the Shanghai municipal authorities in 1984 'to be used for building Chinese-foreign joint ventures, enterprises with sole overseas investment and trading centres'.[31] The Hongqiao development zone covering an area of 65 hectares is earmarked as a 'foreign residence concession'.

The NPCs policy of 'opening coastal cities' has led to the formation of 'an economic development zone' in Huangpu, Guangzhou's international port on the Pearl River. The entire area of Huangpu County is to be developed as a 'special trading area' in which joint ventures, co-operative joint ventures, fully-owned TNC subsidiaries and research institutes are to be set up. Contrary to the procedures envisaged in the Guangdong and Fujian SEZs, which are earmarked as export platforms, foreign capital in the designated coastal cities' development zones will have access to the domestic market.

In the Dalian development zone in north-east China, foreign transnationals are investing in a designated 50 square kilometre area. The Dalian zone will specialise in electronics, precision instruments, machinery and food processing.[32]

Capitalist enclaves in 'socialist' China

Although juridically distinct from the treaty ports (*shang pu*) of the colonial period, the 'development zones' and 'special trading areas' in the designated coastal cities rehabilitate a new form of extraterritoriality under Chinese jurisdiction, but functionally separate from the rest of the Chinese economy, and economically integrated into the world capitalist economy through the granting of customs duty exemptions and special provisions regarding foreign investment. Whereas the modern 'free port' does not imply the surrender of political authority as in the case of the treaty ports, they constitute capitalist enclaves within the territory of the PRC in which foreign enterprises can enter trade and investment transactions 'along capitalist lines'. Whereas title deeds over land are no longer granted to foreigners, the experience of Guangdong's SEZs is that land is leased to large overseas and Hong Kong-based property developers for periods averaging 25 years. The control over industrial, residential and commercial property is concentrated in the hands of foreign real estate and property developers (mainly from Hong Kong) in joint venture arrangements with a provincial government real estate company which develops the necessary infrastructure.

Industrial land is leased to an international property developer who builds the industrial infrastructure and overhead (using Chinese workers) and then *subleases* factory space to potential foreign investors. The control of industrial, residential and tourist land development projects is in the hands of international real estate and property consortia.

The contribution of extraterritoriality to economic modernisation

The balance sheet of economic performance in the special economic zones is somewhat ambiguous. At the time of writing it is too early to evaluate the performance of the 14 coastal free-city ports set up in 1984. Despite the fact that they are identified by the Chinese government as a major component of China's 'economic modernisation', the establishment of SEZs favours neither the transfer of technology nor the adoption of 'scientific management'. Moreover their impact on employment, that is, in terms of generating job opportunities is equally ambiguous: a large proportion of the workers are detached from existing employment in other parts of China; this is particularly the case with regard to professional, managerial, technical and skilled labour.

In this respect the drain of human and material resources towards the development of a foreign trade infrastructure in the SEZs and development zones in particular, and in the coastal regions in general, is likely to have 'backwash effects' on patterns of regional and inter-regional trade, that is, the concentration of investment resources and infrastructure has serious repercussions on the economic development of the inland provinces.

Moreover, investment in the SEZs – theoretically geared towards the transfer of foreign technology and expertise – is concentrated in the 'softer' areas of manufacturing, that is, in many cases in industries in which China is already relatively advanced and has little to gain from foreign capital investment. This situation is, however, different in the designated 14 coastal cities.

Whereas the SEZs constitute regional poles which attract scarce human capital and material resources, the enclave type structure of the SEZ is not conducive to the development of 'forward' and 'backward' sectoral linkages with other parts of the Chinese economy.

It should also be noted that, despite measures taken by the Chinese authorities, the development of the SEZs takes place against a background of economic corruption, bribery and smuggling. The leadership admits in this regard that the opening up of trade is 'a double-edged blade': while it helps China's modernisation, it also constitutes 'a strong incentive to mercenary practices'. Deng Xiaoping reassured foreign investors, however, that despite the fact that corruption 'and other decadent things are slipping in along with foreign capital . . . this will not deter China from pursuing an open door policy'.

The relative importance of smuggling activities, which is partly a consequence of the duty-free import of materials and parts in the over-all flow of goods and capital to the SEZs, is difficult to assess. It, nevertheless, constitutes a serious strain on China's balance of payments. Whether the SEZs contribute to the net inflow of foreign exchange is, in this regard a matter of conjecture.

Foreign Capital in Off-shore Oil

With the 'carving-up' of the Yellow Sea and the East and South China seas into 'concessionary blocks', each to be developed by separate American, European and Japanese petroleum conglomerates in joint venture contracts with the Chinese National Off-Shore Oil Corporation (CNOOC) and its corporate subsidiaries in Tianjin, Shanghai, Guangzhou and Zhanjiang (respectively responsible for joint ventures in different areas of China's coastline) off-shore oil is becoming the most important single area of foreign investment in China.

In addition to the signing of off-shore oil joint ventures respectively with the Japanese National Oil Corporation (JNOC), the French State Corporation Elf-Aquitaine, Atlantic Ritchfield, the British Petroleum, Esso and Shell groups, foreign capital is also involved in major joint ventures both in conventional oil fields as well as in coal mining. In 1984 Arnold Hammer, president of Occidental Petroleum Corporation, was recieved in Beijing by Deng Xiaoping. Hammer's visit in fact coincided with that of Ronald Reagan. The final agreement on joint development of Antaibao at Pingshuo, Shaanxi province, the largest open coal mine in the world, between Occidental and the China National Coal Development Corporation (CNCDC) was signed in Beijing in April 1984.[33] At Daqing oil field, known as a model of 'mass-line leadership' and economic self-reliance during the Cultural Revolution, major agreements have been signed with international petroleum consortia for 'the upgrading' of Daqing's facilities in co-operation with foreign oil transnationals.

China initially envisaged the development of its off-shore oil during the Great Leap Forward.[34] Off-shore exploration was conducted during the 1960s in the Bohai Gulf area where oil was discovered in 1969. The initial development of Bohai, known as *Bohai I*, was entirely self-reliant, based on the use of Chinese built jack-up oil rigs and drilling equipment. Shortly after its construction, *Bohai I* struck oil in 1971 when it completed its first off-shore exploratory well in the Bohai Gulf.[35] From 1971 to 1976, eight off-shore oil wells were opened up in Bohai using a Chinese designed catamaran drillship.[36] The development of off-shore oil until 1976 was essentially carried out according to the principles of 'economic self-reliance' with selective purchases of foreign technology from Japan and France.

The oil crisis in 1973 generated considerable impetus in the development of China's off-shore oil: it encouraged Japan – heavily dependent upon oil supplies from the Middle East and in the face of the 1973 oil embargo – to seek secure supplies of oil in the Far Eastern region. China's first major petroleum exports were in 1973 with the signing of an agreement with Japan. It is worth noting that in 1976 Wang, Yao, Zhang and Jiang (the group of Four) had opposed petroleum exports, charging the foreign trade departments of 'selling out national resources'.[37]

Exploration in the South China Sea was under way in the early 1970s, using Chinese equipment as well as geological and seismic survey equipment from France, Japan and the United States and foreign jack-up rigs for 'over water' drilling which China was not able to produce domestically.

After October 1976, the orientation of China's off-shore oil programme shifted radically from a policy of selective embodiment of advanced foreign technology in support of a sovereign and self-reliant oil industry, to the development of joint ventures and production sharing arrangements with foreign capital. These agreements establish *de facto* foreign ownership over part of China's petroleum reserves in that they entail *appropriation rights* over the future output of the off-shore installations.

Whereas Premier Hua Guofeng had announced that China should build 'some ten more oil fields as big as Daqing', the oil ministers and top communist party officials met in May 1977 to define the scope and direction of China's 'co-operation' with foreign capital both in off-shore and on-shore oil development. The so-called 'petroleum group' made up of prominent Politbureau and Central Committee members Li Xiannian, Yu Qili, Kang Shi'en, Chen Muhua and Gu Mu were, on balance, supporters of the 'Rightist line' with Li Xiannian as the prime mover of the 'petroleum group'.[38] The Minister of Petroleum, Song Zhenming, was, however, dismissed in 1980 and Vice-Premier Kang and Yu Qili were demoted as a result of pressures from Deng supporters who seized upon the death of 72 workers in the capsizing of an off-shore oil rig in 1979 to mount an attack on the 'petroleum group'.[39]

The historic May 1977 meeting was immediately followed by important purchases of American oil-related equipment and, in June 1977, a ten-member Chinese petroleum delegation visited the United States and Japan. The US visit led to a considerable sale of American drilling equipment to China. In the autumn months of 1977 a return high ranking US delegation visited China's petroleum installations and conducted technical seminars for Chinese oil executives in Beijing.[40] In early 1978 Sun Jingwen, Vice-Minister of Petroleum and Chemical Industries, and other top Chinese officials, were invited to the US to tour production and exploration facilities in Texas, Louisiana and California.[41] Also, as a result of the May 1977 Conference, China began long-term sales of crude oil to Japan instead of the previous contracts which were renewed on a year-to-year basis.[42] These developments in the areas of technology purchases were in a sense instrumental and transitional, in that they paved the way for the development of fully-fledged joint ventures and production-sharing agreements with foreign capital.

Joint ventures with the Japan National Oil Corporation

Negotiations with Japan to develop jointly the Bohai Gulf oil deposits were initiated in 1978. In December 1979 China signed its first joint venture with the Japanese National Oil Company (JNOC). The Bohai Gulf agreement is described as a 'no risk formula' which grants the JNOC consortium (made up of the Japan-Arabian Oil Company, Idemitsu, Japan Petroleum Exploration Corporation, Mitsubishi, Mitsui and Teikoku) exploration rights in the southern and western Bohai Gulf.[43] Under the terms of the agreement the Japanese consortium will pay for the costs of exploration although the Chinese side 'will share the losses' if no commercial deposits are found. The development costs will be shared by China (51 per cent) and Japan (49 per cent). Japan will appropriate 42.5 per cent of total production. The deal was negotiated with strong support from the Japanese government, in parallel with a 1.5 billion dollar soft loan by Japan's Overseas Economic Co-operation Fund and a 2 billion dollar loan from Japan's Exim Bank.[44]

The provisions of the contract signed in 1980 with the French State Corporation, Société Nationale Elf-Aquitaine, for the exploration and development of 9400 square kilometres in the northern part of Bohai Bay is remarkably similar to the 'sharing of risks' formula in the Japanese contract.[45] The Compagnie Française des Pétroles (TOTAL) was granted similar exploration and development rights in 1980 in 10 190 square kilometres area in the Gulf of Tonkin.[46]

American oil consortia had a careful eye on the Japanese and French deals because they constituted the basis for the development of 'a model contract' similar to the production-sharing agreements with several Third World oil producers. By 1981, 40 out of the 46 international oil companies organised into several large consortia were eligible for exploration and joint-development of designated 'blocks' of China's coastline in the South China Sea.

In autumn 1981 the US Treasury department rushed a mission of American tax lawyers to Beijing, to resolve the problem of 'double taxation' of US oil companies. New tax rules were adopted 'to encourage co-operative oil exploration' and in February 1982 the State Council approved the 'Regulations of the People's Republic of China on the Exploitation of Off-shore Petroleum Resources in Co-operation with Foreign Enterprises'.[47] These regulations, while not spelling out the specifics of a model contract, identify a contractual framework based on the following general principles:

> [T]he foreign enterprise that is one party to the contract (hereafter 'foreign contractor') shall provide exploration investment, undertake exploration operations and bear all exploration risks. After a commercial oil or gas field is discovered, both the foreign contractor and CNOOC shall make investment in the co-operative development. The foreign contractor shall be responsible for the development and production operations until CNOOC takes over the production operations when conditions permit under the petroleum contract. The foreign contractor may recover its investment and expenses and receive remuneration out of the petroleum produced according to the provisions of the petroleum contract (Article 7).[48]
>
> The foreign contractor may export the petroleum it receives as its share and/or purchases and remit abroad the investment it recovers, its profits and other legitimate income according to law (Article 8).[49]

These provisions are conceptually similar to a form of compensation trade whereby the foreign contractor appropriates a portion of the petroleum produced over a given number of years in exchange for initial investment outlays in oil exploration and development.

The joint ventures between CNOOC (and its regional subsidiaries) and the foreign oil companies are managed by so-called 'joint management committees' (JMCs) made up of representatives from CNOOC and the foreign oil consortium. The JMCs are made up of 11 members, the chairman is appointed by CNOOC and the vice-chairman by the principal contractor of the foreign consortium.[50] For instance, in the South China Sea Eastern division, co-ordinated by CNOOC's regional corporation Nanhai (East) Oil Corporation in Guangzhou, four international consortia had (in 1983) respectively been allocated separate 'contract areas' of the

TABLE 8.1 *Petroleum consortia in the South China Sea*

	Petroleum consortia	*Contract area (in sq. km)*
1.	*The British Petroleum Group*	14 086
	BP Petroleum Development Ltd	3 199
	Petro-Canada Exploration, Inc.	2 256
	Ranger Oil Ltd	1 286
	Petrobras Internacional S.A. – Braspetro	3 209
	The Broken Hill Propriety Company Ltd	4 136
2.	*Occidental Group I*	1 284
	Occidental Eastern Inc.	
	Tricentrol Exploration Overseas	
	Hispanica de Petroleas SA	
	Ampol Exploration Ltd	
	CSR Ltd	
3.	*Occidental Group II*	1 286
	Occidental Eastern	
	Elf-Aquitaine Chine	
	Tricentrol Exploration Overseas Ltd	
	Total Chine	
4.	*Esso – Shell*	5 120
	Esso – China Ltd	2 580
	Shell Exploration (China) Ltd	2 540
5.	*Japan National Oil Corporation I*	2 246
	Japan National Oil Corporation	
	Indemitsu Oil Development Co. Ltd	
	Natomas (Far East) Ltd	
	Cluff Oil PLC	
6.	*Japan National Oil Corporation II*	5 737
	Japan National Oil Corporation	
	Getty Oil International (Orient) Inc.	
	Sun Orient Exploration Company	
	Texas Eastern Orient, Inc.	
	Cluff Oil PLC	

SOURCE *Beijing Review*, XXVII: 16(1984), p. 21.

eastern part of the South China Sea including the Pearl River basin. These consortia are the British Petroleum, Occidental, Esso-Shell and Japanese National Oil Corporation groups. The composition of these four consortia is indicated in Table 8.1.

Competitive bidding and sub-contracting

In fact, the competitive bidding is constrained by the *de facto* formation of a limited number of consortia which have been allocated exploration and development rights in the so-called 'contract areas'.

The joint management committee (JMC) of the joint venture is responsible for establishing the competitive bidding for the provision of exploration, drilling and other services according to a system of tender.[51] Although Chinese companies may also bid, the contracts are often allocated either to international companies or Chinese-foreign joint venture companies dominated by foreign technology.

For instance, off-shore rigs are produced in a (Chinese-foreign) joint venture in Guangzhou Shipyard, which in turn supplies Nanhai (East) Oil Corporation and its joint venture partners. In other words, the development of joint ventures in off-shore exploration has also been conducive to the development of joint ventures with foreign capital in China's off-shore oil equipment industry.

In the western part of the South China Sea, co-operation with foreign capital is co-ordinated by Nanhai (West) Oil Corporation (a regional subsidiary of CNOOC). The latter has established two major joint venture contracts respectively with Atlantic Ritchfield (ARCO) and the Companie Française des Pétroles (TOTAL). Several other consortia established agreements with Nanhai (West) in 1984.[52] Operations are co-ordinated out of Zhanjiang, which was granted the status of a coastal free port in 1984, with designated 'development zones' and foreign residence areas.

In the words of the general manager of Nanhai (West) Oil Corporation Mr Wang Yan:

> The co-operation between China and foreign corporations is wonderful . . . the foreign corporations want to regain their investment and earn early profits and the Chinese wish to provide the drive with oil as soon as possible . . . Since co-operation always involves two sides, their relationship should be equal and beneficial to both of them . . . While implementing the contracts, we always do our best to protect the foreign investors rights and interests concerning specific problems.[53]

When asked 'whether China's rights and interests might be damaged by this co-operation' Wang Yan responded:

> Of course not. We all clearly remember how we suffered in the old days when China lost its sovereignty and dignity. That is why we pay such close attention to protecting the state's rights and interests.[54]

The various institutional modalities which characterise the penetration of the Chinese economy by foreign capital discussed in this chapter encourage China's reintegration into the productive, financial and commercial structure of world capitalism.

The next chapter examines some of the broader implications of China's reinsertion into the capitalist international division of labour.

9

China and World Capitalism

Introduction

China's reintegration into the structure and logic of the world capitalist economy after Mao, and the development of trade and investment relations 'along capitalist lines' constitute a new and crucially important phase in the structure of the post-war international division of labour. This process is characterised by the integration of China's manpower reserves into the 'international reserve pool' of cheap Third World labour and the subordination of China's natural resource base of conventional and strategic raw materials to the needs and requirements of world capitalism. With close to one-quarter of the world's population, unlimited supplies of cheap industrial labour, and a large surplus population in its rural hinterland, China is rapidly becoming the largest world supplier of cheap labour (low technology) industrial exports. Not only is the cost of labour in China more than 30 times lower than in the advanced capitalist countries (for a similar category of skill in the same branch of industry), wages (expressed in US dollars) are several times lower than in many competing cheap labour locations in South-East Asia. Moreover, it should be understood that China's industrial export economy (for example, in textiles) had already achieved a relatively high level of development, prior to Liberation, in Manchuria and the treaty ports. The semi-colonial foreign trade infrastructure which developed historically during the Republican period and Japanese occupation influences the nature of China's reinsertion into the structure of the capitalist international division of labour in the post-Mao period.

The implications of such a reintegration are far-reaching, not only for China's own economic and social development process: the international 'migration' or *relocation* of productive capital to China in a wide range of industries exacerbates the process of structural recession in the advanced capitalist countries because it promotes the decline of the 'old' labour intensive manufacturing industries. Also, the development of China's industrial export base undermines and modifies the underlying economic fabric of competing 'capitalist' Third World suppliers of cheap labour industrial exports, that is, the so-called 'newly-industrialised countries' (NICs).

This chapter examines first the particular role of surplus population and world unemployment in the processes of 'migration' and relocation of industrial capital which were conducive to the development, in the post-Second World War period, of cheap labour industrial exports in the Third World. China's 'reintegration' is discussed in the context of the evolving structure of the international division of labour and its broad implications both for China, as well as for the advanced capitalist countries and the capitalist Third World.

We then proceed to examine a phenomenon which is related to the articulation of the world surplus population, namely the *export of manpower* from China's reserves of cheap labour and the sale of Chinese labour power (in the form of a type of 'indentured labour') to international corporate capital in large scale public works and construction projects located primarily in the 'labour scarce' countries of the Middle East. The export of manpower from China's labour reserves is viewed as the counterpart of the international 'migration' of capital to cheap sources of labour within China: the export of a *mobile* contractual labour force to *immobile* capital (public works, construction, and so on) is the antithetical counterpart of the export of *mobile* capital to *immobile* reserves of cheap labour. The opposite movements of labour and capital belong to a single and united process of world capital accumulation: the development of the post-war international division of labour is conducive to the unity of these two opposing processes, that is, both belong to the unfolding and articulation of an international cheap labour economy.

Finally, this chapter envisages China's reintegration into world capitalism in relation to the problematic of *unequal exchange* and *unequal specialisation* which characterises China's relations with foreign capital under the 'open door' policy.

The International Division of Labour, Historical Perspective on the 'Migration' of Capital and Labour

Historically, the formation of a relative surplus population in the 'old' centres of industrial development of Western Europe played an important role in the national and international migration of labour. In the early nineteenth century, the floating surplus population in the advanced capitalist countries was the lever of capital accumulation which enabled the rapidly expanding branches of industry to appropriate fresh labour power.[1] Both nationally and internationally, the migration of labour followed that of capital:

> Only a very small number continue to find employment in the same branches of industry while the majority are regularly discharged. This

majority forms an element of the floating surplus population growing with the extension of these branches of industry. Part of them emigrate following in fact capital which has emigrated.[2]

The export of capital in the latter part of the nineteenth century and early twentieth century coincides with the waves of emigration: where capital migrates so does labour, the floating surplus population in the 'old' centres flows to the 'new' labour-scarce centres of capital accumulation. The international movement of labour was, therefore, closely related both to the movement of capital and the structure of the international division of labour.

The process of transnationalisation after the Second World War substantially modified the patterns of migration of both capital and labour. The migration of labour (after the Second World War) has become increasingly 'selective', characterised by the movement of professional and skilled manpower from the Third World to the advanced capitalist countries. On the other hand, productive capital will increasingly 'migrate' towards the 'labour reserves; that is, from the advanced centres of capital accumulation to the 'cheap labour reserve countries' of the Third World.

Prior to the Second World War, the industrial and manufacturing base was largely located in the advanced capitalist countries. The movement and structure of wages in these industries was, therefore, 'regulated' by the upward and downward movement of the level of national unemployment. The role of the colonies and overseas territories was essentially to provide raw materials and agricultural staples for the advanced centres of capital accumulation.

The 'new international division of labour'

The transnationalisation of industrial production after the Second World War, characterised by the transfer of the 'old' labour-intensive assembly and transformation industries to the periphery of the world economy, substantially modified the structure of accumulation in the advanced capitalist countries, as well as the role and functions of the national relative surplus population in the national process of capital accumulation.

This process of post-war transnationalisation is characterised by a *tendency* towards the integration of the various phases of commodity production on a world level. In turn, the internationalisation of productive capital is conducive to the integration of the national reserve armies in different countries, that is, the 'national labour reserves' in different social formations are internationalised through the 'integration' of the national markets for labour in different geographical locations. This 'integration' is brought about through the mobility of productive capital (that is, through industrial relocation) rather than through the international mobility of labour.

Off-shore productive capital in the assembly and transformation industries is extremely mobile, moving from one geographical location to another in accordance with the relative scarcity or abundance of cheap Third World industrial labour power. In this process, the national relative surplus population, in distinct Third World countries, not only regulates the internal national wage structure (and hence the cost of labour for international capital) but also the process of 'migration' of international productive capital from one cheap labour location to another, and, therefore, *indirectly* the levels of industrial wages in alternative 'competing' cheap labour locations.

The transnationalisation of productive capital

The transnationalisation of productive capital (and its international relocation), the international 'buying and selling' of labour power in different national labour markets and the international division of labour are parallel and interdependent processes.

The 'migration' of distinct branches of industry from one region of the world to another has proceeded (after the Second World War) through *sequential displacements* in the structure of the international division of labour. In the 1960s many of the 'old' labour-intensive industries, (requiring essentially unskilled labour) of the advanced capitalist countries were relocated to the cheap labour free trade zones of South-East Asia such as Taiwan, Hong Kong, South Korea and Singapore. Rapid capital accumulation in these countries and regions was conducive throughout the 1970s to an increase in the level of wages, in these cheap labour locations, which substantially counteracted the initial impetus of an economic growth process based almost exclusively on the development of cheap labour industrial exports.

The unstable pattern of economic growth and stagnation in the so-called 'newly-industrialised countries' (NICs) of South-East Asia is functionally related to the 'migration' and mobility of productive capital. 'Export-led development' is characterised by a contradictory movement: dynamic growth of the export industries of the semi-industrialised countries of South-East Asia becomes an obstacle to further growth because the increase in industrial wages which accompanies the dynamic development of the export sector modifies the patterns of 'migration' of productive capital. In other words, this process is conducive to the international *relocation* of these 'traditional' cheap labour export industries to yet *cheaper* supplies of unskilled labour in the People's Republic of China as well as in Malaysia, Indonesia, the Philippines, India, and so on.

While this process will gradually displace the traditional labour-intensive industries in South Korea, Singapore, Korea and Taiwan, new (and more sophisticated) areas of economic activity – hitherto exclusively located in the advanced capitalist countries – will 'migrate' towards the NICs of the Third World.

These *sequential* displacements in the structure of the international division of labour not only modify the underlying industrial fabric of the 'newly-industrialised countries' but also that of the advanced capitalist countries. Increasingly, 'skill-intensive' industries, as well as certain areas of heavy industry, are transferred to the Third World's 'industrial periphery'. In Taiwan, for instance, 'skill intensive' industries are being developed in Hsinchu Science Base Industrial Park. Hsinchu belongs to a 'new generation' of export-processing zones in which investment is promoted in areas such as information systems, microprocessors, communications' equipment and computer software. The underlying rationale of the new 'skill-oriented' free trade zones, however, is remarkably similar to the 'vintage cheap labour model', that is, wages for skilled labour are at least four times lower in Taiwan or Singapore than in the advanced capitalist countries.

The World Relative Surplus Population

In each of the national economies, 'the relative surplus population is the pivot upon which the law of demand and supply of labour works'.[3] The national relative surplus population thereby conditions the structure of wages *between* the various branches of a national economy as well as the movement of labour from one branch of activity to another. In Third World social formations, the low wage economy is often sustained through the reproduction of those so-called 'traditional' or 'non-capitalist' sectors which provide and set free their surplus population. The miserable conditions of material existence in so-called 'traditional subsistence agriculture' (and urban petty commodity production) act as an instrumental lever in maintaining low levels of industrial (and agricultural) wages in the 'modern' capitalist sectors.[4]

The *world relative surplus population*, characterised by the juxtaposition and integration of the national industrial reserve armies, becomes the lever of capital accumulation on a world level. On a world level, *the world relative surplus population conditions the international movement (migration) of productive capital in the same branch of industry between different countries*. International capital (the direct or indirect purchaser of labour power) 'moves' from one national labour market to another. From the point of view of capital, the national reserves of labour (in different countries) are integrated into a single 'international reserve pool' where workers in different countries are brought into overt competition with one another.

The maintenance of Third World poverty and underdevelopment constitutes the basis upon which the national and world relative surplus populations are reproduced and sustained. The 'internationalisation' of China's manpower reserves (through their integration into this 'international reserve pool' of cheap labour) substantially modifies the structure of world unemployment and the 'regulating functions' of the world surplus population.

Structural Recession in the Advanced Capitalist Countries

The sequential shifts in the international division of labour after the Second World War, which result from several phases of international relocation of industry, is conducive to a process of *structural recession* in the advanced capitalist countries. *Structural recession* characterised by high unemployment, stagnation and decline of the 'old' labour intensive manufacturing sectors, is an important feature of the economic crisis which is affecting the advanced industrialised countries.

The international division of labour is characterised by a bi-polar structure. In the advanced industrialised countries, the new high technology industries are replacing the 'old' manufacturing base of centre capitalism. The low technology 'hardware' manufacturing industries are transferred to the Third World including China.

The transfer of traditional labour intensive industries to China and other cheap labour locations in the Third World counteracts pressures on the rate of profit evident since the 1960s in the advanced capitalist countries. China's reintegration into the structure of the world economy is, in this regard, of utmost significance because China constitutes the largest Third World 'reserve' of labour, offering an unlimited potential for the international redeployment of labour-intensive transformation industries.

China's 'open door' policy is particularly important in the context of the current economic crisis. Both the structural relocation of manufacturing to China and other Third World countries and the policies of programmed austerity in the advanced capitalist countries contribute to the increase of unemployment and the compression of real wages (in these countries). Moreover, the transfer of labour-intensive industry to China and the Third World also contributes to the phasing out of small- and medium-sized manufacturing, and thereby to increased industrial concentration and centralisation of capital in the advanced capitalist countries.[5]

Given the process of the international relocation of productive capital, the underlying pattern of capital accumulation in the advanced capitalist countries shifts towards those sectors (including high technology, research and development, production designs, and so on) which are less dependent on wage labour. These high technology 'software' sectors (which are the product of intellectual labour and highly-skilled manpower) are inputs (for example, in the form of product designs, licencing agreements, and so on) in the labour-intensive processing and assembly phase of industrial production.

Monopoly control over advanced technology

Monopoly capital tends to disengage itself from production in many areas of manufacturing while maintaining its control over high technology, the use of which is rented out to the sectors of material production), as well as its control in the sphere of international distribution and sale of the commodities produced in manufacturing industry.

This bi-polar structure of the international division of labour, characterised by a clear demarcation between the production of high technology and the phase of *material* production, typifies the relationship between Chinese state industry and their 'foreign partners'. 'Deindustrialisation' in the *material* producing sectors (that is manufacturing) in the advanced capitalist countries accompanied by rapid growth of the high technology industries takes place in parallel with the consolidation of off-shore industrial production based on high technology 'rentals' in China and elsewhere in the Third World.

The Low Wage Economy

Transnationals producing or subcontracting with independent Third World national capitalists or, as in the case of China, with state enterprises, will relocate their productive activities in accordance with the international structure of wage disparities. According to ILO statistics, the cost of industrial labour power in the Third World is, on average, one-tenth that of the advanced capitalist countries.[6] Important disparities in the cost of labour power also exist *between* countries of the Third World: In South and East Asia the effective cost of industrial labour is on average four times higher in Hong Kong, Singapore, Taiwan and South Korea than in China, Sri Lanka, Indonesia, or the Philippines. In China, the average cost of industrial labour (at the official exchange rate) in the state sector is of the order of US$21 a month, in Sri Lanka's Katyunake free trade zone, the average monthly wage is US$36.

Whereas (according to ILO statistics) the over-all average disparity in the industrial wage between centre and peripheral social formations is of the order of one to ten, *the absolute disparity is of the order of one to thirty*. In China the wage rate (1983) for unskilled labour in the state sector was 40 to 60 yuan a month (14 to 21 dollars), that is, less than 13 cents (US) an hour as opposed to 5 to 10 dollars an hour in North America (for the same category of labour and skill). Namely, *the daily cost of labour in the advanced capitalist countries (in the same branch of industry) is often of the same order of magnitude as (or in excess of) the monthly cost of labour in China and other 'labour reserve countries'*. It should, however, be noted that the subsequent devaluation of the Renminbi against the US dollar in 1984–85 has considerably lowered the dollar cost of labour in relation to the 1983 figures recorded in this chapter. This signifies that the effective dollar cost of unskilled labour for multinational capital (at the 1985 exchange rate) is less than 15 US dollars a month.

International disparities in labour costs are also accompanied by important differences in the length of the working week, the intensity of the labour process and the working conditions in industry. In South Korea, Taiwan, Singapore and Hong Kong, the length of the working week (without overtime) varies from 48 to 60 hours. In South Korea, factories in the export garment, footware, electronics assembly, and so on, industries operate on the basis of an 11-hour day (including a one-hour break for lunch) and a six-day working week. In China, the statutory working week is 6 days and 48 hours. Apart from public holidays and Chinese New Year, there are no paid holidays in China.

Third World manufacturing industry reproduces many of the social conditions prevalent historically during the Industrial Revolution in the advanced capitalist countries. The Korean garment and footware industries, for instance, rely heavily on female labour from rural areas in the 15 to 25 year age group; after several years of intensive factory work, long working hours and despotic factory supervision, workers will either abandon employment or be dismissed by the factory. This process enables the frequent replacement of 'used' labour by a fresh supply of 'new' labour which flows into the urban industrial labour market from rural areas.[7]

In the 'labour reserve countries' of China, South Asia and the Far East, the supply of unqualified labour released from the rural hinterland is abundant and the costs of maintenance and upkeep are extremely low. Real wages are often below the level of subsistence, that is, the reproductive process in both peripheral industry and commercial agriculture is characterised by the *non-renewal* of human labour power.[8]

The maintenance of a low wage structure is implemented through the operation of the labour market, as discussed above, as well as through the enforcement of state controls on the level of industrial wages and/or other political instruments which enforce the 'free and competitive' operation of the labour market. The elimination of trade unions as well as the consolidation of traditional techniques of state repression (for example, in the Philippines, South Korea or Indonesia) become the means for enforcing an industrial wage rate substantially below subsistence.

In China, wages are regulated by the state through the statutory wage scale for state enterprises. The effective cost of labour for international capital (in US$ dollars) is also governed by the official exchange rate and the policy of undervaluation of the Renminbi.

Wages and the cost of labour to foreign capital

Conditions for the foreign entrepreneur in 'socialist' China are more favourable than in other 'capitalist' cheap labour locations in South-East Asia. At the official exchange rate, the effective cost of labour (for international capital) is less than one-fifth that paid in Hong Kong, Singapore and South Korea.

Wages in China in the state sector are on average (without bonuses and overtime) of the order of 60 yuan a month (US$21). Industrial wages for unskilled categories (1983) range from approximately 40 yuan (US$14) to 90 yuan (US$32) a month. Wages in joint venture factories are *in principle* established at a rate which is 50 per cent above the average rate in comparable industries. In the co-operative sector (that is, municipal and neighbourhood factories) and in rural factories the level of wages is substantially below that of the state sector.

Foreign capital contracts with a state, municipal or rural enterprise; the 'costs of maintenance and reproduction' of labour power, however, are met by the 'socialist' state, that is, the social distribution of housing and essential social services, which constitute a major achievement of the Chinese revolution, represent in a sense an indirect 'subsidy' to a foreign capitalist enterprise investing (in a joint venture) or subcontracting (for example, with a state enterprise) in China.

Foreign capitalist enterprises do not generally purchase labour power directly in the market: they purchase the services of labour along with the other 'factors of production' (factory space, land, and so on) in a contractual arrangement, joint venture, and so on, with a state enterprise. In this case, no direct money (or social relationship) exists between foreign capitalists and Chinese workers.

The management and supervision of the labour force, the length of the working day, and the reproduction of labour power, are ensured by the state and the various state social programmes. In joint ventures between a foreign company and a Chinese state enterprise the hiring and firing of workers, determination of wages and management of the labour force is entirely under the jurisdiction of the 'Chinese partner'. Moreover, wages in joint ventures and/or enterprises producing for the export sector are regulated with some modifications by the national statutory wage scale.

China's Manpower Exports

As discussed earlier, the post-war international division of labour is characterised by the international 'migration' of productive capital towards the 'labour reserve countries'. Whereas in industrial processing industries capital 'moves' internationally towards cheap sources of labour, in productive activities, which by their very nature (for example, public works, construction, mining, and so on) are not mobile internationally, labour in the form of contractual manpower exports 'moves' from the 'labour reserve countries' to overseas construction and infrastructural projects.

The movement of an internationally *mobile* 'indentured labour force' to *immobile* physical capital is the counterpart of the migration of *mobile capital* to cheap sources of *immobile labour*. The export of manpower is, in this regard, a component part of the development of cheap labour activities in general, and an expression of the changing structure of the international division of labour.

The development of an overseas contractual manpower market is characteristic of the over-all (post-war) process of internationalisation of production, although distinct from the development of cheap labour export processing industries within the geographical boundaries of Third World countries. In other words, the same processes which govern the relocation of industry towards cheap labour locations in the Third World are concurrently conducive to the rapid development of an 'internationally mobile reserve army' of cheap contractual manpower which is used in economic activities, which by their very nature are not mobile internationally.

Manpower exports have taken on different forms in different countries and regions of the world. For instance, Mexico exports a contractual seasonal agricultural work force to southern California; France, West Germany and Switzerland import cheap industrial manpower from southern Europe, North Africa and Turkey. The sale of manpower by the Portuguese colonial authorities (prior to Liberation in Angola and Mozambique) has provided South African mining with cheap supplies of contractual labour, and so on.

The contractual sale of (indentured) manpower after The Second World War should be distinguished from the pre-war international migration of labour. Manpower exports are not generally characterised by the permanent (international) migration of labour. This contractual sale of Third World manpower has played an important role in the development of the 'labour-scarce' economies of the Middle East.

In recent years an important overseas (contractual) manpower market has developed, primarily in the Middle East, in construction and public works projects. China has entered the contractual sale of manpower in competition with Korean, Pakistani, Filipino and other Third World 'suppliers' of cheap labour. The export of Chinese manpower for overseas construction work takes place through:

1. the direct sale of labour power to a foreign construction company;
2. contractual agreements with a Chinese construction company. In this

case, the Chinese company will supply the labour and will undertake part of the construction work.

The manpower export business constitutes one of China's major earners of foreign exchange. Manpower exports were initiated in 1979; by 1981 China had signed close to 300 contracts. In 1982 China had more than 30 000 overseas workers employed either with a Chinese overseas construction company or directly with international construction multinationals:

> They [the workers] are on production and construction projects mainly in the Middle East in co-operation with Middle-East petroleum exporting countries and also from contractor companies from France, West Germany, Italy, Japan and Spain. Competition is strong in the field of supply work forces.[9]

The sale of Chinese labour power to a foreign buyer is often negotiated through the intermediary of a Hong Kong manpower firm. The sale of labour power is conducted both by the central and provincial governments. Guangdong province exports manpower through the Guangdong Manpower Service Corporation. Negotiations with foreign contractors are undertaken by Chronicle Consultants of Hong Kong on behalf of the Guangdong state manpower firm. In Fujian province, Fujian Provincial Investment Enterprise, established in 1979 to promote foreign investment in Fujian, has expanded its activities to include overseas construction contracts and manpower export sales. In Beijing, the central government ministries have also entered the manpower export business: the Ministry of Metallurgical Industry, for instance, supplies manpower to Japanese and US companies as well as to Italy's giant construction multinational IRA.

Labour power for overseas construction projects is generally sold at a contractual price agreed between the Chinese and/or Hong Kong manpower firms and a foreign contractor. The length of the working day and the various conditions of employment are set out in the contract. The contractual price for unskilled, semi-skilled and specialised categories, varies from US$300 to US$450 a month for a six-day week. The actual wages paid to the workers are regulated by the Chinese state manpower company and are somewhat higher than industrial wages paid in China.

Japanese engineering companies which approached the Hong Kong Manpower Firm, Chronicle Consultants, (acting on behalf of the Guangdong government), will in some cases provide Japanese-mandarin speaking supervisory personnel: 'The proposal assures potential employers that the Chinese will be diligent and obedient to their employers' reasonable instructions'.[10]

Rather than purchasing the services of labour directly from a Chinese manpower firm, foreign companies in the multinational construction business often favor direct contractual arrangements with a Chinese construction firm. In this case, the foreign company subcontracts part of the construction work to the Chinese enterprise which, in turn, is responsible for the supervision and management of its overseas work force. For instance, China Construction and Engineering Company (CCEC) and its Hong Kong subsidiary, Overseas Building Company, has a work force of 80 000 workers. CCEC is involved in industrial and construction projects in the Middle East.

There are 14 contracting companies which are subsidiaries of CCEC. CCEC also has a subsidiary in Hong Kong, known as China Overseas Building Development Company Ltd.[11] CCEC also sells Chinese manpower to Japanese construction companies within South-East Asia. In 1981 CCEC, through its Hong Kong subsidiary, provided skilled labour to Ryoden Electric Engineering Company of Japan in the building of an electric power station on Hong Kong's Lamma Island. Ryoden is a subcontractor under the main contractor for the project: Mitsubishi Heavy Industries, Ltd.[12]

Whereas Ryoden purchased the Chinese labour at nearly 500 dollars US a month, the Chinese workers received monthly wages of less than 50 dollars US for their subsistence in Hong Kong. Ryoden provides accommodation for the workers on Lamma Island.[13]

In September 1981, a Hong Kong manpower firm, Zim Chem (Far East Ltd), signed a contract with China's Foreign Construction Company of Fujian Province to negotiate contracts in the manpower export business. Zim Chem has contacts with South Korean construction companies involved in the Middle East, who prefer to purchase the services of Chinese or Filipino workers at a lower cost than to hire Korean nationals. Although the price of Filipino workers is 'more competitive' (That is, as little as 200 US dollars a month), Stephen Chu of Zim Chem (Far East Ltd) admits that whereas

> Filipino workers had a reputation for being difficult to control . . . There will be no problem of control [with the Chinese workers] because contractors know that China has good control over its workers . . . They are accustomed to living away from their families. . .and to labouring in hard working conditions and environments.[14]

Unequal Exchange

The origins of unequal exchange lie in the unequal structure of industrial specialisation which characterises the relationship between China and foreign capital.

Unequal exchange cannot, however, be looked upon narrowly as the result of disparities in wage levels (as well as differences in the levels of labour productivity) between 'rich' and 'poor' countries, because the processes of wage formation both between and within countries are in themselves the result of the structures of economic and political domination and dependency which characterise the world economic system.

Unequal exchange in terms of the 'unequal exchange of value' between China and the advanced capitalist countries (that is, expressed in terms of the number of hours required to produce the commodities exchanged), is the concrete manifestation of the 'unequal' structure of economic specialisation.

But to say that there is 'unequal specialisation, which leads to unequal development' does not advance the debate because this 'unequal international specialisation' develops alongside the unfolding of the institutional and legal fabric of trade, international banking and finance, and so on. These institutional and legal mechanisms (which are the reflection of social production relations), in turn, enable international capital to dominate the spheres of commodity trade and distribution, the development, sale and use of advanced (software) technology, as well as the private and public credit used to fund industrial projects in the 'poor' countries.

It is not our intention to address the interesting and often controversial debate on the theory of unequal exchange. Suffice it to say that whereas this debate has aroused important and crucial issues, it has often taken as its point of departure the abstract process of value formation in Marxian political economy, and Marx's theory of prices of production in *Capital*, with little or no empirical basis to support the analysis of unequal exchange as a concrete phenomenon in the trading relations between 'rich' and 'poor' countries.

Our analysis of unequal exchange and unequal specialisation in this and previous chapters focuses on the institutional and organic nature of China's relationship with foreign capital, as expressed by the unequal structure of trade and investment transactions between China's state enteprises and their foreign partners.

The insertion of the Chinese economy into the capitalist international division of labour should therefore be understood in relation to the various phases of the production, trade, distribution and sale of Chinese exports in world markets. The role of merchant capital in this process enables the large corporate trading corporations to appropriate the greater part of the surplus value without any direct involvement in commodity production. International merchant capital maintains control over the channels of distribution and sale of the commodity. This is a relationship of inequality, whereby the profits of the Chinese enterprise are compressed to a minimum, thereby constraining the capacity of the Chinese industrial export sector to internally finance (without depending on international credit) the capital costs of its 'economic modernisation'.

The division of surplus value: the case of the Chinese export garment industry

What is the quantitative division of surplus value between the Chinese industrial state enterprise and the international mechant capitalist? This question is illustrated in the context of compensation trade and subcontracting in the clothing and garment industry (similar relations exist in other sectors of light industrial exports).

As discussed in the previous chapter, a foreign contractor will establish a long-term agreement with a Chinese manufacturer through the provincial import-export corporation.

In the garment industry, the 'friendship price' is 30 to 40 per cent below the official sale price regulated by the provincial import-export corporation. In turn, the latter is 40 per cent below the factory price in Hong Kong (see Tables 9.1 and 9.2). Moreover, the supply agreement may include a long-term contract which grants China's quota rights (for example) for the US or the EEC) to the foreign contractor. Inasmuch as Hong Kong and Taiwan's quotas have been fully used, compensation trade and/or subcontracting in China constitute an additional 'profit incentive' (that is, in contrast with other established cheap-labour locations in South-East Asia).

The cost-price relations

Tables 9.1 and 9.2 identify the cost-price relations in the Chinese and Hong Kong garment industries, respectively. The data enable us to identify the distribution of surplus value, that is, between the Chinese state enterprise and the various stages of international sale and distribution.

Expenditures on raw materials, (many of which are supplied by the foreign contractor for processing), and equipment, constitute the major element of industrial cost. The factory price negotiated with the provincial export corporation includes transport costs. The data in Table 9.1 suggest that: (a) the net rate of return to the Chinese state enterprise is of the order of 15 per cent; (b) the relationship between the cost price (at the level of the factory) and the retail sale price in the United States is of the order of one to five. In other words, the Chinese state enterprise sells the processed commodity (through the provincial export corporation) to a Hong Kong or international distributor for $3.00 (that is, the factory price of a man's shirt) which in turn is sold in New York for $15.00.

Out of a retail sale price of US$15.00 only 45 cents accrue to Chinese workers in the form of wages. Close to 12 dollars (out of a total retail price of 15 dollars) is appropriated at different stages of the process of international sale and distribution (in the form of commercial profit, the costs of circulation and customs duty). Commercial profit appropriated by the

TABLE 9.1 *Price-cost structure in the Chinese garment export industry*

	Production of a man's shirt (US dollars)
Wages to Chinese workers (variable capital)	0.45
Raw materials and equipment used up (constant capital)	2.10
Industrial profit (portion of surplus value appropriated by the Chinese state enterprise)	0.45
Factory export price (C & F)*	3.00
Insurance	0.10
Customs duty	0.30
Importer's commission (Hong Kong office)	0.15
Handling charges in New York (customs broker, storage, etc.)	0.30
Cost price in New York	3.85
Approximate wholesale price	8.00
Retail price	15.00

*Charges and Freight

SOURCE Interview conducted in China in 1982 with a major US garment importer. The cost structure data was obtained by interviewing the factory manager of the Chinese state enterprise. The other data were provided by the representative of the Hong Kong contractor. These *approximate* figures are representative of the price-cost relations of the garment trade and industry.

international distributor and wholesaler is of the order of US$4.15 (that is, the difference between the cost price in New York and the wholesale price). Another seven dollars are appropriated at the level of retail distribution. Out of a total surplus value of approximately US$12.45, 45 cents are appropriated by the Chinese state enterprise in the form of industrial profit, while another 45 cents accrues to Chinese workers in the form of wages.

It should be noted that the foregoing analysis does not take into account the fact that under compensation trade arrangements, the commodity is sold at a 'friendship price' which is often below the regulated factory price of US$3.00.

China v. Hong Kong price-cost relations

Whereas conventional interpretations invariably suggest that the garment, clothing and related industries are 'labour intensive', it should be noted that labour costs in China constitute a relatively small proportion of total costs. The 'labour-intensive' concept of conventional economics describes the underlying technical relationship. In value terms, however, the organic composition of capital is in fact quite high. In our illustration:

TABLE 9.2 *Price-cost structure in the Hong Kong garment export industry*

	Production of a man's shirt (US dollars)
Factory export price (FOB)	4.80
Freight	0.40
Customs duty	1.32
Importer's commission (Hong Kong office)	0.24
Handling charges in New York (customs broker, storage, etc.)	0.30
Cost price in New York	7.06
Approximate wholesale price	10.00
Approximate retail price	18.00

SOURCE Interview conducted in China in 1982 with a major US garment importer. The cost structure of the Hong Kong garment industry was not available.

$$q = \frac{c}{v} = \frac{2.10}{0.45} = 4.67$$

where c is constant capital (raw materials and equipment used up), v is variable capital (payments to wage-labour) and q is the organic composition of capital.

In other words, not only are wages in China (expressed in US dollars at the official exchange rate) lower than in most other 'capitalist' South-East Asian countries, the proportion of wages in relation to the costs of equipment and raw materials is extremely low.

Comparing now the underlying price-cost relations with those in the Hong Kong garment industry, we notice that the international import-export firm is in a position to increase its commercial profit by approximately 50 per cent through subcontracting in China ($4.15 as opposed to $2.82 as in the case of Hong Kong). These figures do not take into account, however, the fact that an additional cost is incurred to acquire quota rights for Hong Kong merchandise sold in the US market, that is, subcontracting in China implies an increase of commercial profits well *in excess* of 50 per cent in relation to Hong Kong.

While the foregoing figures are approximate, they are nevertheless real. They give us some insight as to the general order of magnitude of cost and price relations in the sector of light industrial exports and the proportion of surplus value which is appropriated by international merchant capital. The empirical illustration also identifies the mechanism whereby China's light industrial sector is brought into competition with other traditional 'capitalist' cheap-labour locations in South-East Asia.

Concluding Remarks

The opening up of trade with international capital (examined in chapters 7, 8 and 9) does not *in itself* constitute 'a capitalist departure'. It is not trade with foreign capital *per se* which is the issue; rather it is the precise nature and institutional framework whereby trade takes place with foreign capital.

During the transition period, capitalist functions continue to prevail. The construction of socialism takes place in a 'a capitalist environment'. 'We must calculate how in the capitalist environment, we can ensure our existence, how we can profit by our enemies, who, of course, will bargain, who have never forgotten to bargain and *who will bargain at our expense*'. Lenin recognised in the context of the New Economic Policy the importance of trade 'as a link in the historical chain of events, in the transitional forms of our socialist construction'.[15] Trade in this context is a transitional strategy subject to regulation and control by the proletarian state. Lenin in the early 1920s, however, was acutely aware of the dangers and contradictions of state capitalism as a transitory form.

Under a state monopoly of foreign trade and investment, concessions to foreign capitalists would be geared towards selective transfers of advanced technology in accordance with clearly specified economic objectives. This was indeed the basis of the establishment of foreign concessions in Soviet Russia in the aftermath of the First World War, and during the years of the New Economic Policy (NEP). The policy of foreign capitalist concessions was viewed, in this context, by Lenin, as a necessary basis for the transfer of science, technology and managerial expertise at a time when the Soviet economy had been disrupted by the First World War, the October Revolution and the Civil War. (China's circumstances after 1976 are, in this regard, in no way comparable to those of Soviet Russia in 1918.) The establishment of foreign concessions was to contribute to the development of productive forces in carefully identified key priority areas of the Soviet economy. In the debate with Bukharin on the role of state capitalism during the transition to socialism, Lenin stressed:

> The need for a specific type of 'buy out' which the workers must offer to the most cultured, the most skilled, the most capable organisers among the capitalists . . . '[M]anagement' is entrusted by the Soviet Power to capitalists, not as capitalists, but as technicians or organisers for higher salaries. . . [I]t is precisely these people whom we the proletarian party must appoint to 'manage' the labour process and the organisation of production, for there are *no* other people who have practical experience in this matter.[16]

But there is a difference between 'buy out' and 'sell out': China's 'open door' bears no resemblance to Lenin's policy of foreign concessions, because under present arrangements it is essentially the foreign capitalist *who decides*. Namely, inasmuch as the establishment of joint ventures and trade agreements are not subordinated to clearly defined priorities, and that foreign capital can enter virtually any sector of the Chinese economy, the transfer of technology will essentially be governed by the laws of profit and the capitalist free market.

Trade with foreign capitalists is, therefore, established in the context of particular social relations. What sectors of Chinese society control trade and foreign investment relations with international capital? How is the class structure modified as a result of trade? How does the underlying process affect the distribution of income and patterns of consumption in China? In short, does the opening up of trade affect the basis of socialist construction in China? *None of these issues is critically discussed or debated in China today*.

The 'open door' policy is presented by the Chinese leadership as a technical economic problem which has no direct bearing on the class struggle. Marxist critique of the political economy is replaced by a cost engineering economism pertaining to efficiency, labour performance and productivity. Trade in the context of the 'open door' policy is not a strategy of the proletariat; rather trade and foreign investment relations with international capital are restored by a bureaucratic élite operating from within the managerial structures of the state in close association with expatriate Chinese and foreign capital.

It is worth noting in this context that Wang, Zhang, Jiang and Yao (the group of Four) had, in 1976, a few months before they were deposed, warned against comprador tendencies in the party and foreign trade departments: 'Inside the party, and primarily inside the Politbureau, there are bourgeois compradors.' In April 1976 an article by Fang Hai (presumably commissioned by the group of Four), entitled 'A Critique of the Foreigners' Slave Philosophy', published in the communist party journal *Hongqi* (Red Flag), describes the 'opening up' to foreign trade as 'slavery to the foreigners. . .crawling behind the foreigners at snail pace'.[17]

The following year after the group of Four had been deposed, Guo Manyen (Kuo Man-yen) responded to Fang Hai (on behalf of the 'Rightist' leadership) in an article in *Hongqi* (April 1977) thereby 'rectifying' and establishing the party's official position on foreign trade. Kuo Man-yen accused the 'Gang of Four' of fabricating:

> Wild fairy tales, saying we had 'unlimitedly imported what could be domestically produced'. . .[They] labelled our foreign trade departments as 'unlimitedly exporting goods', even those much needed at home.[18]

To the accusations of 'selling out to the foreigners', Kuo Man-yen responded that China's foreign trade policy:

is normal trade conducted in conformity with the principle of equity and mutual benefit; it has nothing to do with the fabrication that we sold out our national resources. Ours is an independent and sovereign state. We have never allowed, *nor will we ever allow, foreign capital to invest in our country. We have never joined capitalist countries in exploiting our national resources. . .We never did, nor will we ever, embark on joint ventures with foreign capitalists. Even less will we lease our land or waters to foreign powers.*[19]

10

Sino-US Strategic Relations

Mao's Paper Tiger Diplomacy

In 1956, Mao Zedong denounced US imperialism as a 'paper tiger', accusing the Eisenhower administration of 'flaunting the anti-communist banner everywhere in order to perpetrate aggression against other countries':

> When we say US imperialism is a paper tiger, we are speaking in terms of strategy. . . It has claws and fangs, we have to destroy it peacemeal. For instance, if it has ten fangs, knock off one and there will be nine left, knock off another and there will be eight left. When all the fangs are gone it will still have claws. . . Strategically we must utterly despise US imperialism, tactically we must take it seriously.[1]

In 1984 Chinese Premier Zhao Ziyang visited Ronald Reagan at the White House, stressing 'the need to strengthen ties between China and the United States. . . We share common grounds in opposing foreign expansionism and interference in the internal affairs of independent states'.[2] This statement was made only a few months after the US military invasion of Grenada.

China's leaders after Mao have had a change of mind; the 'paper tigers' had 'not been battered by the wind and the rain'.[3] Henry Kissinger, a 'paper tiger' in his own right, invited by the Communist weekly *Beijing Review* to express his views on Sino-American relations, wrote in early 1984, prior to Premier Zhao Ziyang's visit to the White House:

> [T]he new [Reagan] administration overcoming earlier preconceptions, has committed itself to a firm and close relationship with Beijing. . . China and the US represent different ideologies, but they are brought together by important common interests.[4]

Zbigniew Brzezinski, National Security Advisor to the Carter Administration, also writing in the *Beijing Review*, was more candid that Kissinger:

> Continued Soviet strategic deployments targeted against both Western Europe and the Far East. . . [have] become a truly interpendent concern *and a very appropriate subject for discussion between US and Chinese leaders*.[5]

The 'earlier preconceptions' of the Chinese communist party had also been overcome at a time when China was celebrating the ninetieth anniversary of the birth of Mao Zedong. Mao's critical writings on US imperialism, contained in Volume Five of his *Selected Works*, however, had been carefully removed from bookstores across China (pending a newly-prepared edition) and replaced by the recently edited works of Liu Shaoqi, Mao's principal opponent during the Cultural Revolution and the major ideologue of the so-called 'capitalist road'.

Sino-US Strategic Rapprochement

The pledging of US military aid to China after Mao should be understood in relation to US global strategic interests. As of the late 1960s, Henry Kissinger, under the Nixon administration, had favoured Sino-US *détente* at a time of tense relations between Moscow and Beijing.

In 1969, the Sino-Soviet crisis led to armed border clashes along the Ussuri River. The initial Sino-US *rapprochement* occurred at a meeting in Warsaw in the face of a Soviet military build-up along the north-west and Mongolian borders.

The signing of the Shanghai Communiqué in 1972, and the power struggle after Mao's death in 1976, paved the way for the development of both US foreign investment in China, as well as Sino-US strategic *rapprochement*. Concurrently with the economic and social reforms, adopted since 1977–8, the 'Rightist' leadership after Mao has redefined its military and strategic relations with the United States.

Whereas the Sino-Vietnamese War and Soviet support for Vietnam played an important role, the development of Sino-US strategic relations were also influenced by the 'open door' to American business and financial interests. Arms sales agreements and US investment in China's defence industries were to become an integral part of China's bilateral trade relations with the United States.

Deng Xiaoping's 1979 White House visit constitutes, in this regard, an important turning point in Sino-US strategic and military relations to be followed – with the Zhao and Reagan visits in 1984 – by the development of close bilateral relations in the areas of conventional and strategic arms' sales, military and logistical training of PLA officers by US military advisers, US co-operation and 'advice' in the restructuring of the People's

Liberation Army, and bilateral consultations between the Pentagon and the PLA.

Military and strategic issues and US-Soviet relations were reviewed in the 1979 Deng-Carter White House meetings attended by Vice-President Mondale, Secretary of State Cyrus Vance, and National Security Advisor Zbigniew Brzezinski. Deng Xiaoping was explicitly anti-Soviet, urging the development of a Sino-US 'alliance' against Moscow. One thing had converted itself into its opposite: the United States was no longer considered an 'imperialist threat'. In the words of Deng Xiaoping:

> The true hotbed of war is the Soviet Union, not the United States. . . The first characteristic of the Soviet Union is that it always adopts the attitude of bullying the soft and fearing the strong. . . The question: After setting up this relationship between China, Japan and the US [normalisation of relations between China and the US and the peace and co-operation treaty signed between China and Japan] we must further develop the relationship in a deepening way. *If we really want to place curbs on the polar bear, the only realistic thing is for us to unite.*[6]

Upgrading China's military hardware

In May 1980 China successfully tested its first full-range intercontinental ballistic missile, fired from test sites in Xinjiang to target areas in the South Pacific. China's CSSX-4 is a two-stage liquid fuel missile with single target warhead devices. According to the International Institute for Strategic Studies, China's nuclear arsenal consists of the new CSSX-4 ICBM, 50 to 70 intermediate-range ballistic missiles (IRBMs) with a range of 1500-1700 miles, and 40 medium-range ballistic missiles (MRBMs) with a range of about 700 miles. 'China's delivery systems are directed overwhelmingly towards the USSR'.[7] Despite its stated policy of 'self-reliance' in military production, China was none the less anxious to upgrade and modernise its military arsenal with US help – although this was never stated explicitly in official announcements until 1984.

In 1981 Secretary of State, Alexander Haig, invited China's deputy chief of staff, General Liu Huaqing, to visit Washington with proposals for American arms and technology sales. The Pentagon had previously, under the Carter administration, 'analysed China's defence needs', in terms of a shopping list of 52 strategic and conventional items including ground-to-air missiles, anti-tank weapons, armoured personnel carriers and radar equipment.[8]

In the US Munitions Control Newsletter published by the State Department in March 1980, and sent to 1500 US suppliers of weapons and high technology, Washington identified close to 30 types of 'support equipment designated in the US Munitions Control List available for licenced export to the PRC'.[9] These included tanks and military vehicles, aircraft and spacecraft equipment, military training equipment, military and space electronics. This constituted the first step towards the subsequent development of more sophisticated arms sales.

In August 1981, Reagan had indeed agreed to include a 'conservative' 30 out of the Pentagon's 52 items proposed by the Carter administration. General Liu's visit to Washington was postponed, however, because of Reagan's persistence in supplying arms to Taiwan.[10]

Reagan's August 1981 decision to liberalise arms' sales was, none the less, fruitful. At the Geneva Disarmament talks on 17 August 1981, the Chinese delegation passively supported the US decision to produce neutron bombs. Yu Peiwen, head of the Chinese delegation to the meetings, stated, in this context, that

> production of neutron bombs by the United States will offset the 'tank advantage' enjoyed by the Soviet Union in the European theatre, as the neutron bomb is an effective anti-tank weapon. . . In the final analysis. . . production of the neutron bomb is in fact a product of the nuclear arms race between the two superpowers.[11]

China's position prior to the November 1981 Soviet-US negotiations in Geneva, was remarkably consistent with that of Washington, stating that 'the Soviet Union has attained a nuclear superiority over NATO in Europe'.[12] The Chinese press echoed Washington's 'nuclear balance' argument. While rhetorically condemning both 'super powers', the Reagan administration was portrayed as committed to genuine arms reduction:

> The Reagan administration's anti-inflation and lower expenditure programme is in conflict with expanding arms expenditures. . . In September [1982] the US administration had to lop off 13 billion dollars for military spending from its 1982 budget. . . Therefore, Reagan has opted to resume negotiations with the Soviet Union on the reduction of theatre nuclear weapons. . . Specifically, [the Soviet Zero option] looks like 'withdrawal' by both sides, but in reality, NATO is to be effectively prevented from deploying new type missiles, while the Soviet Union keeps its SS-20 missiles out of Soviet territory in the West. Of course, this is unacceptable to the West.[13]

Quoting Alexander Haig, the article concludes:

> It is unthinkable to let the Soviets retain their mobile missiles while the United States has to cut down the number of their missiles.[14]

The Geneva talks led to a stalemate: Pershing and Cruise missiles were deployed in Western Europe.

In June 1984 Premier Zhao Ziyang reasserted China's position. While sympathetic to the Peace Movement in Western Europe, Zhao expressed his apprehension because 'other countries may take advantage of this movement to serve their own interests. . . The Western European countries' efforts to strengthen their defences for the sake of their own security are not contradictory to their efforts to safeguard peace'.[15]

Whereas Secretary of State Alexander Haig had said privately that 'China was an unofficial member of NATO', and, therefore, essential to a coherent western defence structure, the Taiwan issue and arms sales to Taiwan remained 'an obstacle' to the development of what Chinese Premier Zhao Ziyang described as, at his 1984 press conference at Washington's Madison Hotel, 'a strategic partnership'.[16]

In May 1984, Zbigniew Brzezinski, former presidential advisor on National Security to the Carter Administration, confirmed the existence of a *de facto* strategic alliance in his statement to a congressional committee:

> There is now in effect an emergence of a *de facto* alliance, or, if you will, an alliance of stealth between the United States and China because of certain common and enduring geopolitical interests. . . China, Japan and the United States form an iron triangle of security in the Far East.[17]

High level Sino-US discussions were conducted throughout 1982–3, leading to Defence Secretary Casper Weinberger's visit to Beijing in September 1983. This visit, which was geared towards the sale and transfer of military technology, was followed by that to the US of Zhang Ping, a senior official of China's Commission on Military Technology, and the son of Defence Minister Zhang Aiping. Zhang Ping 'made a month-long, secrecy enshrouded trip to the United States, touring numerous aircraft, missile, tank and other armaments factories. The secrecy was at the request of Peking, which in general, has insisted that the exchanges of military delegations occur with a minimum of publicity'.[18]

A few months later Ronald Reagan stated that China was no longer considered among the list of 'unfriendly nations'. In other words, China is no longer a 'communist threat'. The signing in January 1984 of an agreement for the supply and production (in China) of US-designed nuclear reactors 'for peaceful use' represented a further step, contributing to the liberalisation of arms sales pending an 'acceptable' solution (to both China and the United States) for the 'peaceful reunification' of Taiwan with the motherland.

The Chinese position was officially clarified in a statement by Premier Zhao Ziyang at a luncheon hosted by the Mayor of New York City during his 1984 visit: '*China is prepared to buy from the United States some weapons which the US is willing to sell and which China needs and can afford*'.[19] Something had changed in China's *Real Politik* since Mao's 'paper tiger diplomacy' of the mid-1950s. Mao had warned the Chinese people of the threat of armed US aggression of the Chinese mainland: 'The Chinese people cannot be cowed by the Atomic Bomb [and] by US atomic blackmail.'[20]

The 'Open Door' to Military Technology

After Reagan's visit to Beijing in April 1984, and his discussions with Deng Xiaoping, two Chinese delegations visited the US 'to look at military training and logistics' and a US military delegation travelled to China to examine various areas of co-operation in the military field. In June 1984 Chinese Defence Minister Zhang Aiping visited Washington, and had high level discussions at the White House and the Pentagon, as well as visits to major US military installations. While emphasising that the visit 'was not directed against any third nation', Defence Minister Zhang stressed that '*prospects will broaden for expanding the friendship of the two peoples [US and China] and the exchange of military personnel*'. He further stated that the visit '*is aimed at strengthening mutual understanding between the defence institutions of the two countries and promoting friendly relations with the American people and army*'.[21]

Defence Minister Zhang Aiping also visited Canada for talks with the Canadian Defence Minister and senior officials of the Canadian military establishment. Negotiations with Canada pertained to the purchase of Canadian built weapons (under the Canada-US joint military production agreement) as well as satellite technology.

Upgrading and 'streamlining' the PLA

Zhang Aiping's visit to the United States and Canada in June 1984 took place only a few days after the announcement by Yang Dezhi, Chief of the PLA general staff, of a further reform of the People's Liberation Army which covered – in addition to PLA 'streamlining' and the restoration of military rank and hierarchy – provisions regarding 'training, weaponry reserve service and military theory'. Whereas 'the PLA will depend mainly on itself to modernise its equipment. . .*we will introduce advanced [military] technologies from abroad*':[22]

> Modernisation of national defence cannot rely on purchase of weapons from foreign countries. . . [this] does not mean that we should not learn from the experience of foreign countries in army building, or import

advanced military technology from industrialised countries. [*A form of 'open door policy' in the sphere of military technology*.][23]

Zhang Aiping's mission was followed up a few months later with the visit to China of the US Naval Secretary, John F. Lehman. Lehman's mission paved the way for supplying China with American naval equipment and weaponry including HAWK surface-to-air-missiles and TOW anti-tank missiles. The latter would be produced in China under a Sino-US co-production agreement, and in the context of the Pentagon's 'guide-lines' on the transfer of military technology, that is, agreements of this nature are reached after careful analysis by the Pentagon's International Technology Transfer Group.[24] The Group is responsible, *inter alia*, for establishing 'guide-lines' regulating the transfer of military technology to the other major western arms producers as well as – in the context of co-production agreements – to countries such as Brazil, South Africa, Israel, Egypt, South Korea and China.[25] The US is evidently not the only partner in military co-production agreements with China. Other partners include France's Aerospatiale and Britain's Rolls Royce.

In December, 1984 General John W. Vessey, Chairman of the US Joint Chiefs of Staff, paid a 12-day official visit to China. General Vessey's arrival in Beijing coincided with the announcement by the Reagan administration that it had reached agreement to help modernise China's naval fleet by supplying China with 'sonars, torpedoes, gas turbine engines and the Phalanx rapid firing gun that can be used to shoot down anti-ship missiles such as the French-made Exocet'. During General Vessey's visit, high level discussions were held at the senior military and CCP Politbureau levels. Vessey also attended military manoeuvres and lectured at China's top military academy.[26]

Defence Spending and the International Division of Labour

The production of arms and military equipment are part of the structure of the international division of labour. Third World countries are invariably inserted into this structure as exporters of raw materials, agricultural staples and cheap labour manufactured goods, and importers of equipment, technology and large quantities of advanced weaponry and military hardware from the advanced capitalist countries. Part of the revenues which result from the low-wage export economy are thereby 'recycled' into the purchase of military equipment. The latter in turn supports the maintenance of client authoritarian Third World regimes which are 'friendly' to the US and to the western alliance.

China's circumstances, however, are (for many reasons) not comparable to those of a *client* capitalist Third World country (for example, a former political colony) which is integrated into the economic and political network of neo-colonialism. The integration of the Chinese economy into the structures of world trade and finance, its integration into the structure of international banking, and its membership in the World Bank and IMF none the less contribute indirectly to the shaping of institutional relations at the strategic and political levels. China's 'open door' to imported US and western military technology should, therefore, be considered both in the context of its foreign trade and investment policy and consequent reinsertion into the capitalist international division of labour, as well as in relation to its strategic and geopolitical *rapprochement* with the West.

The liberalisation of controls on strategic exports to China proceeds alongside the development of bilateral trade and investment relations. In the words of Ronald Reagan, speaking at the Great Hall of the People in Beijing in April 1984:

> Last June [1983], I instructed our government to liberalise controls over the export to China of high technology products. . .the relaxing of export controls reflects my determination that China be treated as a friendly non-aligned nation and that the United States be fully prepared to co-operate in your modernisation. . .I am particularly proud that the United States and China have reached agreement on co-operation in the peaceful use of atomic energy.[27]

The term 'friendly non-aligned nation' when used by Ronald Reagan is by no means the antonym of the term 'aligned'.

China's *Real Politik* in South-East Asia

In parallel with its strategic *rapprochement* with the US, China has redefined its foreign policy *vis-à-vis* the Third World. Although officially non-aligned, and in principle committed to revolutionary change in the Third World, Beijing's position has, in practice, on a number of issues coincided with that of Washington. In South-East Asia, for instance, China's new rapport with Thailand, the Philippines and Malaysia is geared towards a 'friendly' *rapprochement* with the national bourgeoisies of Chinese extraction. As a result, China will no longer give support to insurgent communist parties. In the words of Zhao Ziyang:

> The relations between China and communist parties in these countries are only political and moral ones. . .The communist parties in various countries are purely internal matters of these countries. How each and

every country handles such a matter is an affair of its own and China does not want to interfere.[28]

Communist insurgency has been weakened in Thailand and Malaysia as a direct consequence of Chinese pressures. As a result, the communist party of Thailand was involved in secret negotiations with the Bangkok government in 1981–2, and a similar process is taking place in Malaysia and Burma.[29]

China's position not only constitutes an implicit apology of the repressive and authoritarian regimes prevalent in South-East Asia, the shift in its foreign diplomacy has important geopolitical implications. Beijing's foreign diplomacy in the region must be understood in relation to regional patterns of trade and capital accumulation. Beijing's new *Real Politik* in South-East Asia is based on the existence of dominant national ethnic Chinese bourgeoisies which are favourable to the direction of economic and social change in China.

China's foreign policy in South-East Asia, therefore, is not only a geopolitical and diplomatic umbrella, it is the expression of economic and social ties with the national bourgeoisies of Chinese extraction. New patterns of political, geopolitical and economic integration are likely to unfold in the South-East Asia region which are conducive to the transnational integration of the interests of the Overseas Chinese bourgeoisies in the different countries of the region. This integration of class interests depends heavily on the direction of economic and social change in China itself.

Concluding Remarks

Clearly, China's economic, political and strategic relations with the United States have little to do with the concept of 'normalisation' which led to the signing of the Shanghai Communiqué in 1972, and thereby ended an economic and political isolation initially imposed upon China during the Eisenhower administration. Moreover, China's frequent rhetorical condemnation of the US on a number of international issues should not be a pretext to confound the problem of China's realignment. These statements are at odds with the realities of China's foreign policy.

China's strategic *rapprochement* with the US and its anti-Soviet stance are not in themselves indicative of a process of 'capitalist restoration'. None the less, when viewed in conjunction with the decollectivisation of agriculture, the reforms in industrial management and the 'open door' to foreign capital, they are indeed consonant with the general picture of economic, social and political change in China. Moreover, China's strategic *rapprochement* with the US is remarkably consistent with its diplomatic stance in other areas of its foreign policy, for example, its 'friendly' relations with authoritarian regimes in South-East Asia, the shift in its policy regarding insurgent communist movements against these authoritarian regimes, its relations with Chile's Pinochet government, and so on.

The important developments discussed in this chapter are, therefore, of extreme significance, not only for the future of socialism within China itself, but also in the context of the East-West conflict and the arms race. China's strategic relations with Washington exacerbate the East-West conflict, because they signify the deployment of a pro-American People's Liberation Army along the Sino-Soviet border from Central Asia to the Far-East.

Looking on the other hand at the future development of world capitalism (for example, in the context of North-South relations), China's reintegration into the capitalist international division of labour and its strategic *rapprochement* with the West strengthens the advanced capitalist countries' economic and political hold over the Third World, weakens the movement of the so-called 'non-aligned' nations, and to some extent also impairs the chances of successful revolutionary change in other (smaller) countries of the Third World.

China's strategic *rapprochement* and 'reintegration' should also be taken into account when assessing the relative significance of revolutionary change in Central America or elsewhere in the Third World. Next to China, Central America is a drop in the ocean. China's 'friendly' *rapprochement* with the US and its 'open door' to foreign capital constitute potential gains for the US and western capitalism which amply compensate for the 'weaknesses' and losses attributable to revolutionary change in other parts of the capitalist Third World.

11

Towards the Restoration of Capitalism?

Introduction

Capitalist farming based on the rich peasant economy is restored alongside the rehabilitation of authoritarian forms of management and the development of state capitalism in industry. The internal economic reforms interact with the development of trade and foreign investment 'along capitalist lines' characterised by the penetration of the Chinese economy by international corporate capital and its concurrent reintegration into the logic and structure of the world capitalist economy. The 'open door' policy in turn modifies the structure of corporate ownership as well as the unfolding of social class relations after Mao. The existence of foreign ownership in the form of joint ventures and fully-owned subsidiaries of transnational corporations *legitimises* the restoration of property rights to members of both the national and expatriate bourgeoisie, thereby contributing to the development of a property-owning class within 'socialist China'.

The 'open door', however, extends beyond the sphere of strictly economic relations. It permeates, along with the entry of foreign capital, the very fabric of Chinese society through the transfer of western social, cultural and intellectual values. In the field of education, the élitist system of key schools is rehabilitated in parallel with the development of an 'open door' in university teaching and research. Many features of the 1920s Kuomintang educational reforms modelled on the US college system have re-emerged, along with the development of university pairing arrangements with the US, Western Europe and Japan, and the setting up, with the help of the World Bank and USAID, of fully-fledged 'academic subsidiaries' in China's key universities. Moreover, the 'transfer of intellectual technology', that is, the transfer of theoretical thought structures, particularly in the social sciences and management education, constitutes a powerful lever which subordinates China's educational system to the material and social requirements of international corporate capital. In turn, western concepts of 'modernisation' based on individual entrepreneurship, private property and the market mechanism, provide 'suitable' intellectual and ideological rationalisations of China's 'socialist construction'.

The post-Mao economic system, characterised by the triangular and self-reinforcing interaction of the reforms in agriculture, industry and foreign trade, is supported by major changes in political, institutional and ideological relations. As discussed in chapter 1, the elimination and repression of Maoist opposition in all spheres of political and social life have been conducive to the development of a monolithic party system which admits neither dissent nor opposing views to the regime's political project. Whereas the formal ideological underpinnings of the leadership's programme of economic and social reforms are rooted in Marxism-Leninism, the actual class content, which identifies entrepreneurship, western technology and foreign capital as 'the instruments of socialist construction', is increasingly at odds with the party's rhetorical commitment to the principles of scientific socialism. This pseudo-proletarian ideology is primarily intended to distort the truth and confuse the realities of the class struggle. The 'two line' struggle within the party is pushed to the background. 'The transition from new democracy to socialism' in the 1950s (that is, 'the new democratic revolution') is viewed (for example, in the Central Committee's *Resolution on Party History*) as essentially characterised by the elimination of the national bourgeoisie, as a class, resulting from the so-called 'socialisation of ownership of the means of production'. This interpretation follows almost verbatim that put forth in the Soviet Union by Stalin in the early 1930s, that is, the class struggle does not exist because state ownership of the means of production signifies the absence of a property-owning class and, therefore, *pari passu* the absence of class conflict:

> The capitalist class in the sphere of industry has ceased to exist. The kulak class [that is, rich peasants] in the sphere of agriculture have ceased to exist, and the merchants and profiteers in the sphere of trade have ceased to exist. Thus all exploiting classes have now been eliminated.[1]

Mao Zedong Thought is cited by the new regime, in support of the thesis first put forth by Stalin, by distorting and quoting out of context Mao's analysis 'On the Correct Handling of Contradictions among the People: Antagonistic class contradictions have been eliminated as a result of the new democratic revolution, the 'patriotic capitalists' have been transformed into working people, *therefore*, 'according to Mao Zedong' 'contradictions among the people' are essentially of a non-antagonistic nature.[2] The *Resolution on CCP History* (although upholding its commitment to Mao Zedong Thought) evidently denies Mao's position put forth in the 1957 Anti-Rightist Campaign and subsequently at the Tenth Plenary of the Eighth Central Committee in 1962, that is, that contradictions between the proletariat and the bourgeoisie remained the principal contradiction in Chinese society and 'that the bourgeoisie would attempt a comeback and become the source of revisionism inside the Party'.[3] Mao's position is categorised by the party leadership as one of 'Left error':

> [H]is theoretical and practical mistakes concerning class struggle in a socialist society became increasingly serious, his personal arbitrariness gradually undermined democratic centralism in Party life. . .*These erroneous 'Left' theses upon which Comrade Mao Zedong based himself in initiating the 'cultural revolution' were obviously inconsistent with the system of Mao Zedong Thought.*[4]

Which presumably means that the CCP after Mao upholds its commitment to Mao Zedong Thought independently of what Mao actually wrote or thought or his concrete actions in particular phases of the Chinese revolution.

From a line of reasoning which denies the existence of social classes (and therefore that of the bourgeoisie), the communist party becomes the sole repository of the mass movement. The party carries out the revolution under the dictatorship of the proletariat, in the name of the proletariat; obedience to the 'party line' is acceptance of the 'revolutionary line', opposition to it is 'counterrevolutionary'. Official party ideology distorts the underlying structures of class domination and state power: The party embodies the collective wisdom of the proletariat; decisions taken by those actually in power (that is, the state bourgeoisie) are taken on behalf of the proletariat.

But this deceit can only be temporary because the unfolding of events will ultimately force the leadership to reveal its true face. Increasingly the facts of Chinese reality will undermine the unity of the party's ideological discourse, and reconciliation of actual policy with the theoretical principles of Marxism-Leninism and Mao Zedong Thought will become increasingly difficult to sustain. This is evident in many of the leadership's pronouncements which attempt to 'explain' or 'justify', for instance, the role of the coastal cities' extraterritorial capitalist development zones in the construction of socialism, or the presence of US military advisers and logistical support to the PLA in the process of 'modernising' a People's Army, and so on. Clearly none of this stands up when confronted with reality. 'The four modernisations', in all their essential features, constitute a programme which goes against the very foundations of revolutionary socialism and against the interests of the working class.

Class Relations After Mao

To what extent was revolutionary socialism firmly established in China as a result of the 1949 Revolution? To what extent was the pre-1976 period characterised by a fundamentally different set of social relations to that in existence prior to 1949 during the Republican period? These questions, which have been raised at various points in previous chapters, are important in identifying the nature of the political and economic transition since 1976. Inasmuch as social relations were not modified in a fundamental and permanent way as a result of the 1949 Revolution and the struggles waged during the Great Leap and the Cultural Revolution, it might be argued that the 're-emergence' of capitalism after Mao does not constitute a *new* departure in terms of a new economic and social system but rather is the expression of historical continuity (from the pre-1949 period) in the fabric of Chinese society. This does not, however, signify that 'capitalism has existed all along': such an interpretation denies the attempt of socialist construction characterised by the fundamental and far-reaching social and economic transformations of the 1950s and 1960s. None the less, a critical historical assessment of this question must be based on an understanding of the fragile and contradictory nature of proletarian state power during the entire transition period since 1949.

The state bourgeoisie in China and the Soviet Union

Proletarian state power is fragile because the working class fails to effectively take over the political and party apparatus; as mentioned earlier, the dictatorship of the proletariat is not achieved simply as a result of the abolition of private ownership of the means of production. Bettelheim suggests (in the context of the debate on class formation in the Soviet Union) that the existence of social classes is not rooted in legal forms of ownership but in social production relations which are not abolished as a result of the elimination of private property:

> The existence of the dictatorship of the proletariat and of state and collective forms of property is not enough to 'abolish' capitalist production relations and for the antagonistic classes, proletariat and bourgeoisie to 'disappear'. The bourgeoisie can continue to exist in different forms, and, in particular, can assume the form of a state bourgeoisie.[5]

In opposition to Bettelheim, Ernest Mandel identifies the counter-revolution of the late 1920s and early 1930s in the Soviet Union as associated with the development of bureaucratism and the unfoldment of 'a materially privileged social layer' which took over the state apparatus.[6] The development of this 'social stratum' is (according to Mandel) the result of objective conditions in the aftermath of the October Revolution, that is, the inexperience of the masses in running the state apparatus and managing state industry, the necessity of these privileged groups for carrying out these functions. Mandel describes contemporary Soviet society as characterised by 'bureaucratic deformation' or 'degeneration'.[7] This 'social layer' is not viewed as a social class, (that is, a '*real bourgeoisie*') but as a 'bureaucratic stratum'; the contradictions of Soviet society cannot, therefore, (according to Mandel) be attributed to a distinct phase of the class struggle under a system of state ownership of the means of production.

According to Mandel, state ownership of industry, trade and commerce, together with 'the suppression of the right of their private appropriation', centralised economic planning and state monopoly of foreign trade implies 'the absence of generalised commodity production and of the rule of the law of value in the USSR'.[8] It follows that the Soviet economy is 'no longer capitalist' because 'there is neither a market for large means of production nor for manpower, and labour power has ceased to be a commodity'.[9] The main contradiction of Soviet Society (according to Mandel) is 'the unfolding conflict between the logic of the plan and the influence of the law of value attributable to the partial survival of partial commodity production'.[10] This 'contradiction', however, is derived without direct reference to the class struggle and the evolution of social production relations under a system of state ownership, that is, it is formulated and expressed within the realm of 'pure' 'economic laws of motion'.

In Sweezy's analysis (in his review of Bettelheim's *Class Struggle in the USSR*), the forced requisitioning of 1927–8 destroyed the worker-peasant alliance and:

> barred the road to the socialist development of Soviet society. The surplus which could be squeezed out of the peasantry was too little to sustain the projected rate of industrialisation and it soon became necessary to add the working class itself to the sources of tribute. This left the party with only the rising state bourgeoisie as a social base, and gave the latter the opportunity to infiltrate the party gradually taking it over as its own instrument of rule.[11]

Whereas the 'state bourgeoisie' developed on the basis of the remnants of tsarist bureaucracy, it emerged and took systematic expression (according to Bettelheim and Chavance) in the political and economic transformations of the late 1920s and early 1930s: 'This transformation was produced by the class struggles of that period, which made the state bourgeoisie a class in itself and consolidated the conditions in which that class exploited and oppressed the working masses'.[12]

To what extent is the debate on the state bourgeoisie and class formation in the Soviet Union useful in our understanding of the post-Mao period? The terms of reference of 'capitalist restoration' in China after Mao rest, in our opinion, on entirely different analytical premises which are the result of the specific and distinct character of the 1949 Revolution (that is, in relation to the Bolshevik Revolution of 1917). Moreover, as discussed in chapter 4, the historical origins of the state bourgeoisie in China are to be found in the structures of bureaucratic and comprador capitalism transposed and incorporated at Liberation into the economic and social fabric of the state and party apparatus. The semi-colonial character of pre-Liberation China, as expressed by an extraterritorial enclave economy dominated by foreign capital, an important bureaucratic state capitalist structure (as well as a corporate state-supported economy in the regions occupied by Japan), influenced the scope and direction of economic and social change during the new democratic (bourgeois) revolution of the early 1950s. Contrary to the development of the state bourgeoisie in Soviet Russia, which had no relationship or association with the Russian bourgeoisie of the tsarist period, the Chinese state bourgeoisie originates from the old social order of the Kuomintang period. The state bourgeoisie in China can, therefore, under no circumstances be considered a 'bureaucratic stratum' or a 'social layer' which originated and took expression under socialism in the aftermath of the 1949 Revolution.

In the Soviet Union, the development of the state bourgeoisie was intimately related to the unfolding of the state sector under a system of central economic planning. Precisely the opposite conditions prevailed in China after Mao, that is, the consolidation of the state bourgeoisie as a class proceeds alongside the development of private capital, and joint (state-private) capital, and the partial collapse of the system of central planning. The state bourgeoisie's association with the national ('former capitalists') and expatriate bourgeoisie determines the precise unfolding of social production relations as well as the precise boundaries of state planning. The Central Committee's political project does not consist, therefore, in consolidating the monopoly of the state and strengthening the structures of bureaucratism (that is, 'along Stalinist lines') but in promoting the development of state capitalism in close association with that of private capital under a system of predominantly public (state) ownership of the means of production. In other words, the very existence of the state bourgeoisie as a class, hinges upon that of a 'classical' private property-owning class which develops concurrently with the unfolding of state capitalism. As mentioned earlier, this process contrasts with the development of the state bourgeoisie in the Soviet Union under Stalinism:

(a) The Soviet state bourgeoisie did not originate from the pre-1917 Russian bourgeoisie (although the structures of tsarist bureaucracy did influence the development of the Stalinist state apparatus).
(b) The Soviet state bourgeoisie developed alongside the concurrent elimination of a private property-owning class and the consolidation of the state sector in the years after the New Economic Policy, that is, the elimination of private property, was the very basis upon which the state bourgeoisie took systematic expression as a social class.

The new democratic revolution

In China, the social reproduction of the state bourgeoisie after Liberation (as a class) was sustained as a result of the essentially reformist character of New Democracy and the fragility of proletarian state power in carrying out the democratic (bourgeois) revolution in the transition towards socialism. The question remains, therefore, as to whether these (bourgeois-democratic) reforms of the early to mid-1950s were cohesively and forcefully led by the proletariat or by the state bourgeoisie.

According to Trotsky, the revolution begins as a bourgeois-democratic revolution, but with the proletariat in power it must necessarily be superseded by more radical reforms.[13] Lenin in '*Two Tactics of Social Democracy in the Democratic Revolution*' identifies the role of the proletariat and peasantry in the democratic revolution (over Tsarism) as essentially geared towards 'intermediary stages of revolutionary development' which bring about a 'radical redistribution of landed property in favour of the peasantry, establish consistent and full democracy including the formation of a republic, eradicate all oppressive features of Asiatic bondage [and so on]'.[14] The bourgeois-democratic revolution must, however, be led by what Lenin identified as 'the revolutionary democratic dictatorship of the proletariat, and the peasantry':[15]

> *But if the proletariat is not strong enough, the bourgeoisie will be at the head of the democratic revolution and will impart to it an inconsistent and self-seeking nature. Nothing short of a revolutionary democratic dictatorship of the proletariat and peasantry can prevent this.*[16]

What were the precise conditions of the development of proletarian state power after 1949? In China, the communist party was divided (both prior and after Liberation). These divisions, which became increasingly manifest after the founding of the People's Republic, were the reflection of the social divisions within Chinese society. None the less, the achievements of the 1950s, leading up to the Great Leap Forward, would not have been possible without the alliance of workers and peasants and some cohesive *element* of proletarian state power. The reforms of the new democratic period, however, were achieved through various forms of political accommodation and *de facto* 'alliance' (of a populist-reformist nature) in which the 'national patriotic bourgeoisie' and the state bourgeoisie played an important role. This temporary *convivance* of 'Left' and 'Right' within the party exhibited the fragile and contradictory unity of opposite class interests which ultimately evolved, with the 1957 Anti-Rightist Campaign, the Great Leap, and the Cultural Revolution towards open confrontation.

The confrontations of the 1950s and 1960s expressed the failure of the proletariat and the communist party in leading the democratic revolution to its completion in the transition period as well as in carrying out more radical economic and social reforms built upon the foundations of a successful democratic revolution. The 'taking over' of state power by the state bourgeoisie in the aftermath of October 1976 constitutes, in this regard, not only the demise of the Cultural Revolution but the triumph of the state bourgeoisie's political project. The latter, in all its essential features, is one of bourgeois reform, to use Bettelheim's expression, a '*Great Leap Backward*', in relation to the achievements of the Chinese revolution.

The regime's political project

What underlies this political project is so-called 'socialist construction' led by the state bourgeoisie in alliance with the rich peasantry and in association with the 'patriotic' expatriate bourgeoisie and foreign capital.

The political antithesis of the worker-peasant alliance is the alliance of the state bourgeoisie with the rich peasantry which took systematic expression after October 1976, and in particular after the adoption of the Central Committee's farm policies in late 1978. The consolidation of private commercial farming through decollectivisation constitutes the basis for appropriating the agricultural surplus. The latter endorses the growth of the urban state industrial sector, as well as that of the export economy (that is, through the impetus given to cash crops, industrial crops and agro-business). In parallel, state industry subordinates an important rural industrial base through the functional integration of the system of rural factories into the urban economy. The control of rural industries is transferred to the state bureaucracy; the division of economic activity between the city and the countryside is controlled by the state apparatus and the social class which controls it.

The development of commercial agriculture based on privately-owned means of production and the concentration of resources in the rich agricultural regions are conducive to the empoverishment and proletarianisation of an important sector of the peasantry. From 1979 to 1983 (according to official sources), 32 million farm workers (approximately 10 per cent of the rural work force) 'made redundant by the rural responsibility system' were absorbed into township level industrial enterprises.[17] This process of 'redundancy' accompanies the concentration of arable land and the development of the rich peasant economy which sets free its surplus population. In some regions up to one-third of the rural labour force had (between 1979 and 1984) drifted off the land into rural as well as city-based enterprises.[18] Moreover, the state's support to the development of commercial agriculture (based on the 'specialised household') encourages the formation (in the countryside) of an (often contractual and seasonal) agricultural wage labour force and the concentration of agricultural land in the hands of the rich peasantry. (This process contrasts with that of the Soviet Union where forced collectivisation of *agriculture in support of urban industry* in the 1930s was the basis for the development of the state bourgeoisie).

Collective institutions in rural areas break down, commune administration under self-government is integrated into the state bureaucratic apparatus, the provision of social services in rural areas is increasingly based on economism and the 'ability to pay' of the recipients. The reforms in the educational system, which channel students from rural areas into a socially separate compartment of the educational system, contributes to the social reproduction of the peasantry as a subordinate class.

The state bourgeoisie's association with foreign and expatriate Chinese capital

The 'open door' policy has established the unity of (class) interests of the 'national' and 'expatriate' (for example, Hong Kong-based) segments of the bourgeoisie by encouraging the social and economic intercourse of 'former national capitalists' in state industry, banking and commerce, with their expatriate counter-parts in Hong Kong and elsewhere. China's state banking system is dominated by 'former capitalists' – this is particularly evident with regard to the Bank of China group in Hong Kong and the 'mixed' financial undertakings between the Bank of China (and its subsidiary banks) and banking interests controlled by the expatriate Chinese bourgeoisie.

The nationalisation of state industry in the mid-1950s, while constraining the development of the 'national bourgeoisie' as a property-owning class, does not signify, in the words of Deng Xiaoping, 'the transformation of that class into working people':

1. 'Former capitalists' hold positions of authority in state industry, banking and commerce.
2. 'Former capitalists' have been granted the 'right' to own capital and invest in private capitalist undertakings in specific areas of the economy (for example, in the construction industry and services). These investments are often carried out in association with members of the expatriate bourgeoisie (for example, with their relatives from Hong Kong).
3. The interest payments on the value of the industrial assets of 'former capitalists' were restored after 1976. These accumulated earnings do not, however, constitute on their own (that is, in the absence of foreign and expatriate Chinese investment) an 'investment fund' of significant magnitude, which is capable of restoring the national bourgeoisie as an independent property owning class.
4. Whereas the private industrial and financial capabilities of 'former

capitalists' are limited in magnitude, the Central Committee's Policy *vis à vis* 'former capitalists', together with the granting of 'special rights' to the expatriate bourgeoisie, are conducive to a process of *de facto class integration*, between the national and expatriate segments, of the bourgeoisie characterised by a common interest and purpose and in many cases the same family background.

5. This process is, none the less gradual: the political solution regarding the status of Hong Kong after 1997 will unquestionably play an important role in furthering and legitimising the 'rights' of the Hong Kong-based Chinese bourgeoisie as a *national* as opposed to an *expatriate* social class with the ability to own and accumulate capital on the mainland.
6. In this process, the *social class distinction* between the state bourgeoisie, 'former capitalists' and the expatriate bourgeoisie will gradually fade with the unfolding of 'mixed' and 'joint' forms of state-private as well as fully-private undertakings under a system of predominantly public state ownership.
7. The agreement reached between Britain and China regarding the economic and political status of Hong Kong after the expiry of the 99-year lease of the New Territories, grants economic and political legitimacy to the Hong Kong Chinese bourgeoisie as the ruling class in Hong Kong. Hong Kong will become 'an autonomous capitalist region' of the People's Republic under local self government. At the same time, Hong Kong is to gradually become – under Deng Xiaoping's '*One Country*, *Two Systems*' – China's international banking centre, controlled jointly by the Hong Kong Chinese bourgeoisie and the state bourgeoisie through the operation of the Bank of China and other PRC-controlled banking institutions in Hong Kong.

Comprador relations after Mao

Relations with foreign capital unfold in the context of an articulate and well-developed state industrial sector characterised by the advancements achieved in heavy industry, technology and capital construction since 1949. With the opening up of trade, comprador relations have developed within the state bureaucratic apparatus: the later constitutes the institutional link with foreign capital. At the same time, these comprador links are decentralised from the central government ministries to the provincial, municipal and enterprise levels. This decentralisation enables foreign capital to penetrate virtually any sector or region of the Chinese economy by striking individual deals with state officials at the regional and local levels.[19] In no way is foreign capitalist penetration constrained to the designated coastal cities' development zones: township, county and city governments can, under these institutional arrangements, establish direct contractual links with foreign capital. Evidently, these links take time to develop due to various bureaucratic impediments, the lack of a foreign trade infrastructure, as well as a relatively cautious attitude on the part of foreign capital.

The comprador nature of the state bureaucracy at the provincial and municipal levels is manifest in the relations established with the expatriate bourgeoisie and foreign capital. In Shanghai, for instance, the municipal government is integrated by so-called 'former capitalists': The All China Federation of Industry and Commerce and the China Democratic National Construction Association (both controlled by 'former capitalists') exert a decisive influence in municipal affairs and in the establishment of trade and joint-venture relations with foreign and Hong Kong-based capital.

Regions and localities 'compete' with one another for the 'favours of foreign capital', which in turn tends to negotiate with government trade bodies in several provinces and municipalities before finalising a foreign trade or investment contract. This process of 'competition' is viewed by the leadership as healthy because it forces regions to be more 'efficient'.

The comprador character of the regional state bourgeoisie is also apparent in the pronouncements of provincial communist party bosses in offering, for instance, 'even better conditions', that is, than in other (competing) provinces, to foreign and Hong Kong capitalists (for example, the numerous statements of the provincial communist party first secretaries of Guangdong and Fujian regarding the granting of 'preferential treatment' to foreign capital).

Undermining economic self-reliance

The liberalisation of trade, and the establishment of comprador links at the regional level have been conducive to the *economic balkanisation* of China's regions, each of which is involved in distinct and separate investment and trading arrangements with foreign capital. While liberalising foreign trade, some provinces have erected trade barriers against commodities from other provinces.

This balkanised form of 'integration' of China's economic regions with the world economy undermines the structures of economic self-reliance. In turn, these regional poles of capital accumulation constitute the basis for the development of a regional *'war-lord' type political power* in the hands of comprador officials at the provincial and city levels. The tendency, already prevalent in southern Guangdong, Shanghai and north-eastern China, is towards regional polarisation and economic subordination of the hinterland regions of China's interior.

Whereas the 'open door' undermines economic self-reliance and weakens the internal backward and forward sectoral linkages, the forces of 'extraversion' (that is, which gear the Chinese economy towards the World market) only partially undermine the structure of national accumulation: the size of internal demand is such that the external sector is incapable of totally reversing the 'auto-centred' structure of China's economy. Moreover, the size of the export sector determines, in the absence of external indebtedness, the importance of economic penetration of the internal market by foreign capital.

The nature of the various joint venture and trade transactions (discussed in chapter 8), which imply the balancing (or compensation) of the export of finished commodities for imports of machinery and technology at the microeconomic level, signifies that the penetration of the internal market by transnational capital unfolds concurrently and simultaneously with the growth of the export sector and China's reintegration into the capitalist international division of labour, that is, exports of finished output are used to 'compensate' the foreign partner for the joint ventures' purchases of technology, designs, production licences and brand names used to develop the foreign product (or an equivalent Chinese prototype) in the internal market. Moreover, the extent to which foreign capital penetrates the Chinese economy also depends on the extent to which Chinese (cheap labour) exports manage to overcome trade barriers and the protective trade structure prevalent in the EEC and North America.

Towards peripheral or centre capitalism?

Whereas the open door policy redefines China's relationship to the world capitalist economy, this process is not directly comparable to the position of a typical Third World country integrated into the prevailing structures of 'peripheral' capitalist development. The nature of the Chinese economy, the size of China's population, and its historical antecedents (both prior and after 1949), make simple 'centre-periphery' model-oriented comparisons misleading.

The process of class formation in China is, in this regard, *sui generis*: the state bourgeoisie cannot be viewed (for example) as in the Philippines, Indonesia or Brazil) as a *client social class* whose existence and development depends on foreign capital. The Central Committee's project, including the 'open door' policy, was initiated by the state bourgeoisie. While its political project implies the collaboration of foreign capital, it is free of the underlying patterns of interference and economic domination (by transnational capital) prevalent in many countries of the Third World.

None the less, this does not mean that patterns of economic and technological dependency could not develop as a *de facto* result of the 'open door' policy. China's advanced technology producing sectors which produce the *software* inputs into the production of physical means of production (that is, industrial hardware and equipment), is undermined by the 'open door' policy. The latter destroys the *linkages* between the national production of advanced technology on the one hand and the use of indigeneous advanced technology in the production of physical capital on the other hand. With the 'open door' to foreign capital, the phases of material hardware production are increasingly sustained through the import of advanced technology. This process evidently weakens the structure of a self-reliant economy characterised by the intercourse and 'exchange' between the various sectors of the national economy. In other words, China's heavy and capital goods industries are increasingly subordinated to foreign advanced technology through the import of software production licences, know-how, and so on.

The analysis of economic self-reliance based on an '*auto-centred*' as opposed to an '*extraverted*' structure is developed in various texts of Samir Amin, including his book on China entitled *L' Avenir du Maoïsme*. Amin characterises the 'Maoist model' as based on the worker-peasant alliance and the withdrawal of China's economy from the capitalist international division of labour. These two conditions which are linked with one another, constitute, according to Amin, the strategy upon which socialist transition is brought about during the age of imperialism.[20] Amin's book (first published in 1981) does not pinpoint the historical circumstances under which these two interrelated conditions (that is, the worker-peasant alliance and the withdrawal from the capitalist international division of labour) are systematically undermined by the post-Mao CCP leadership. Our analysis in previous chapters suggests that the conditions of the 'Maoist model' have been replaced by their opposite: (1) the dictatorship of the state bourgeoisie in alliance with the rich peasantry; (2) the reintegration of China's economy (via the 'open door') into the capitalist international division of labour.

The future of the Open Door

The future of China's position in the World capitalist system, however, largely depends on the ability of the central state bourgeoisie to master and control its relationship with international corporate capital. Whereas the party leadership has stressed its commitment to the 'open door' policy, some observers have suggested that the 'open door' is but 'half-opened' as a result of a movement within the central leadership against comprador elements at the provincial level and in the 14 designated coastal city ports and special economic zones. The future scope and direction of the 'open door' could radically shift, therefore, as a result of the conflicts between different segments of the state bourgeoisie. This could take the form, for instance, of a greater degree of centralisation, institutional control and central government interference in the contractual arrangements with foreign capital at the regional level.

More fundamentally this question relates to the development of a genuine national political and economic project by a cohesive central state bourgeoisie *capable of adopting foreign technology without becoming an 'economic satellite' of Western capitalism*. Although this development is a distinct possibility, the relatively mild criticism voiced within the party against 'several bad consequences' of the 'open door' do not in any way convey a weakening of the official party line as contained in Prime Minister Zhao Ziyang's 1985 'guidelines' for the seventh Five year plan. Moreover, the shifts in the political power structure in the aftermath of the September 1985 'Special Conference' of the communist party reinforce (at least in the immediate future) the party's stance on the 'open door' by bringing into the Politbureau and the Central Committee a new team of 'pro-Western' technocrats and protegés of Deng Xiaoping.

Transition towards Capitalism?

In which direction is the post-Mao economic and social system evolving? The official CCP position, which indeed is shared by many western Marxists, is that the reforms constitute a necessary phase in 'the transition between capitalism and socialism'. The Chinese Communist Party states, in this regard, that '*it is necessary to take one step back*' so as to take '*one step forward towards socialism*' at a later date. Although not referring explicitly to the New Economic Policy put forth by Lenin in Soviet Russia in the early 1920s, the reforms are justified, without this being the object of serious debate or discussion, as a strategy of transition towards socialism: 'Decollectivise now so as to recollectivise on solid grounds later', and so on. The arguments presented rhetorically and dogmatically by the Central Committee have no theoretical or practical justification because the policy of 'taking one step backward' is neither motivated nor controlled by the working class. This process should, therefore, be distinguished from the adoption of specific policies, with the proletariat in control of the political process, which temporarily rehabilitates the interests of the national bourgeoisie, the Kulaks, and foreign capital, in view of mobilising and developing the productive forces. Reforms of this nature, characteristic of the New Economic Policy adopted in Soviet Russia in the early 1920s, require critical debate, discussion and careful regulatory measures. Lenin recognised in the context of the debate on foreign concessions (at a time when the Soviet economy was in a shambles in the aftermath of the First World War and the Civil War) that these policies also 'created new dangers' which required the stipulation of very careful conditions and safeguards regulating foreign corporate capital:

> Every concessionnaire remains a capitalist and he will try to trip up the Soviet power while we for our part make use of his rapacity . . . each

clause of a concession agreement records some aspects of a war, and we should organise things in such a way as to safeguard our interests in that war.[21]

Whether this type of discussion regarding China's foreign investment legislation is actually held behind closed doors within the inner group of the CCP Politbureau is doubtful. The provisions regulating foreign capital do not in any respects express the critical concern for safeguards, and so on. Neither is there any discussion concerning the history of foreign domination in China's treaty ports in relation to the development of new extraterritorial arrangements in China's coastal cities. In other words, there is no historical perspective on China's colonial development during the Qing and Republican periods, no sensitivity to the fact that:

(a) The interests of foreign capital after Mao are broadly similar to those prevalent during the late Republican period;
(b) the same corporate interests which were present in China's treaty ports are actively in the process of re-establishing themselves in the 14 designated coastal cities.

It should also be noted that the CCP's assessment of the role of the post-Mao reforms 'in the transition towards socialism' is in contradiction with its own official interpretation of the new democratic period of the early to mid–1950s. These earlier policies – characterised as 'bourgeois democratic' in nature – required (according to the post-Mao CCP) the collaboration of the 'patriotic national bourgeoisie' as a necessary basis for the development of productive forces in the form of private and mixed (state–private) forms of ownership. The 'bourgeois democratic' revolution having been 'successfully completed', it is then superseded (again according to official party interpretations) by the development of 'socialist public ownership of the means of production, namely ownership by the whole people and collective ownership by the working people'.[22] What justifies then – *after* the 'successful completion' of the bourgeois–democratic revolution in the mid–1950s the return, that is, 'a step backwards' 30 years later, to NEP type reforms similar in nature to those *already* applied in the early 1950s. Inasmuch as the latter were 'successful' (according to the post-Mao leadership) in establishing the basis of socialism, what is the role of the post-Mao reforms in the historical sequence of socialist construction? Is it now necessary to re-establish private and mixed forms of ownership, free markets, and so on, in the name of socialist construction? Is it now necessary for the development of socialist production relations to undermine and destroy socialist production relations so as to rebuild them 'on solid grounds later'?

The post-Mao economic and social system

In the words of Lenin (in the context of the debate on foreign concessions): 'Growing capitalism will be under control and supervision while political power will remain in the hands of the working class and the workers' state'.[23] *But this does not describe the political process in China after Mao: these reforms are not under the control and supervision of the Chinese working class. So the transition cannot be towards socialism.*

Whereas many western Marxists fail to perceive the nature of class relations in post-Mao China, the latter is by now understood by various sectors of (conservative) western political and business opinion (including Ronald Reagan and David Rockefeller): 'China watchers', business analysts and the representatives of international corporate capital have understood that there is no workers' state in post-Mao China. These sectors are largely supportive of the Central Committee's political project because the post-Mao regime's particular blend of Chinese 'communism' is ultimately compatible with their long-run economic, financial and political interests. Whereas moderate progressive reforms in Chile (under Allende), Nicaragua and other parts of the Third World are considered 'a communist threat' (that is, a threat to US imperialism), Chinese 'communism' has converted itself into a major ally of the United States. This strategic alliance, ironically, contributes to a more effective US strategy of 'combating the spread of communism' in the Third World.

Curiously, the White House and the CCP Politbureau, together with the CIA, Wall Street and the US media, share a common *Weltanschauung*, that is, in the way in which they represent and express economic and social change in post-Mao China. US foreign policy and the interests of American corporate capital are not confounded by words: Chinese 'communism' is by now recognised not by its official label but for what it is in reality.

As discussed earlier, the nature of social production relations (rather than legal forms of ownership) and the precise expression of proletarian state power are central to an understanding of the post-Mao economic and social system. These social production relations are expressed by the restoration of despotic management in industry and the separation of the direct producers from the means of production. The social subordination of workers to senior management is the concrete expression of 'exploitation' of the proletariat by the state bourgeoisie: so-called 'scientific management' not only denies decision-making powers to workers, it subordinates the activity of working people to production, profit and accumulation.

'Scientific management' in post-Mao China combines Confucian authoritarianism with western Taylorism. The latter consists in the fragmentation of the labour process and its control by 'scientific' management. Workers are not only subordinated to the structure of factory discipline and authority, management controls, and dictates, each step of the labour process including its mode of performance.[24] Challenge to Taylorism and the capitalist division of labour emerged initially in China during the Great Leap in the form of the *duo mian shou* movement – 'every machine must be multipurpose'.[25] The *duo mian shou* movement called for the diversification of skills: workers should learn a variety of skills and perform a range of production tasks.[26] The movement thus constituted a reaction against: (a) the prevailing social division of labour; (b) the fragmentation of the labour process, and its separation or divorce from the direct producers.

The *duo mian shou* movement implied transforming the division between mental and manual labour which constitutes the very basis of Taylorism and which prescribes the separation of the skills and knowledge of the labourer from the labour process.[27] Namely, the science and knowledge activities which characterise production are separated from the manual tasks of production. Similarly, the underlying (capitalist) division of labour under Taylorism *separates* production tasks from administrative, managerial and co-ordinating tasks: the separation of the direct producers from production means that workers have no say in the conception, design and co-ordination of the productive process: *workers are simply objects of control, supervision and discipline.* [28]

Labour power as a commodity

According to Chavance, the constitution of a ruling stratum (that is, a state bourgeoisie) is characterised by the appropriation by the ruling stratum of the unpaid surplus labour of the direct producers.[29] The consequence of this appropriation under despotic management is characteristic of the restoration of labour power as a commodity. Workers are viewed, alongside machinery and raw materials, as a 'factor input' which entails a cost of production. It is in this context that the services of labour become a commodity which are bought and sold much in the same way as the other material 'factors of production'.

Wage labour in commodity form was partially restored in the early 1980s in agriculture and industry. This tendency became fully pervasive with the 1984 reform in the eight-grade wage-scale system and the adoption of a 'the flexible wage system' under the authority of the factory director. Moreover, the reforms in the system of state-assigned jobs, increased 'flexibility' in hiring and firing, personnel management, labour discipline, and so on, further contributed to the unfolding of wage labour in commodity form.

The separation of the direct producers from the means of production is also accompanied by the restoration of economic calculus based on profit maximisation. The appropriation of the unpaid surplus labour of the direct producers signifies the concurrent transformation of the enterprise's cost concepts. In agriculture, the separation of the direct producers from the means of production is characterised by the collapse of collective property, the development of the rich peasant economy and a tendency towards the proletarianisation and semi-proletarianisation of the poor and middle peasantry.

The constitution of a ruling state bourgeoisie

As discussed above, the establishment of a ruling state bourgeoisie is determined by the appropriation (by the state bourgeoisie) of the unpaid labour of the direct producers. The extent of material privilege of the state bourgeoisie is not, however, the primary issue in defining its existence as a social class. *The dictatorship of the state bourgeoisie is determined by the 'collective ownership' of state industry, commerce and finance by a social minority*: state capital is the collectively-owned property of the state bourgeoisie. The state controls the precise forms of appropriation and accumulation on behalf of the 'collective interests' of the ruling class as well as the various forms of 'mixed' or 'joint' ownership and accumulation which result from the reinstatement of the expatriate bourgeoisie and former capitalists as a private property-owning class within 'socialist' China.

Social class relations are reproduced through an élitist and compartmentalised educational system. A pro-western stratum of intellectuals, socially associated with the interests of the state bourgeoisie and foreign capital, strengthens the reproduction of social relations through the emulation of bourgeois values and western concepts of modernisation. The reforms of the universities and research institutions after Mao, heavily influenced by overseas Chinese intellectuals, embody (via the transfer of intellectual technology) western concepts of 'objective science' and western norms of scholarly achievement. Similarly, the 'open door' policy and the development of consumerism contribute to the commercialisation of cultural art forms and the development of the visual arts, the mass media, and so on, in commodity form. This tendency is particularly visible in the numerous joint venture TV and film productions with Hong Kong-based companies.

Social inequality and the distribution of income

At present, the levels of consumption and material privilege enjoyed by the Chinese state bourgeoisie are relatively low, for example, in relation to those enjoyed by capitalists in western (or other Third World) countries. This form of comparison, as mentioned earlier, is misleading: the development of social life styles enjoyed by the dominant social class in a particular social formation must be analysed in relation to the historical evolution of social production relations and the concurrent changes in the distribution of income and wealth which accompany the development of a privileged social class. The underlying *duality in consumption* and material life styles between the privileged class, and the masses of workers and peasants, must necessarily relate to China's particular conditions, that is, in a country of more than one billion population, average per capita income (less than 300 US dollars per capita) is scarcely above the level of materials subsistence. Thus, these small social pockets of material privilege and luxury consumption are indeed indicative of growing social and income inequalities. Relative income inequalities in China after Mao are indeed high even in relation to those prevalent in the advanced capitalist countries.

The collective interests of the state bourgeoisie

In China after Mao, the state appropriates the surplus value on behalf of the *collective interests of the ruling class*. It allocates one portion to accumulation, the other portion to the state bourgeoisie's 'consumption fund'. The proportions governing the relationship between accumulation and consumption are decided upon 'collectively' by the state bourgeoisie. The state bourgeoisie's 'consumption fund' is not only appropriated collectively, it is also divided (and split up) collectively (according to certain rules) by the state. Invariably, the (Confucian) structure of hierarchy, social position and authority (within the state bureaucracy) will determine the *social distribution* of consumption and privileges (that is, the way in which the 'consumption fund' is divided and distributed).

The middle stratum

The changing structure of income distribution not only expresses the social privileges enjoyed by the ruling élite, it also reveals the formation of an essentially urban 'middle stratum' which enjoys the 'fruits of economic modernisation' brought about through the changes in the structure of national accumulation. (This middle stratum may represent 20 per cent of the urban population or 6 per cent of total population). The development of this 'middle stratum' is an essential component of the CCP's project because it represents the regime's basis of political support and, therefore, a means for its political and ideological legitimation. The formation of a 'middle stratum' also supports the restructuring of demand and supply relations by channelling economic resources into the production of consumer goods for the upper end of the income scale. In other words, the formation of a 'middle stratum' accompanies both the changes in social and political relations as well as the shifts in the structure and composition of economic growth.

Pseudo-collectivism

The leadership's political project signifies the replacement of collective property and institutions by a 'pseudo-collectivism' which supports the 'collective' interests of a social minority. In rural areas, for instance, this pseudo-collectivism is expressed by the development of new co-operative forms essentially characterised by the 'co-operative' association of well-to-do farmers. The new producers' co-operatives contribute to the development of commercial farming by consolidating the collective interests of the rich peasantry.

The Future of Socialism

In the aftermath of October 1976, articulate opposition both within and outside the communist party to the 'bourgeois line' has been considerably weakened. The 'Rightist' leadership is well established and in control of the party and state apparatus. This means that the direction of economic and social change, which underlies the regime's political project, will not be radically modified in the foreseeable future: Changes in the course and pace of the reforms are indeed possible, but *a major reversal of the regime's political project will not originate from within the communist party itself.* Such a reversal must of necessity originate from the class struggle in the form of a major revolutionary upheaval directed against the party establishment.

With the 'bourgeois line' firmly in control of the party, it is unlikely, however, that a major upheaval in economic, political and social relations will occur in the immediate and foreseeable future. This is important because, in the meantime, and in the absence of an articulate and forceful mass movement capable of challenging the post-Mao regime, the reforms will gain in impetus and progress considerably towards dismantling the economic and social achievements of Chinese socialism. In the few years since the 1976 *coup d'état*, many achievements of the Chinese revolution have been forcefully undone: the decollectivisation of agriculture, the 'open door' to foreign capital and the reforms in industry have proceeded at a very rapid pace.

We should not, therefore, underestimate the strength of the 'Rightist' leadership in carrying out these reforms: in addition to the endorsement of those articulate and organised groups within Chinese society which ultimately will benefit socially and materially from the reforms, and the regime has the support of expatriate Chinese and foreign capital. The regime's social basis of support among a small (although significant) sector of the urban and rural population constitutes the means for its political legitimation. Moreover, after the social strife of the Cultural Revolution, the post-Mao leadership presented itself to the masses as having restored 'order', 'normality' and 'political stability'. Consequently, in the first years after the 1976 downfall of the so-called 'Gang of Four', there was indeed evidence of significant popular support for the new leadership. This initial support, however, has been largely eroded as a consequence of the increased rural poverty, urban unemployment, inflation and so on which have resulted from the reforms. As the reforms unfold, therefore, and reveal the falsity of 'socialist construction via the capitalist road', they also unleash those social forces which confront and challenge the regime's authority.

October 1976 marks the beginning of a new phase of the class struggle which, of necessity, will express itself under very different circumstances. The political purges and repression conducted by the regime in the aftermath of October 1976 against supporters of Mao Zedong have destroyed the party's revolutionary base. Opposition based on the mass movement will, therefore, necessarily unfold under very difficult and unfavourable circumstances before emerging as a decisive force in the political and social struggle against the 'bourgeois line'. This is something which we have to recognise and accept because there are no 'historical laws' which ensure that a successful 'Second Cultural Revolution' will of necessity take place at a time and in way which *necessarily* undermines the regime's political authority, thereby excluding the possibility of 'capitalist restoration' outright. In China after Mao, the revolutionary line can only operate underground as a clandestine organisation directed against the seat of authority and the party establishment.

A longer historical view of the class struggle from the middle of the nineteenth century reveals the fundamental nature of the Chinese people's struggle against oppression and foreign domination. This longer view is required in our understanding of the class struggle after Mao. The history of China is the history of the class struggle: in the aftermath of 1976, however, this struggle will be a long and drawn out process. In the words of Mao:

> The victory or defeat of the revolution can be determined only over a long period of time. If it is badly handled, there is always the danger of a capitalist restoration. All members of the party and all the people of our country must not think that after one, two, three or four cultural revolutions there will be peace and quiet.[30]

For those committed to progressive economic and social change in the contemporary Third World, Chinese socialism represented the means for overcoming the poverty, social misery and oppression of the rural and urban masses. The lessons of the Chinese Revolution must be drawn. The setbacks and failures of the 'revolutionary line' must be understood and fully assessed. This book constitutes an initial reflection on the complex political, economic, and social process unfolding in post-Mao China.

References

1 The Political Transition

1. Charles Bettelheim, 'The Great Leap Backward', *Monthly Review*, XXX:3 (1978), p. 42.
2. Roger Howard, *Mao Tse-tung and the Chinese People* (New York: Monthly Review Press, 1977) p. 355.
3. Ibid., p. 356.
4. Quoted in Roger Howard, *Mao-Tse-tung and the Chinese People*, p. 356.
5. Parris Chang, 'Chinese Politics, Deng's Turbulent Quest', *Problems of Communism* (January-February 1981), p. 102.
6. Speech by Hua Guofeng on 18 September 1976, *Beijing Review*, XIX:39 (1976), quoted in Charles Bettelheim, 'The Great Leap Backward', *Monthly Review*, XXX:3 (1978), p. 88.
7. Charles Bettelheim, 'The Great Leap Backward', *Monthly Review*, XXX:3 (1978), pp. 88–9.
8. Ibid., p. 89.
9. Parris Chang, 'Chinese Politics, Deng's Turbulent Quest', *Problems of Communism* (January-February 1981), p. 4.
10. Ibid., p. 4.
11. Ibid., p. 9.
12. Ibid., p. 9.
13. Ibid., p. 13.
14. Ibid., p. 13.
15. Deng Xiaoping, *Selected Works* (Beijing: Foreign Languages Press, 1984), p. 238.
16. Amnesty International, *China*, *Violations of Human Rights* (London: Amnesty International Publications, 1984) pp. 12–13.
17. Ibid., p. 12.
18. Deng Xiaoping, *Selected Works*, pp. 238–339 (my italics).
19. Amnesty International, *China*, *Violations of Human Rights*, p. 14.
20. Ibid., pp. 6–7.
21. Ibid., p. 7.
22. Ibid., p. 9.
23. Ibid., p. 9.
24. *Hongqi* (Red Flag), No. 2 (February 1982) quoted in *China Daily*, 12 February 1982.
25. Deng Xiaoping, *Selected Works*, pp. 375–6.
26. Ibid., p. 376.
27. Ibid., p. 378 (my italics).

28. Amnesty International, *China Briefing* (London: Amnesty International Publications, 1984) p. 7.
29. Ibid., p. 7 (my italics).
30. Ibid., p. 6.
31. Ibid., p. 6.
32. Deng Xiaoping, *Selected Works*, pp. 88–9.
33. Ibid., p. 89.
34. Ibid., p. 89.
35. For further details, see Amnesty International, *China Briefing*, p. 7.
36. Parris Chang, 'Chinese Politics, Deng's Turbulent Quest', *Problems of Communism* (January-February, 1981), p. 16.
37. *Resolution on Certain Questions in the History of our Party, 1949–1981: Authoritative Assessment of Mao Zedong, The Cultural Revolution, Achievements of the People's Republic* (Beijing: Foreign Languages Press, 1981). The draft of this document was under the direct supervision of Deng Xiaoping.
38. Ibid., pp. 46, 56.
39. Ibid., p. 72.
40. Ibid., p. 21.
41. Sun Xiacun, 'Seeking the Truth from Facts', *China Reconstructs*, XXX:11 (1981), p. 30.
42. *Renmin Ribao* (People's Daily), 10 October 1981.
43. Ye Jianying, (former) Chairman of the Standing Committee of the NPC, speech on the occasion of the 32nd anniversary of the People's Republic of China, quoted in *South China Morning Post*, 2 October 1981 (my italics).
44. Richard Pascoe, 'Ex Nationalists Get Top Posts', *South China Morning Post*, 15 December 1981.
45. Speech by Kuomintang Premier Sun Yunsuan, 11th Sino-American Conference on Mainland China, Taipei, 10 June 1982.
46. Deng Xiaoping, *Selected Works*, p. 202.

2 Land Reform and Collectivisation

1. Edgar Snow, *Red China Today* (Harmondsworth: Penguin, 1971), p. 415.
2. Alfred Lin, 'Agrarian Crisis in Pre-Communist China', in S. S. K. Chin and C. K. Leung (eds), *China, Development and Challenge*, vol. I (Hong Kong: Centre of Asian Studies, University of Hong Kong, 1979) p. 90.
3. Ibid., p. 90.
4. Cf. Mao Zedong, *Selected Works*, vol. I (Beijing: Foreign Languages Press, 1975) pp. 137–9.
5. Alfred Lin, 'Agrarian Crisis in Pre-Communist China', p. 90.
6. Ibid., p. 90.
7. Ibid., p. 93.
8. Du Jing, 'On the Question of Land Confiscation and Distribution in the Agrarian Reform', *Social Sciences in China*, III:3 (1982) p. 107.
9. Alfred Lin, 'Agrarian Crisis in Pre-Communist China', p. 96.
10. Mao Zedong, 'The Struggle in Chingkang Mountains', *Selected Works*, vol. I; cf. also Tung Chi-ming, *An Outline History of China* (Hong Kong: Joint Publishing Co., 1979) p. 354.
11. John Wong, *Chinese Land Reform in Retrospect*, (Hong Kong: Centre of Asian Studies, University of Hongkong, 1979) p. 3.

12. Mao Zedong, 'Report on an Investigation of the Peasant Movement in Hunan', *Selected Works*, vol. I, p. 24.
13. John Wong, *Chinese Land Reform in Retrospect*, p. 3.
14. Tung Chi-ming, *An Outline History of China*, pp. 425–6.
15. Mao Zedong, *Selected Works*, vol. IV, p. 203.
16. Ibid., pp. 203–4 (my italics).
17. Du Jing, 'On the Question of Land Confiscation and Distribution in the Agrarian Reform', p. 116.
18. Ibid., p. 116.
19. Ibid., pp. 116–17.
20. Ibid., p. 116.
21. Ibid., p. 117.
22. Ibid., p. 117.
23. Ibid., p. 118.
24. V. I. Lenin, *The Development of Capitalism in Russia* (Moscow: Progress Publishers, 1967) chapter 2.
25. Ibid., pp. 72, 129–30, 180.
26. Ibid., p. 180.
27. C. Bettelheim, *Class Struggles in the USSR, First Period, 1917–1923* (New York: Monthly Review Press, 1976) p. 83.
28. Ibid., p. 223.
29. Quoted in Bettelheim, *Class Struggles in the USSR, First Period, 1917–1923*, p. 83.
30. Mao Zedong, *Selected Works*, vol. IV, p. 368.
31. Immanuel Hsu, *The Rise of Modern China* (Hong Kong: Oxford University Press, 1970) p. 34.
32. Mao Zedong, *Selected Works*, vol. V, p. 257.
33. Xue Muqiao, *China's Socialist Economy* (Beijing: Foreign Languages Press, 1980) p. 34.
34. W. Burchett and R. Alley, *China, The Quality of Life*, (Harmondsworth: Penguin, 1976) p. 17.
35. Immanuel Hsu, *The Rise of Modern China*, pp. 784–5.
36. Ibid., p. 787.
37. Mao Zedong, 'The Debate on the Cooperative Transformation of Agriculture', *Selected Works*, vol. V, p. 224.
38. Ibid., p. 224.
39. Mao responded with 'The Four Clean-Ups' with respect to political, ideological, organisational and economic aspects of the People's Commune. See Joan Robinson, *The Cultural Revolution in China* (Harmondsworth: Penguin, 1969) p. 36.
40. W.A.C. Adie, 'China's Second Liberation' in Educational Foundation for Nuclear Science (eds), *China After the Cultural Revolution* (Clinton, Mass.: Vintage Books) p. 42.
41. Ibid., p. 40.
42. K. S. Karol, *La deuxième revolution chinoise* (Paris: Editions Robert Laffont, 1973), p. 190.
43. Joan Robinson, *The Cultural Revolution in China*, pp. 35–7.
44. The 'Sixteen-Point Decision' adopted by the Central Committee of the Chinese Communist Party, 8 August 1966, quoted in R. Howard, *Mao Tse-tung and the Chinese People* (New York: Monthly Review Press, 1977) pp. 326–7.
45. *The Great Power Struggle in China* (Hong Kong: Asian Research Centre,

1969) pp. 52–5, quoted in R. Howard, *Mao Tse-tung and the Chinese People*, pp. 331–2.
46. Jean Esmein, *La révolution culturelle chinoise* (Paris: Editions du Seuil, 1970) chapter 8.
47. Ibid., p. 265.
48. Mao Zedong, 'On the Cooperative Transformation of Agriculture', *Selected Works*, vol. V, pp. 201–2.

3 The Decollectivisation of Agriculture

1. Quoted in H. Yamamoto, 'Three Forms of the Agricultural Responsibility System', in C. K. Leung and S. S. K. Chin (eds), *China in Readjustment* (Hong Kong: Centre of Asian Studies, University of Hong Kong, 1983) pp. 129–30.
2. For further details see H. Yamamoto, ibid.
3. *Ta Kung Pao*, Hong Kong (16 December 1982).
4. W. H. Hinton, 'More on China's New Family Contract System', *Monthly Review*, XXXV:11 (1984), p. 43.
5. Ibid., pp. 114–46.
6. Ibid., p. 146.
7. *China Daily*, 22 January 1984, p. 1.
8. *China Daily*, 18 January 1984, p. 4.
9. *Beijing Review*, 24:34 (1981), p. 18.
10. See CCP Central Committee 'Circular on Rural Work in 1984', *China Daily*, 4 February 1984.
11. Friedrich Engels, 'On Russia', in Karl Marx, *Selected Works*, vol. II (London: Lawrence & Wishart, 1942) p. 680.
12. Li Chien-nung, *The Political History of China, 1840–1929* (Stanford: Stanford University Press, 1956) p. 63.
13. Quoted in C. Bettelheim, *Class Struggles in the USSR, First Period, 1917–1923* (New York: Monthly Review Press, 1976) p. 214.
14. Friedrich Engels, 'On Russia', p. 683 (my italics).
15. Ibid., p. 683.
16. Interview conducted by the author in Daqing Township, Yuhongqu County, Liaoning Province in September 1983.
17. According to *Xinhua* (New China News Agency) 15 January 1983, more than a quarter of the total loans to the rural economy in 1982 was channelled to individual households.
18. Interview conducted by the author in Dali Commune, Nanhai County, Guangdong Province in September 1983.
19. Interview conducted by the author in Ninguan Village, Yangshe Township, Yuhonqu County, Liaoning Province in September 1983.
20. R. Stavenhagen, *Agrarian Reform in Structures and Underdevelopment in Africa and Latin American*, Conference on Strategies for Economic Development, Africa versus Latin America, United Nations African Institute for Economic Development and Planning, Dakar, September 1972, pp. 15–17.
21. Mao Zedong, 'On the Co-operative Transformation of Agriculture', *Selected Works*, vol. V, p. 197.
22. See Michel Chossudovsky, 'Capitalist Development and Agriculture in Latin America', in L. Alschuler (ed.), *Dependent Agricultural Development and Agrarian Reform in Latin America* (Ottawa: University of Ottawa Press, 1981).

23. Interview conducted by the author in Daqing Township, Yuhongqu County, Liaoning Province, September 1983.
24. Ibid.
25. Interview conducted by the author in Ninguan Brigade (village), Yangshe Township, Yuhongqu County, Liaoning Province, September 1983.
26. Ibid.
27. Interview in Dali (see note 18).
28. 'Why Land is Concentrated in Shanxi', *China Daily*, 6 September 1983 (my italics).
29. Ibid.
30. 'One Peasant Outdid Whole Brigade', *China Daily*, 9 September 1983 (my italics).
31. W. H. Hinton, 'More on China's New Family Contract System', p. 45.
32. *China Daily*, 6 September 1983.
33. Statement by Wan Li, a member of the CCP Politbureau, quoted in *China Daily*, 19 January 1984.
34. *China Daily*, 6 September 1983.
35. Ibid.
36. *China Daily*, 21 November 1983.
37. 'Let's Use Rural Surplus Labour Well', *China Daily*, 22 October 1981 (my italics).
38. 'Peasants Income Rises During 1983', *Beijing Review*, XXVII:21 (1984), p. 9.
39. Ibid., p. 9.
40. *China Daily*, 19 April 1984, p. 1.
41. Interview in Daqing Township, September 1983.
42. Ibid.
43. Interview in Yuhongqu County, Liaoning Province, September 1983.
44. Interview in Dali Township, Guangdong Province, September 1983.
45. *Beijing Review*, XXVI:48 (1983), p. 18.
46. Ibid., p. 19 (my italics).
47. Ibid., pp. 19–20 (my italics).
48. Statement by Du Runsheng, director of the CCP Rural Policy Research Centre, quoted in *China Daily*, 8 March 1984, p. 3 (my italics). The Rural Policy Research Centre is directly under the authority of the Central Committee Secretariat.
49. *Beijing Review*, XXVI:48 (1983), p. 21.
50. Ibid., p. 20.
51. *Renmin Ribao*, 17 November 1983, quoted in *China Daily*, 18 November 1983 (my italics).
52. *Beijing Review*, XXVI:48, 1983, p. 20.
53. Statement by Cui Yuef, Minister of Public Health, quoted in *Beijing Review*, XXVI:20 (1983), p. 20.
54. 'Funds for Public Health Inadequate', *Beijing Review*, XXVI:20 (1983), p. 11.
55. For further details see H. Yamamoto, 'Three Forms of the Agricultural Responsibility System'.
56. Ibid.
57. Ibid.
58. Ibid.
59. Interview of factory workers in a rural township export-processing factory, Dali Township, Guangdong Province, September 1983.
60. *China Daily*, 29 February 1983, p. 1.
61. Ibid., p. 1.

62. Interview conducted by the author, Shenyang Free Market, Liaoning Province, September 1983.
63. Xue Muqiao, *China's Socialist Economy*, pp. 148–9.
64. Quoted in *Far Eastern Economic Review*, CXXX:39 (1985) p. 11.
65. 'Report on the Arrangements for the National Economic Plans', *Main Documents of the Third Session of the Fifth National People's Congress* (Beijing: Foreign Languages Press, 1980) p. 27.
66. 'Beatrice, Two Chinese Organisations Form Joint-Venture Firm to Make Canned Food', *The Asian Wall Street Journal*, 23 November 1981.
67. Ibid.
68. Interviews with Liaoning Province foreign trade officials conducted by the author in Shenyang, September 1983.
69. Ibid.
70. Ibid.
71. *China Daily*, 28 April 1984, p. 2.
72. Ibid., p. 2.
73. Ibid., p. 2.
74. In north-east China, foreign funds channelled into livestock production are encouraging the development of privately-owned enterprises involved in large-scale animal husbandry.

4 State Capitalism in Industry

1. Hou Chi-ming, *Foreign Investment and Economic Development in China, 1840–1937* (Cambridge, Mass.: Harvard University Press, 1965) p. 136.
2. Wang Jingyu, 'The Birth of the Chinese Bourgeoisie', *Social Sciences in China*, III:1 (1982), p. 220.
3. Ibid., p. 220.
4. Ibid., p. 229.
5. Hou Chi-ming, *Foreign Investment and Economic Development*, p. 136.
6. Ibid., p. 142.
7. Quoted in *Lishi Yanjiu* (Editorial Board for Modern and Contemporary Chinese History), 'Chinese Historical Studies of the Early Modern China's Bourgeoisie', *Social Sciences in China*, IV:1 (1983), p. 13.
8. Ibid., p. 13.
9. Ibid., p. 15.
10. Ibid., p. 17.
11. Ibid., p. 19.
12. Mao Zedong, 'The Only Road for the Transformation of Capitalist Industry and Commerce, *Selected Works*, vol. V, p. 112.
13. Ibid., p. 114.
14. Mao Zedong, 'On the Correct Handling of Contradictions among the People', *Selected Works*, vol. V, p. 403.
15. Mao Zedong, 'Combat Bourgeois Ideas in the Party', *Selected Works*, vol. V, pp. 103–104.
16. Immanuel Hsu, *The Rise of Modern China* (Hong Kong: Oxford University Press, 1975), p. 830.
17. Ibid., p. 830.
18. Ibid., p. 831.
19. Lee Nan-shong, 'Industrial Development and Mass-Line Leadership in China', in

E. K. Y Chen and S. S. K. Chin (eds), *Development and Change in China*, vol. IV (Hong Kong: Centre of Asian Studies, University of Hong Kong, 1981) p. 104.
20. Li Hsueh-feng, 'Strengthen the Party's Leadership and Implement the Mass Line', *People's Handbook*, (1957), speech delivered at Eighth Party Congress, 24 September 1956, reprinted in *Chinese Law and Government*, no. 1 (1980), p. 27.
21. Lee Nan-shong, 'Industrial Development and Mass-Line Leadership in China', p. 105.
22. Li Hsueh-feng, 'Strengthen the Party's Leadership', pp. 30–31.
23. Lee Nan-shong, 'China's Managerial Modernisation, Three Basic Models, 1956–1978', *Chinese Law and Government*, no. 1 (1980), p. 3.
24. Yang Shih-chieh, 'The Great Leap Victory of the Party's Leadership and the Extensive Mass Movement at the Anshan Iron and Steel Works', *Renmin Ribao*, 11 February 1960, reprinted in *Chinese Law and Government*, no. 1 (1980), pp. 54–5.
25. Lee Nan-shong 'China's Managerial Modernisation', p. 80.
26. Ibid., p. 81.
27. Ibid., p. 81.
28. Ibid., p. 119.
29. Yang Shih-chieh, 'The Great Leap Victory of the Party's Leadership', pp. 58–9.
30. The text of this document is contained in *Almanac of the Chinese Economy, 1981* (Hong Kong: Modern Cultural Company, 1982) pp. 175–8. See also the analysis of Chen Yu-shen, 'The 30-Point Decision on Industry: An Analysis', *Issues and Studies* (January 1979) p. 62.
31. Chen Yu-shen, ibid., p. 62.
32. Ibid., p. 59.
33. *Almanac of the Chinese Economy, 1981*, p. 179.
34. *South China Morning Post*, 28 December 1981.
35. Quoted from a *Renmin Ribao* editorial by J. Mirsky 'Daqing's Image as a Model Restored', *South China Morning Post*, 3 February 1983.
36. *Almanac of the Chinese Economy, 1981*, pp. 176–7.
37. Ibid., p. 179.
38. Ibid., p. 179.
39. A few of the summary executions of 'delinquents' and 'embezzlers' were reported in the Chinese press. Unofficial reports suggest that mass executions of more than 100 individuals took place in 1983–4 on the same day.
40. Editorial, *China Daily*, 12 February 1982.
41. Interview with Ni Zhifu, President of the All China Federation of Trade Unions, *Beijing Review*, XXVII:7 (1984), p. 18.
42. Interview with Chen Yu (Vice-Chairman of the All China Federation of Trade Unions) *China Reconstructs*, XXVIII:5 (1979), p. 9 (my italics).
43. Charles Bettelheim, 'The Great Leap Backward' (1978). Bettelheim's analysis and quote of a Shandong communist party broadcast on Radio Jinan, 1 February 1977 (italics in the original).
44. Interview with the factory director, Shenyang Small Tractor Factory, Shenyang, Liaoning Province, September 1983 (my italics).
45. Interview with the director of Chang Zheng Municipal Garment Factory, Shenyang, Liaoning Province, September 1983.
46. Interview with the director of Guangzhou Shipyard Container Factory, Guangdong Province, September 1983.

47. Interview with the director (chairman of the board of directors) of Parker Hubei, Wuhan, Hubei Province, September 1983.
48. Mao Zedong, *Selected Works*, vol. V, p. 305.
49. 'How U.S. Soft Drink Giant Breaks into China's Consumer Market', *Economic Reporter*, no. 9 (September 1981) p. 20.
50. *China Daily*, 20 June 1984.
51. See, for instance, Gao Liang, 'Annoted Survey of China's Major Economics Periodicals', in *Almanac of China's Economy, 1981*, pp. 1077–85.
52. *China Reconstructs*, XXXIII:1 (1984), p. 60.
53. Ibid., p. 60.
54. Ibid., p. 60.
55. Ibid., p. 61 (my italics).
56. Ibid., p. 61 (my italics).
57. Ibid., p. 60.
58. Ibid., p. 61.
59. Ibid., p. 63.
60. Ibid., p. 63.
61. Ruth Hayhoe, 'Chinese Higher Education: The Challenge of the Eighties', *Canadian Association of University Teachers Bulletin* (February 1984) p. 19.
62. Ibid., p. 19.

5 Wages and the Labour Process

1. Christopher Howe, *Wage Patterns and Wage Policy in Modern China, 1919–1972* (Cambridge: Cambridge University Press, 1973) p. 36.
2. Ibid., p. 36.
3. Ibid., p. 85.
4. Ibid., pp. 89–95.
5. Ibid., p. 29.
6. Chen Po-wèn, 'Rising Prices and Wages in Mainland China', *Issues and Studies* (February 1980) pp. 42–4.
7. Christopher Howe, *Wage Patterns and Wage Policy in Modern China*, p. 94.
8. W. Parish, 'Egalitarianism in Chinese Society', *Problems of Communism* (January–February 1981), p. 39.
9. Ibid., p. 39.
10. 'Oppose Economism and Smash the Latest Counter-Attack by the Bourgeois Reactionary Line', *Honggi* (Red Flag), 12 January 1967, reprinted in Joan Robinson, *The Cultural Revolution in China* (Harmondsworth: Penguin, 1969) pp. 112–13.
11. W. Burchett and R. Alley, *China, The Quality of Life* (Harmondsworth: Penguin, 1976) p. 175.
12. Ibid., p. 175.
13. Ibid., p. 175.
14. Christopher Howe, *Wage Patterns and Wage Policy in Modern China*, pp. 146–7.
15. For further details see Christopher Howe's analysis, ibid., p. 96.
16. Chen Po-wen, 'Rising Prices and Wages in Mainland China'. In November 1979 the government removed price controls on more than 10 000 farm and manufactured products. The prices of meat, fish, eggs, milk vegetables and other non-stable foods (sold in the free market) increased by 33 per cent in a

matter of months. To offset the higher cost of food, the government allocated a monthly allowance of 5 yuan to supplement urban industrial wages (*Review*, The Economist Intelligence Unit, London (Spring 1980).
17. Chen Po-wen, ibid., p. 40.
18. Ibid., p. 40. Chen does not, however, identify the basis upon which this calculation was made.
19. Ibid., p. 40.
20. Jing Qi, 'New Bonus System Lifts Limits', *Beijing Review*, XXVII:26 (1984), p. 4.
21. Ibid., p. 4.
22. Zhao Ziyang, 'Report on the Work of the Government', Second Session of the Sixth National People's Congress (NPC), 15 May 1984, *Beijing Review*, XXVII:24 (1984), p. iv.
23. Jonathan Sharp, 'Surplus Workers and Shirkers but No Sackings', *South China Morning Post*, 2 February 1982.
24. Quoted in *South China Morning Post*, 3 December 1981 (my italics).

6 'Market Socialism' or 'Market Capitalism'?

1. Premier Zhao Ziyang's 'Report on the Work of the Government', Second Session of the Sixth National People's Congress (NPC), 15 May 1984, *Beijing Review*, XXVII:24 (1984), p. iv.
2. Mao Zedong, *Selected Works*, vol. V, p. 290.
3. 'Provisional Regulations Concerning the Development and Protection of Socialist Competition' adopted by the Executive Meeting of the State Council, 27 October 1980, in *Almanac of China's Economy, 1981* (Hong Kong: Modern Cultural Company, 1982) p. 220.
4. Ibid., p. 221.
5. Ibid., p. 221.
6. P. M. Christensen, 'Plan, Market or Cultural Revolution in China', *Economic and Political Weekly* (Bombay), XVIII (7 May 1983), p. 649.
7. Ibid., p. 649.
8. Ma Hong, 'On China's New Strategy for Economic Development' in *Almanac of China's Economy, 1981*, p. 314.
9. Mao Zedong, *Selected Works*, vol. V, p. 287.
10. 'Provisional Regulations Concerning the Development and Protection of Socialist Competition', p. 221 (see note 3).
11. For further details see our analysis in chapters 7 and 8.
12. Under 'socialist competition' this process is said to lead to 'socialist combination' through consolidation, mergers, and so on, of 'backward enterprises, that is, as part of the process of socialisation of production which 'lays the material foundation for the consolidation and strengthening of the socialist system'. See Ma Hong, 'On China's New Strategy for Economic Development', p. 315.
13. Oskar Lange and Fred M. Taylor, *On the Economic Theory of Socialism* (Minneapolis: University of Minnesota Press, 1938) reprinted in Wayne A. Leeman, *Capitalism, Market Socialism and Central Planning* (Boston: Houghton Mifflin, 1963) p. 23.
14. Ibid., p. 23.
15. K. Marx, *Capital*, Book III (Moscow: Progress Publishers, 1959) chapter 4.

16. Liao Jili, 'Restructuring China's Economic System', in *Almanac of China's Economy, 1981*, pp. 335–6 (my italics).
17. Ibid., p. 336.
18. See Zhao Ziyang 'Report on the Sixth Five Year Plan', Fifth Session of the Fifth National People's Congress, 30 November 1982, in *Fifth Session of the Fifth National People's Congress(main documents)* (Beijing: Foreign Languages Press, 1983) pp. 113–5.
19. 'Mr. Cardin Goes to China', *China Daily*, 10 October 1981.
20. *Economic Reporter* (Hong Kong) (several issues), *The China Business Review* (several issues), see also State Statistical Bureau, *Statistical Yearbook of China 1981* (English edition) (Hong Kong: Economic Information and Agency, 1982) pp. 5–21.
21. Ibid.
22. Ibid.
23. Ibid.
24. Ibid.
25. K. Marx, *Capital*, Book II (Moscow: Progress Publishers, 1954), p. 407.
26. See P. Salama, 'Vers un nouveau modèle d' accumulation', *Critiques de l'économie politique*, nos 16–17 (1974).
27. For further details, see Michel Chossudovsky 'Underdevelopment and the Political Economy of Malnutrition and Ill Health', *International Journal of Health Services*, XIII:1 (1983) pp. 69–73.

7 The Open Door to Foreign Capital

1. On the reorientation of China's transportation network, see the article by C. K. Leung and Claude Comtois, 'Transport Reorientation Towards the Eighties', in C. K. Leung and S. S. K. Chin (ed), *China in Readjustment* (Hong Kong: Centre of Asian Studies, University of Hong Kong, 1983) pp. 216–33.
2. See Immanuel Hsu, *The Rise of Modern China* (Hong Kong: Oxford University Press, revised edition, 1975) pp. 225–8.
3. Hu Sheng, *Imperialism and Chinese Politics* (Beijing: Foreign Languages Press, 1981) p. 10.
4. Hu Sheng, ibid., p. 10; Immanuel Hsu, *The Rise of Modern China*, p. 244.
5. Immanuel Hsu, *The Rise of Modern China*, p. 429.
6. Quoted in Hu Sheng, *Imperialism and Chinese Politics*, p. 53.
7. Immanuel Hsu, *The Rise of Modern China*, p. 534.
8. A. Feuerwerker, *The Foreign Establishment in China in the Early 20th Century*, Michigan Papers in Chinese Studies (Ann Arbor: University of Michigan Press, 1976) p. 11.
9. Ibid., p. 11.
10. For further details on American Interests in China see C. F. Remer, *Foreign Investments in China* (New York: Macmillan, 1933) chapter 5.
11. Ibid., p. 53.
12. Feuerwerker, *The Foreign Establishment in China in the Early 20th Century*, pp. 2–3.
13. Ibid., p. 3.
14. Hu Sheng, *Imperialism and Chinese Politics*, p. 63.
15. For an analysis of contemporary Japanese imperialism in South-East Asia see

the excellent study by Jon Halliday and G. McCormack, *Japanese Imperialism Today* (Harmondsworth: Penguin, 1973).
16. 'Premier Zhao on Sino-US Relations and World Situation', *Beijing Review*, XXVII:4 (1984), pp. 18–19.
17. 'The Law of the People's Republic of China on Chinese-Foreign Joint Ventures', in *China's Foreign Economic Legislation* vol. 1 (Beijing: Foreign Languages Press, 1982) pp. 1–7.
18. 'Provisions of the People's Republic of China for Labour Management in Chinese-Foreign Joint Ventures', in *China's Foreign Economic Legislation*, vol. 1, p. 20.
19. The Central Government retained authority in certain key areas of the economy as well as in large-scale capital construction projects.
20. 'Chairman of the Board of Directors of CITIC Interviewed', *Beijing Review*, XXIII:17 (1980), p. 24 (my italics).
21. 'An American Bank Pioneer in China', *Economic Reporter* (Hong Kong), (May 1982), p. 16.
22. Ibid., p. 16.
23. 'Rockefeller Meets Rong', *Far Eastern Economic Review*, CIX:19 (11 July 1980), p. 48.
24. Ibid., p. 48.
25. For further details on the Bank of China group in Hong Kong see Lau Pui-king, 'The Recent Development of Non Trade Relations between China and Hong Kong', Contemporary China Studies Seminar, Centre of Asian Studies, University of Hong Kong, 26–28 February 1981.
26. *Wide Angle* (Hong Kong) June 1980, quoted in *China News Analysis*, no. 1184 (4 July 1980), p. 6.
27. *China Daily*, 25 November 1981.
28. Interview with Guo Di-huo, *Far-Eastern Economic Review*, CIV:22 (1 June 1979), p. 26.
29. *China Daily*, 27 September 1983.
30. Ibid.
31. *Constitution of the People's Republic of China*, adopted on 4 December 1982 by the National People's Congress at its Fifth Session (Beijing: Foreign Languages Press, 1983).
32. Ibid.
33. *Wen Hui Bao*, August 1979.
34. Michael Anderson, 'China's Greap Leap Towards Madison Avenue', *Journal of Communication*, XXXII (Spring 1982), p. 10.
35. Ding Yunpeng, 'Put Advertising in its Proper Perspective', *Wen Hui Bao*, 14 January 1979, quoted in Michael Anderson, 'China's Great Leap Towards Madison Avenue, p. 1.
36. Michael Anderson, p. 11.
37. Ibid., p. 16.
38. 'China Plans to Closely Supervise Domestic and Foreign Advertising', *Asian Wall Street Journal*, 19 February 1982.
39. Ibid.
40. Ibid.
41. Quoted in *South China Morning Post*, 30 December 1981 (my italics).
42. Xu Dixin, 'Salient Feature: State Capitalism', *Beijing Review*, XXVII:4 (1984), p. 31.
43. Ibid., p. 29.
44. Ibid.

8 Transnational Capital in Socialist China

1. The text of the law is published in *China's Foreign Economic Legislation*, vol. I (Beijing: Foreign Languages Press, 1982). See also A. Rawley, 'Cracking the Cryptic Code', *Far Eastern Economic Review*, CV:29 (20 July 1979), pp. 49–50.
2. Anthony Rawley, 'Cracking the Cryptic Code', ibid., p. 52.
3. Excerpts of Yu Qiuli's press conference in Tokyo were published in *Beijing Review*, XXIII:16 (1980), p. 4.
4. *China's Foreign Economic Legislation*, vol. I, pp. 20–1 (my italics).
5. Ibid., pp. 20–1.
6. Liu Zhicheng and Wu Qichang, 'How China Employs Foreign Investment', *China Reconstructs*, XXXII:12 (1983), p. 5.
7. See the various provisions concerning payment of income tax of Chinese-Foreign joint ventures and foreign enterprises, in *China's Foreign Economic Legislation*, vol. I, pp. 36–70.
8. Interview conducted by author at Changzheng Municipal Garment Factory, Shenyang, Liaoning Province in September 1983.
9. Ibid.
10. Interview conducted by the author with the factory director of White Crane Garment Factory and the Hong Kong based sales' representative of the American Export Corporation of California (Amerex) in July 1982.
11. Interview conducted by the author with the factory director of Guangzhou Shipyard Container Factory, Guangdong Province, in September 1983.
12. Ibid.
13. Ibid.
14. See Wen Tianshen, 'Auto Industry – Growth and Problems', *China Reconstructs*, XXXIII:2 (1984), pp. 4–7.
15. Ibid., p. 6.
16. Interview with the director of No. 2 Automobile Factory in Beijing in September 1983.
17. Interview with the chairman of the board of directors of Parker-Hubei Seals Ltd. in September 1983. The management structure of Parker-Hubei is discussed in Chapter 4.
18. Ibid.
19. Ibid.
20. Ibid.
21. Ibid. (my italics).
22. Frank Ching, 'China, US Firms Sign Partnership Pacts', *Asian Wall Street Journal*, 15 September 1981.
23. Ibid.
24. *Regulations of PRC on Special Economic Zones* (Hong Kong: Wen Wei Po, 1981) chapter I, Article 1.
25. 'Zhao Ziyang on SEZ Management', *Ta Kung Pao*, weekly supplement, no. 789 (20–26 August 1981), p. 1.
26. *China Daily*, 12 September 1981, p. 1.
27. 'Regulations of PRC on Special Economic Zones', chapter IV, Articles 19, 20.
28. 'Zhao Ziyang on SEZ Management', *Ta Kung Pao*, weekly supplement, no. 789, p. 1.
29. Melinda Liu, 'China Puts Hong Kong Investors at Ease', *Far Eastern Economic Review*, CIV:16 (20 April 1979).
30. 'Extensive Foreign Co-operation Vital', *China Daily*, 12 June 1984, p. 2.

31. *China Daily*, 7 June 1984, p. 1.
32. *China Daily*, 15 June 1984, p. 1.
33. *Beijing Review*, XXVII:20 (1984), p. 10.
34. John B. Leach, 'Offshore: The Petroleum Industry in the People's Republic of China, 1969–1978', *Chinese Economic Studies* (Fall–Winter 1979–80) p. 116.
35. Ibid., p. 119.
36. Ibid., p. 120.
37. Quoted in Kuo Man-yen, 'Expose the Gang of Four in Attacking Foreign Trade Policy', *Hongqi* (Red Flag), no. 4 (April 1977), pp. 57–61, English version published in *Chinese Economic Studies* (Fall 1977) p. 13.
38. Parris H. Chang, 'Chinese Politics, Deng's Turbulent Quest' *Problems of Communism* (January–February 1981), pp. 4–6.
39. Ibid., p. 16.
40. Leach, 'Offshore', p. 135.
41. Ibid., p. 135.
42. Ibid., p. 141.
43. 'What Kind of Contract Will China Accept', *The China Business Review* (January–February 1980), p. 24.
44. Dori Jones, 'The Dawning of Coal's "Second Golden Age"', *The China Business Review* (May–June 1980), p. 42.
45. Dori Jones, 'China's Offshore Oil', *The China Business Review* (July–August 1980), p. 52.
46. Ibid., p. 52.
47. The English text of these regulations was published in the *Economic Reporter* (Hong Kong) (March 1982), pp. 10–13.
48. Ibid., Article 7.
49. Ibid., Article 8.
50. Interview conducted by the author with officials of Nan Hai (East) Oil Corporation, Guangzhou, September 1983.
51. Ibid.
52. See Jing Wei, 'Oil Exploration South China Sea, Co-operation with Foreign Countries', *Beijing Review*, XXVII:6 (1984).
53. Ibid., pp. 26–7.
54. Ibid., p. 27.

9 China and World Capitalism

1. Karl Marx, *Capital*, Book I (New York: Random House, The Modern Library, 1907) p. 704.
2. Ibid., p. 704.
3. Ibid., p. 701.
4. For further analysis on structural recession see M. Chossudovsky, 'The Politics of World Capital Accumulation', *Canadian Journal of Development Studies*, II:1 (1981), p. 9–40.
5. Ibid.
6. According to data published in the *Bulletin of Labour Statistics* (Quarterly), International Labour Office, Geneva. See also F. Fröbel, J. Heinrichs and O. Kreye, *Die neue internationale Arbeitsteilung* (Reinbeck bei Hamburg: Rowohlt, 1977) pp. 633–4, and Michael Sharpston, 'International Subcontracting', *Oxford Economic Papers* (March 1975), p. 105.

7. For details see M. Chossudovsky, 'The Politics of World Capital Accumulation'.
8. Ibid.
9. *China Daily*, 4 November 1981.
10. Richard Breeze, 'Peking's People Exports', *Far Eastern Economic Review*, CIV (30 November 1979), p. 69.
11. Peter Humphrey, 'China's Massive Labour Earnings', *South China Morning Post*, 16 February 1982.
12. Peter Humphrey, 'China Has Advisors on PWD Jobs', *South China Morning Post*, 15 January 1982.
13. Ibid.
14. Peter Humphrey, 'Social Firm to Employ Chinese', *South China Morning Post*, 2 February 1982.
15. V. I. Lenin, 'The Importance of Gold Now and After the Complete Victory of Socialism', *Pravda*, 6–7 November, 1921; *Selected Works* (Moscow: Progress Publishers, 1971) pp. 656–8.
16. V. I. Lenin, 'Left Wing Childishness and the Petty Bourgeois Mentality', in *On State Capitalism during the Transition to Socialism* (Moscow: Progress Publishers, 1984) pp. 48–52.
17. Quoted in Kuo Man-yen, 'Expose the Gang of Four in Attacking Foreign Trade Policy', *Hongqi* (Red Flag), no. 4, (April 1977), English version published in *Chinese Economic Studies* (Fall 1977) p. 13.
18. Ibid.
19. Ibid.

10 Sino-US Strategic Relations

1. Mao Zedong, 'US Imperialism is a Paper Tiger', *Selected Works*, vol. V, p. 310.
2. Zhao Ziyang, quoted in *The New York Times*, January 1984.
3. Mao Zedong, *Selected Works*, vol. V, p. 310.
4. *Beijing Review*, XXVII:2 (1984), pp. 20–21.
5. Ibid. (my italics).
6. Interview with Deng, *Time* (5 February 1979), pp. 14–15.
7. The Economist Intelligence Unit, *Review* (Fall 1980), p. 6.
8. K. Chern, 'The Impact of the Taiwan Issue on Sino-American Relations, 1980–82', in C. K. Leung and S. S. K. Chin (eds), *China in Readjustment* (Hong Kong: Centre of Asian Studies, University of Hong Kong, 1983) p. 380.
9. Quoted in *The China Business Review* (March–April 1980).
10. K. Chern, 'The Impact of the Taiwan Issue on Sino-American Relations', p. 380.
11. 'Neutron Bombs and Soviet Slander', *Beijing Review*, XXIV:35 (1981), p. 10.
12. 'A Look At US-USSR Nuclear Negotiation', *Beijing Review*, XXIV:45 (1981), p. 10. See also the speech of China's representative Mr Liang Yufan to the UN General Assembly meeting of 22 October 1981 in the same issue of *Beijing Review*.
13. Ibid., p. 11.
14. Ibid., p. 11.
15. Press conference held in Beijing on 23 May 1984, prior to Zhao's official visit

to France, Italy, Denmark, Norway and Sweden, *Beijing Review*, XXVII:3 (1984).
16. *China Daily*, 17 January 1984.
17. Richard Ward, 'China: US Arms and Strategic Calculations', *Africa-Asia* (no. 15, March 1985), p. 10.
18. Ibid., p. 10.
19. Ibid. (my italics).
20. *Selected Works*, vol. V, p. 152.
21. *China Daily*, 5 June 1984, p. 1 (my italics).
22. Statement by Yang Dezhi, Chief of PLA General Staff, quoted in *China Daily*, 2 June 1984, p. 1.
23. Statement of China's Defence Minister, Zhang Aiping, quoted in *China Daily*, 5 June 1984.
24. Richard Ward, 'China: US Arms and Strategic Calculations', p. 10.
25. G. Aronson, 'Quand le Tiers-monde devient partie prenante dans la fabrication et le commerce des armements', *Le Monde Diplomatique* (no. 372, March 1985), p. 11.
26. Richard Ward, 'China: US Arms and Strategic Calculations', p. 10.
27. President Ronald Reagan's speech delivered in the Great Hall of the People, 27 April 1984 in *Beijing Review*, XXVII:19 (1984), p. 19.
28. Premier Zhao Ziyang quoted in *Ta Kung Pao*, no. 788, 13–19 August 1981.
29. For further details see M. Chossudovsky, 'Asean Communist Parties and China', *Economic and Political Weekly*, XVI:39 (1981), p. 1571.

11 Towards the Restoration of Capitalism?

1. J. V. Stalin, *Leninism* (London: Lawrence & Wishart, 1940), p. 561, quoted in Bettelheim, *Class Struggles in the USSR, First Period: 1917–1923*, p. 21.
2. Mao Zedong, 'On the Correct Handling of Contradictions among the People', *Selected Works*, vol. V, pp. 384–419.
3. *Resolution on CPC History*, p. 30.
4. Ibid., pp. 32–3 (my italics).
5. Charles Bettelheim, *Class Struggles in the USSR, First Period: 1917–1923*, pp. 21–2.
6. Ernest Mandel, 'The Laws of Motion of the Soviet Economy', *Review of Radical Political Economics*, XIII:1 (1981), p. 36. See also Ernest Mandel, 'The Nature of the Soviet State', *New Left Review*, no. 108 (March–April 1978), and Sweezy's critique of Mandel in Paul M. Sweezy, 'Is There a Ruling Class in the USSR?' *Monthly Review*, XXX:5 (1978), pp. 1–18.
7. Ernest Mandel, 'The Laws of Motion of the Soviet Economy', pp. 35–6.
8. Ibid., p. 35.
9. Ibid., p. 35.
10. Ibid., p. 35. Mandel's characterisation of *individual conditions* (with reference to the Soviet Union) focusing on the establishment of so-called 'general laws for the existing societies in transition between capitalism and socialism' is, in our opinion, based on a narrow typification of Marxian economic categories, that is, the so-called 'laws of motion of the Soviet economy' are arrived at from the observation of economic phenomena in separation from the social class relations which underly these phenomena.
11. Paul M. Sweezy, 'Revolution from Above: the USSR in the 1920s', *Monthly Review*, XXIX:5 (1977), p. 11.

12. Charles Bettelheim and Bernard Chavance, 'Stalinism as the Ideology of State Capitalism', *Review of Radical Political Economics*, XIII:1 (1980), p. 40.
13. See L. Trotsky's analysis of this question in the 1919 preface to the reissue of *The Permanent Revolution* (New York: Merit Publishers, third edition, 1969).
14. V. I. Lenin, 'Two Tactics of Social Democracy in the Democratic Revolution', (Beijing: Foreign Languages Press, 1970) p. 53.
15. Ibid., p. 56.
16. Ibid., p. 58 (my italics).
17. 'Peasants Flock to Join Town Enterprises', *China Daily*, 10 August 1984.
18. Ibid.
19. In 1984, municipalities could sign contracts with foreign capital (without higher level provincial approval) for amounts not exceeding one million yuan (500 000 dollars). Provincial government bodies required central government approval for contracts in excess of one million dollars. In practice, municipal and provincial authorities are often in a position to bypass these ceilings.
20. Samir Amin, *L'avenir du Maoïme* (Paris: Les Éditions de Minuit, 1981) p. 148.
21. V. I. Lenin, 'Reply to the Debate on the Report on Concessions' in *On State Capitalism during the Transition to Socialism* (Moscow: Progress Publishers, 1984), p. 123.
22. The 1982 Constitution of the People's Republic of China, Article 6, p. 4.
23. V. I. Lenin, 'From Report on the Political Work of the Central Committee of the RCP(B)', March 8–16, 1921, in *On State Capitalism during the Transition to Socialism*, p. 108.
24. Tse Ka-kui, 'Challenging the Bourgeois Division of Labour: Perspective on the Chinese Experience of Industrial Transformation since the Great Leap Forward', *Social Praxis*, V:3 (1978), p. 248.
25. Ibid., p. 257.
26. Ibid., p. 257.
27. Ibid., p. 257.
28. Ibid., p. 258.
29. See Chavance's analysis in 'On the Relations of Production in the USSR', *Monthly Review*, XIX:1 (1977), p. 2.
30. In Jerome Chen, *Mao's Papers* (London: Oxford University Press, 1970), p. 139.

Bibliography

Adie, W.A.C., 'China's Second Liberation', in Educational Foundation for Nuclear Science (eds), *China After The Cultural Revolution* (Clinton, Mass.: Vintage Books Year).
Amin, S., *L'avenir du Maoïsme* (Paris: Les Éditions de Minuit, 1981).
Amnesty International, *China, Violations of Human Rights* (London: Amnesty International Publications, 1984).
Amnesty International, *China Briefing* (London: Amnesty International Publications, 1984).
Anderson, M., 'China's Great Leap Towards Madison Avenue', *Journal of Communication* XXXII (Spring 1982).
Andors, Stephen, 'The Political and Organisational Implications of China's New Economic Policies', *Bulletin of Concerned Asian Scholars*, no. 1 (1980) pp. 44–57.
Benny, K. and D. Jones, 'China's Activities in IMF and World Bank', *The China Business Review* (March-April, 1981) pp. 47–9.
Benny, K. and D. Jones, 'Communications Satellite Program', *The China Business Review* (March-April, 1981) pp. 30–35.
Benny, K. and D. Jones', 'Doing Business With China's Defence Industries', *The China Business Review* (May-June, 1981) pp. 23–8.
Bettelheim, C., *Révolution culturelle et organisation industrielle en Chine* (Paris: François Maspero, 1975).
Bettelheim, C., *Class Struggles in the USSR, First Period, 1917–1923* (New York: Monthly Review Press, 1976).
Bettelheim, C., *Class Struggles in the USSR, Second Period, 1923–1930* (New York: Monthly Review Press, 1978).
Bettelheim, C., *Questions sur la Chine après la mort de Mao* (Paris: Maspero, 1978).
Bettelheim, C., 'Letter of Resignation to the Franco-Chinese Friendship Association', *Monthly Review*, XXX:3 (1978), pp. 9–13.
Bettelheim, C., 'The Great Leap Backward', *Monthly Review*, XXX:3 (1978).
Bettelheim, C. and B. Chavance, 'Stalinism as the Ideology of State Capitalism', *Review of Radical Political Economics*, XIII:1 (1980).
Blecher, M., 'Income Distribution in Small Rural Chinese Communities', *The China Quarterly*, no. 68 (December 1976), pp. 797–816.
Breeze, R., 'Peking's People Exports', *Far Eastern Economic Review*, CIV, 30 November 1979.
Breeze, R., 'The Price of Modernisation', *Far Eastern Economic Review*, 6 June 1980, pp. 51–2.
Burchett, W. and R. Alley, *China, The Quality of Life* (Harmondsworth: Penguin, 1976).

Burns, J. P., 'The Election of Production Team Cadres in Rural China: 1958–74', *The China Quarterly*, no. 74 (June 1978), pp. 273–96.
Burton, N., 'In Defence of the New Regime', *Monthly Review*, XXX:3 (1978), pp. 15–36.
Cai, Beihua, 'Shanghai's Foreign Trade and its Prospects', *Chinese Economic Studies* (Fall 1980), pp. 79–93.
Central Committee of the Chinese Communist Party, *Socialist Upsurge in China's Countryside* (Beijing: Foreign Languages Press, 1978).
Central Committee of the Chinese Communist Party, *Resolution on CPC History* 1949–1981 (Beijing: Foreign Languages Press, 1981).
Chang, C. Y., 'Modernisation and Overseas Chinese', in S. S. K. Chin (ed.), *Modernisation in China* (Hong Kong: Centre of Asian Studies, University of Hong Kong, 1979).
Chang, C. Y., 'Overseas Chinese in China's Policy', *The China Quarterly*, no. 82 (June 1980), pp. 281–323.
Chang, P. H., 'Chinese Politics, Deng's Turbulent Quest', *Problems of Communism* (January-February 1981), pp. 1–21.
Chang, S. D., 'Urbanisation and Economic Readjustment in China', in C. K. Leung and S. S. K. Chin (eds); *China in Readjustment* (Hong Kong: Centre of Asian Studies, University of Hong Kong, 1983).
Chavance, B., 'On the Relations of Production in the USSR', *Monthly Review*, XIX:1 (1977), pp. 1–12.
Chen, Baoling, 'Party Committees Study Elimination of Leftist Influences', *Hebei Ribao* (Shijiazhuang), 20 April 1981.
Chen, E. K. Y., 'Post-Mao Economic Readjustment and Reform in China: An Ideological Interpretation within a Stalinist Framework', in C. K. Leung and S. S. K. Chin (eds), *China in Readjustment* (Hong Kong: Centre of Asian Studies, University of Hong Kong, 1983).
Chen, Hsi-huang, 'Agricultural Development and Its Problems in Mainland China', *Issues and Studies* (August 1980), pp. 63–77.
Ch'en, I-ch'eng, 'Controversy over Forms of Ownership in Communist China', *Issues and Studies* (October 1980), pp. 49–59.
Ch'en, I-ch'eng, 'The Latest Economic Crisis in Mainland China', *Issues and Studies* (February 1981), pp. 11–12.
Chen, J., *Mao's Papers* (London: Oxford University Press, 1970).
Chen, Po-wen, 'Rising Prices and Wages in Mainland China', *Issues and Studies* (February 1980).
Ch'en, Ting-chung, 'From "Private Plot to Private Labour Force"', *Issues and Studies* (May 1981), pp. 5–9.
Ch'en, Ting-chung, 'New Switch in Peiping's Agricultural Policy', *Issues and Studies* (June 1981), pp. 24–40.
Chen, Yu-shen, 'The 30-Point Decision on Industry: An Analysis', *Issues and Studies* (January 1979).
Chern, K., 'The Impact of the Taiwan Issue on Sino-American Relations, 1980–82', in C. K. Leung and S. S. K. Chin (eds), *China in Readjustment* (Hong Kong: Centre of Asian Studies, University of Hong Kong, 1983).
Chi, Fu, 'China's Newborn SEZs and their Strategic Significance', *Economic Reporter* (August 1981), pp. 11–22.
Chin, S. S. K., (ed.), *Modernisation in China* (Hong Kong: Centre of Asian Studies, University of Hong Kong, 1973).
Chin, S. S. K., 'Mao Tse-tung Thought and Modernisation', in S. S. K. Chin (ed.), *Modernisation in China* (Hong Kong: Centre of Asian Studies, University of Hong Kong, 1973).

Chin, S. S. K., *The Thought of Mao Tse-Tung* (Hong Kong: Centre of Asian Studies, University of Hong Kong, 1979).
Ching, F., 'The Current Political Scene in China', *The China Quarterly*, no. 80 (December 1979), pp. 691–715.
Ching, F., 'China, US Firms Sign Partnership Pacts', *Asian Wall Street Journal* (Hong Kong), 15 September 1981.
Chinn, D. L., 'Basic Commodity Distribution in the People's Republic of China', *The China Quarterly*, no. 84 (December 1980), pp. 744–54.
Chossudovsky, M., 'The Politics of World Capital Accumulation', *Canadian Journal of Development Studies*, II:1 (1981), pp. 9–40.
Chossudovsky, M., 'Capitalist Development and Agriculture in Latin America', in L. Alschuler (ed.), *Dependent Agricultural Development and Agrarian Reform in Latin America* (Ottawa: University of Ottawa Press, 1981).
Chossudovsky, M., 'Asean Communist Parties and China', *Economic and Political Weekly* (Bombay), XVI:39 (1981), pp. 1571–2.
Chossudovsky, M., 'China's Manpower Exports', *Economic and Political Weekly* (Bombay), XVII:3 (1982), pp. 63–4.
Chossudovsky, M., 'China: Changing Consumption Patterns', *Economic and Political Weekly* (Bombay), XVII:8 (1982), pp. 277–9.
Chossudovsky, M., 'China's Free Trade Zones' *Co-existence*, no. 1 (1983), pp. 41–55.
Chossudovsky, M., 'China and the International Division of Labour', *Studies in Political Economy*, no. 1 (1983), pp. 73–97.
Chossudovsky, M., 'China's Open Door Policy' in C. K. Leung and S. S. K. Chin (eds), *China in Readjustment* (Hong Kong: Centre of Asian Studies, University of Hong Kong, 1983).
Chossudovsky, M., 'Underdevelopment and the Political Economy of Malnutrition and Ill Health', *International Journal of Health Services*, XIII:1 (1983).
Christensen, P. M., 'Plan, Market or Cultural Revolution in China', *Economic and Political Weekly* (Bombay), XVIII:19 (1983).
Clarke, Christopher M., 'Leadership Divisions', *The China Business Review* (March-April 1981), pp. 43–6.
Congress of the United States, *Chinese Economy Post-Mao*, vol. 1, A compendium of papers submitted to the Joint Economic Committee (Washington: US Government Printing Office, 1978).
Cummings, Bruce, 'The Political Economy of Chinese Foreign Policy', *Modern China*, V:4 (1979), pp. 411–61.
Deleyne, Jan, *The Chinese Economy* (London: André Deutsch Ltd, 1973).
Deng, Xiaoping, *Selected Works* (Beijing: Foreign Languages Press, 1984).
Ding, Yunpeng, 'Put Advertising in its Proper Perspective', *Wen Hui Bao*, 14 January 1979.
Dobb, Maurice, 'The October Revolution and Half a Century', *Monthly Review*, XXIX:6 (1967), pp. 38–44.
Dong, Furen, 'China's Economy Undergoes a Sharp Change', *Chinese Economic Studies* (Summer 1980), pp. 19–37.
Du, Jing, 'On the Question of Land Confiscation and Distribution in the Agrarian Reform', *Social Sciences in China*, III:3 (1982).
Eckstein, Alexander, *China's Economic Development* (Michigan: University of Michigan Press, 1975).
Economic Information and Agency (eds), *China's Foreign Trade and its Management* (Hong Kong: Chung Hwa Book Co., 1978).
Engels, F., 'On Russia', in K. Marx, *Selected Works*, vol. II (London: Lawrence & Wishart, 1942).

Engels, F., *Socialism Utopian and Scientific* (New York: International Publishers, 1972).
Esherick, Joseph W., 'On the "Restoration of Capitalism"', *Modern China*, V:1 (1979), pp. 41–78.
Esmein, Jean, *La révolution culturelle chinoise* (Paris: Editions du Seuil, 1970).
Feuerwerker, A., *The Foreign Establishment in China in the Early 20th Century*, Michigan Papers in Chinese Studies (Ann Arbor, University of Michigan Press, 1976).
Fröbel, F., J. Heinrichs and O. Kreye, *Die neue internationale Arbeitsteilung* (Reinbeck bei Hamburg: Rowohlt, 1977).
Gao, Liang, 'Annoted Survey of China's Major Economics Periodicals', in *Almanac of China's Economy, 1981*' (Hong Kong: Modern Cultural Company, 1982).
Green, Stephanie, 'The Off-shore Oil Race', *The China Business Review* (July-August 1981).
Gu, Nianling, 'China's Current Effort to Import Technology and its Prospects', *Chinese Economic Studies* (Summer 1980), pp. 54–78.
Halliday, J., 'The Struggle for East Asia', *New Left Review*, no. 124 (November-December 1980), pp. 3–24.
Halliday, J. and G. McCormick, *Japanese Imperialism Today* (Harmondsworth: Penguin, 1973).
He, Jianzhang, 'Problems Involving the System of Planned Management of the Economy', *Jingji yanjiu* Economic Research), no. 5 (1979), pp. 35–45. In English in *Chinese Economic Studies* (Summer 1980), pp. 32–62.
He, Jianzhang, 'More on Planned Economy and Market Regulations', *Social Sciences in China*, III:4 (1982), pp. 46–59.
Hinton, W. H., 'More on China's New Family Contract System', *Monthly Review*, XXXV:11 (1984).
Ho, Kwon Ping, 'Birth of the Second Generation', *Far Eastern Economic Review*, 18 May 1979, pp. 76–80.
Hou, Chi-ming, *Foreign Investment and Economic Development in China, 1840–1937* (Cambridge, Mass.: Harvard University Press, 1965).
Howard, R., *Mao Tse-tung and the Chinese People* (New York: Monthly Review Press, 1977).
Howe, C., *Wage Patterns and Wage Policy in Modern China, 1919–1972* (Cambridge: Cambridge University Press, 1973).
Hsia, Tao-tai and Kathryn A. Haun, 'China's Joint Venture Law', *China Law Reporter*, I:2 (1980), pp. 61–83.
Hsu, Immanuel, *The Rise of Modern China* (Hong Kong: Oxford University Press, revised edition, 1975).
Hsueh, T. T. and T. O. Woo, 'China's Foreign Trade Since Deng Xiaoping's Rise to Power', in C. K. Leung and S. S. K. Chin (eds), *China in Readjustment* (Hong Kong: Centre of Asian Studies, University of Hong Kong, 1983).
Hu, Sheng, *Imperialism and Chinese Politics* (Beijing: Foreign Languages Press, 1981).
Hung, Yu Chiao, 'Chinese Communist Policy on Finance and Trade', *Issues and Studies* (March 79), pp. 30–43.
Ji, Chongwei, 'A Brief Account of China's Absorption of Foreign Funds', *Economic Reporter* (April 1981), pp. 8–12.
Ji, Chongwei, China's Policy on Joint Ventures and their Management', *Economic Reporter* (September 1981), pp. 3–8.
Jia, Shi, 'China's Foreign Trade Prospects', *China's Foreign Trade*, no. 4 (1981), pp. 2–3.

Jin, Qi, 'New Bonus System Lifts Limits', *Beijing Review* XXVII:26 (1984).
Jing, Wei, 'Oil Exploration South China Sea: Co-operation with Foreign Countries', *Beijing Review*, XXVII:6 (1984).
Jones, D., 'What Kind of Contract Will China Accept?', *The China Business Review* (January-February 1980).
Jones, D., 'The Dawning of Coal's "Second Golden Age"', *The China Business Review* (May-June 1980).
Jones, D., 'China's Offshore Oil', *The China Business Review* (July-August 1980).
Jones, D., 'The Baoshan Contracts', *The China Business Review* (July-August 1980), pp. 47–9.
Karol, K. S., *La deuxième révolution chinoise* (Paris: Editions Robert LaFont, 1973).
Kissinger, C. C., 'China and Angola', *Monthly Review*, XXVIII:1 (1976), pp. 1–24.
Kraar, Louis, 'The Wealth and Power of the Overseas Chinese', *Fortune* (March 1971).
Kuo, Man-yen, 'Expose the Gang of Four in Attacking Foreign Trade Policy', *Hongqi* (Red Flag), no. 4 (April 1977) pp. 57–61. English version in *Chinese Economic Studies* (Fall 1977) pp. 6–15.
Laibman, David, '"The State Capitalist" and "Bureaucratic – Exploitative" Interpretations of the Soviet Social Formation: A Critique', *Review of Radical Political Economics*, XX:4 (1978), pp. 24–34.
Lange, O. and F. M. Taylor, *On the Economic Theory of Socialism* (Minneapolis: University of Minnesota Press, 1938).
Lau, Pui-king, 'The Recent Development of Non Trade Relations between China and Hong Kong', Contemporary China Studies Seminar, Centre of Asian Studies, University of Hong Kong 26–28 February 1981.
Leach, J. B., 'Offshore: The Petroleum Industry in the People's Republic of China', *Chinese Economic Studies* (Fall-Winter 1979–80) pp. 105–51.
Lee, N., 'The Militia in People's War under Modern Conditions', in C. K. Leung and S. S. K. Chin (eds), *China in Readjustment* (Hong Kong: Centre of Asian Studies, University of Hong Kong, 1983).
Lee, Nan-shong, 'Modernisation and Managerial Power in China, 1956–1966', in S. S. K. Chin (ed.), *Modernisation in China* (Hong Kong: Centre of Asian Studies, University of Hong Kong, 1979).
Lee, Nan-shong, 'China's Managerial Modernisation, Three Basic Models, 1956–1978', *Chinese Law and Government* no. 1 (1980).
Lee, Nan-shong, 'Industrial Development and Mass-Line Leadership in China', in E. K. Y. Chen and S. S. K. Chin (eds), *Development and Change in China*, vol. IV (Hong Kong: Centre of Asian Studies, University of Hong Kong, 1981).
Leeman, W. A., *Capitalism, Market Socialism and Central Planning* (Boston: Houghton Mifflin, 1963).
Lenin, V. I., 'The Importance of Gold Now and After the Complete Victory of Socialism', *Pravda*, 6–7 November, 1921, *Selected Works* (Moscow: Progress Publishers, 1952).
Lenin, V. I., 'The Proletarian Revolution and the Renegade Kautsky', in *Selected Works*, vol. II (Moscow: Foreign Languages Publishing House, 1952).
Lenin, V. I., 'The State and the Revolution', in *Selected Works* (Moscow: Foreign Languages Publishing House, 1952).
Lenin, V. I., 'Two Tactics of Social Democracy in the Democratic Revolution', in *Selected Works* (Moscow: Foreign Languages Publishing House, 1952).
Lenin, V. I., *The Development of Capitalism in Russia* (Moscow: Progress Publishers, 1967).
Lenin, V. I., *On State Capitalism During the Transition to Socialism* (Moscow: Progress Publishers, 1984).

Leung, C. K. and C. Comtois, 'Transport Reorientation Towards the Eighties', in C. K. Leung and S. S. K. Chin (eds), *China in Readjustment* (Hong Kong: Centre of Asian Studies, University of Hong Kong, 1983).
Leung, C. K. and S. S. K. Chin, *China in Readjustment* (Hong Kong: Centre of Asian Studies, University of Hong Kong, 1983).
Li, Chien-nung, *The Political History of China, 1840–1929* (Stanford: Stanford University Press, 1956).
Li, Chuang, 'Ex Capitalists Aid Economy', *China Reconstructs*, XXX:9 (1981).
Li, Hsueh-feng, 'Strengthen the Party's Leadership over Enterprises and Implement the Mass Line', *Jen-min shouts'e* (People's Handbook) (1957), pp. 111–13, reprinted in *Chinese Law and Government*, no. 1 (1980).
Li, Xin, 'The 1911 Revolution, *China Reconstructs*, XXX:9 (1981).
Liao, Jili, 'Restructuring China's Economic System', in *Almanac of China's Economy, 1981* (Hong Kong: Modern Cultural Company, 1982).
Lin, A., 'Agrarian Crisis in Pre-Communist China', in S. S. K. Chin and C. K. Leung (eds), *China Development and Challenge*, vol. I (Hong Kong: Centre of Asian Studies, University of Hong Kong, 1979).
Lin, C. C., 'The Reinstatement of Economics in China Today', *The China Quarterly*, no. 85 (March 1981), pp. 1–48.
Lin, Zili, 'Socialism, Theory and Practice', *Beijing Review*, XXIV:34 (1981), pp. 14–17.
Lin, Zili, 'On the Distinctively Chinese Path of Socialist, Agricultural Development', *Social Sciences in China*, IV:3 (1983), pp. 111–46.
Lishi Yanjiu (Editorial Board for Contemporary Chinese History), 'Chinese Historical Studies of the Early Modern China's Bourgeoisie', *Social Sciences in China*, IV:1 (1983).
Liu, Guoguang and Zhao, Renwei, 'On the Relations Between Planning and the Market in the Socialist Economy', *Jingji yanjiu* (Economic Research), no. 5 (1979), pp. 46–55.
Liu, Kuaguang, 'on Reforming China's Management System', *Chinese Economic Studies* (Summer 1980), pp. 38–53.
Liu, M., 'Welcoming Back the Bourgeoisie', *Far Eastern Economic Review*, CIV:22 (1979), pp. 24–6.
Liu, Mingfu, 'On the Economic Forms of Socialist Economy', *Jingji yanjiu* (Economic Research), no. 4 (1979), pp. 52–7.
Liu, Shaoqi, *Three Essays on Party Building* (Beijing: Foreign Languages Press, 1980).
Liu, Shaoqi, *Selected Works*, vol. I (Beijing: Foreign Languages Press, 1984).
Liu, Zhicheng and Wu Qichang, 'How China Employs Foreign Investment', *China Reconstructs*, XXXII:12 (1983).
Lohi, C., 'Learning How Best to Run a Chinese Factory', *Modern Asia* (January-February 1981), pp. 46–48.
Luk, M. Y. L., 'New Perspectives or Party History', in C. K. Leung and S. S. K. Chin (eds), *China in Readjustment* (Hong Kong: Centre of Asian Studies, University of Hong Kong, 1983).
Luxemburg, R., *The Russian Revolution, Leninism or Marxism* (Ann Arbor: The University of Michigan Press, 1961).
Ma, Hong, 'On China's New Strategy for Economic Development', in *Almanac of China's Economy, 1981* (Hong Kong: Modern Cultural Company, 1982).
Ma, Hong, 'Marxism and China's Socialist Economic Construction', *Social Sciences in China* IV:3 (1983), pp. 95–110.
Mandel E., 'The Nature of the Soviet State', *New Left Review*, no. 108 (March-April 1978).

Mandel, E., 'The Laws of Motion of the Soviet Economy', *Review of Radical Political Economics*, XIII:1 (1981).
Mandel, E., 'The Class Nature of the Soviet Union', *Review of Radical Political Economics*, XIV:1 (1982), pp. 55–67.
Mao Zedong, *Selected Works*, in five volumes (Beijing: Foreign Languages Press, 1977).
Marx, K., *Capital*, in 3 vols (Moscow: Progress Publishers, 1959).
Monthly Review Editors, 'The Cultural Revolution in China', *Monthly Review*, XVIII:8 (1967), pp. 1–17.
Nakagane, K., 'Structural Changes in Agricultural Production in China: Three Northeastern Provinces', *The Developing Economies*, XX:4 (1982), pp. 414–36.
Nickum, J. E. and D. C. Shak, 'Living Standards and Economic Development in Shanghai and Taiwan', *The China Quarterly*, no. 77 (March 79), pp. 25–49.
Onoye, E., 'Readjustment and Reform in the Chinese Economy: A Comparison of the Post-Mao and Post-Great Leap Forward Periods', *The Developing Economies*, XX:4 (1982), pp. 359–3.
Paine, S., 'Spatial Aspects of Chinese Development', *Journal of Development Studies*, XVII:2 (1981), pp. 133–95.
Parish, W., 'Egalitarianism in Chinese Society', *Problems of Communism* (January-February 1981), pp. 37–53.
People's Republic of China, 'Provisional Regulations Concerning the Development and Protection of Socialist Competition', adopted by the Executive Meeting of the State Council, 27 October 1980, in *Almanac of China's Economy, 1981* (Hong Kong: Modern Cultural Company, 1982).
People's Republic of China, *Regulations of PRC on Special Economic Zones* (Hong Kong: Wen Wei Po, 1981).
People's Republic of China, *Regulations of PRC on Special Zones* (Hong Kong: Wen Wei Po, 1981).
People's Republic of China, *China's Foreign Economic Legislation*, vol. I (Beijing: Foreign Languages Press, 1982).
Pepper, S., 'Chinese Education after Mao: Two Steps Forward, Two Steps Back and Begin Again?', *The China Quarterly*, no. 81 (March 1980), pp. 1–65.
Perkins, D. W., *China's Modern Economy in Historical Perspective* (Stanford: Standford University Press, 1975).
Perkins, D. W. (ed.), *Rural Small Scale Industry in the People's Republic of China* (Berkeley: University of California and Los Angeles Press, 1981).
Pincus, F. L., 'Higher Education and Socialist Transformation in the People's Republic of China since 1970: A Critical Analysis', *Review of Radical Political Economics*, XI:1 (1979), pp. 24–37.
Pyle, T., 'Reforming Chinese Management', *The China Business Review* (May-June 1979), pp. 7–19.
Qiu Qihua, 'Research on the World Economy in China', *The China Quarterly*, no. 84 (December 1980), pp. 720–6.
Rakovski, M., *Towards An East European Marxism* (London: Alison & Busby, 1978).
Rawley, A., 'Cracking the Cryptic Code', *Far Eastern Economic Review*, CV:29 (1979).
Remer, C. F., *Foreign Investments in China* (New York: Macmillan, 1933).
Reynolds, B. L., 'Two Models of Agricultural Development: A Context for Current Chinese Policy', *The China Quarterly*, no. 76 (December 1978), pp. 842–72.
Robinson, J., *The Cultural Revolution in China* (Harmondsworth: Penguin, 1969).
Rousset, D., *The Legacy of the Bolshevik Revolution* (London: Alison & Busby, 1982).

Schuman, F. *et al.*, 'More on Soviet Society', *Monthly Review*, XXVII:10 (1976), pp. 1–24.
Shapiro, S., *Experiment in Sichuan* (Beijing: New World Press, 1981).
Sharpston, M., 'International Subcontracting', *Oxford Economic Papers* (March 1975).
Shum, K. K., 'Ideological Origins of the "Capitalist Roaders"', in C. K. Leung and S. S. K. Chin (eds), *China in Readjustment* (Hong Kong: Centre of Asia Studies, University of Hong Kong, 1983).
Silver, G. A. and G. Tarpinian, 'Class Analysis and the Transition to Socialism: A Rejoinder to Ernest Mandel', *Review of Radical Political Economics*, XIV:1 (1982), pp. 68–73.
Sit, V. Fung-shuen, 'Neighbourhood Workshops in the Socialist Transformation of Chinese Cities', in S. S. K. Chin (ed.), *Modernisation in China* (Hong Kong: Centre of Asian Studies, University of Hong Kong, 1973).
Smil, V., 'Energy in China: Achievements and Prospects', *The China Quarterly*, no. 65 (January 1976), pp. 54–82.
Snow, E., *Red China Today* (Harmondsworth: Penguin, 1971).
Stalin, J. V., *Leninism* (London: Lawrence & Wishart, 1940).
Stalin, J. V., *Economic Problems of Socialism in the USSR* (Beijing: Foreign Languages Press, 1972).
Stavenhagen, R., *Agrarian Reform in Structures and Underdevelopment in Africa and Latin America*, Conference on Strategies for Economic Development, Africa versus Latin America (Dakar: United Nations African Institute for Economic Development and Planning, September 1972).
Strong, A. L., '*The Rise of the Chinese People's Commune*' (Beijing: New World Press, 1954).
Su, Wenming (ed.), *Economic Readjustment and Reform*, China Today Series (Beijing: *Beijing Review*, 1982).
Subramanian, S., 'The Economic Distance between China and India, 1955–73', *The China Quarterly*, no. 70 (June 1977), pp. 371–82.
Sun, Xiacun, 'Seeking the Truth from Facts, the Party and China's National Capitalists', *China Reconstructs*, XXX:11 (1981).
Sun, Xiangjian, 'On the Question of the Profitability of China's Foreign Trade to the National Economy', *Social Sciences in China*, III:1 (1982), pp. 35–60.
Sweezy, P. M., 'Theory and Practice in the Mao Period', *Monthly Review* XXVIII:9 (1977), pp. 1–12.
Sweezy, P. M., 'Revolution from above: the USSR in the 1920s', *Monthly Review*, XXIX:5 (1977), pp. 1–19.
Sweezy, P. M., 'Is There a Ruling Class in the USSR?', *Monthly Review*, XXX:5 (1978), pp. 1–18.
Sweezy, P. M., and Bettelheim, *Lettres sur quelques problèmes actuels du socialisme* (Paris: Maspero, 1972).
Tabata, I. B., 'From October to the Cultural Revolution', *Monthly Review*, XIX:6 (1967), pp. 59–70.
Tao, Tai Hsia and K. A. Haun, 'China's Joint Venture Law, Part II', *China Law Reporter*, no. 2 (Fall 1980), pp. 61–83.
Tissier, P., *Les communes populaires chinoises* (Paris: éditions 10–18, 1976).
Tissier, P., *La Chine, transformations rurales et développement socialiste* (Paris: Maspero, 1976).
Tretiak, D., China's Vietnam War and its Consequence', *The China Quarterly*, no. 8 (December 1979), pp. 740–67.
Trotsky, L., *The Revolution Betrayed* (London: New York Publications, 1957).

Trotsky, L., *The Permanent Revolution*, 3rd edn (New York: Merit Publishers Pathfinder Press, 1969).
Tse, Ka-kui, 'Challenging the Bourgeois Division of Labour: Perspective on the Chinese Experience of Industrial Transformation since the Great Leap Forward', *Social Praxis*, V:3 (1978), pp. 235–75.
Tung, Chi-ming, *An Outline History of China* (Hong Kong: Joint Publishing Co., 1979).
Vienet, R., 'Human Rights, What Rating for China?', *Far Eastern Economic Review*, CV (11 May 1979).
Wang, Jingyu, 'The Birth of the Chinese Bourgeoisie', *Social Sciences in China*, III:1 (1982), pp. 220–40.
Weil, M., 'Technology Transfers', *The China Business Review* (March-April 1981), pp. 21–8.
Weil, M., 'Readjustment, Phase II', *The China Business Review* (July-August 1981), pp. 18–25.
Wen, Tianshen, 'Auto Industry – Growth and Problems', *China Reconstructs*, XXXIII:2 (1984).
Whiting A. S., Sino-American Détente', *The China Quarterly*, no. 82 (June 1980), pp. 334–41.
Womack, B., 'Politics and Epistemology in China since Mao', *The China Quarterly*, no. 80 (December 1979), pp. 768–92.
Wong, J., *Chinese Land Reform in Retrospect* (Hong Kong: Centre Asian Studies, University of Hong Kong, 1979).
Wong, K. Y., 'The Environment of Shenzhen Special Economic Zone and its Potentials', in C. K. Leung and S. S. K. Chin (eds), *China in Readjustment* (Hong Kong; Centre of Asian Studies, University of Hong Kong, 1983).
Wu, Yuanli and Chun hsi Wu, *Economic Development in Southeast Asia* (Standford: Hoover Institution, 1980).
Wu, Yuzhang, *Recollections of the 1911 Revolution*, 4th edn (Beijing: Foreign Languages Press, 1981).
Xu, Dixin, 'Prospects of China's Economy in the 1980s', *Chinese Economic Studies* (Summer 1980), pp. 6–18.
Xu, Dixin *et al.*, *China's Search for Economic Growth* (Beijing: New World Press, 1982).
Xu, Dixin *et al.*, 'Salient Feature: State Capitalism', *Beijing Review*, XXVII:4 (1984).
Xu, Li, 'Report on the 1982 Annual Meeting of the Association for the Study of Contemporary Chinese History', *Social Sciences in China*, IV:4 (1983), pp. 26–38.
Xue, Muqiao, *China's Socialist Economy* (Beijing: Foreign Languages Press, 1980).
Xue, Muqiao, 'On Reforming the Economic Management System', *Beijing Review*, XXIII:5 (1980), pp. 16–20.
Xue, Muqiao, 'Another Discourse on Regulation by Planning Mechanism and Regulation by Market Mechanism', *Hongqi* (Red Flag), no. 1 (January 1981), pp. 18–22.
Xue, Xin, 'Scientific Socialism or Agrarian Socialism?', *Social Sciences in China*, III:1 (1982), pp. 70–93.
Yamamoto H., 'Three Forms of the Agricultural Responsibility System', in C. K. Leung and S. S. K. Chin (eds), *China in Readjustment* (Hong Kong: Centre of Asian Studies, University of Hong Kong, 1983).

Yan, Lin, 'The Necessity, Possibility and Realisation of Socialist Transformation of China's Agriculture', *Social Sciences in China*, III:1 (1982), pp. 94–122.
Yang, Shih-chieh, 'The Great Leap Victory of the Party's Leadership and the Extensive Mass Movement at the Anshan Iron and Steel Works', *Renmin Ribao* (People's Daily) 11 February 1960, reprinted in *Chinese Law and Government* no. 1 (1980).
Ye, Jianying, *Speech at the Meeting in Celebration of the 30th Anniversary of the Founding of the People's Republic of China* (Beijing: Foreign Languages Press, 1979).
Zhang, Shuguang, 'Reform the Economic Structure and Increase the Macroeconomic Results', *Social Sciences in China*, III:1 (1982), pp. 40–69.
Zhao Ziyang, 'Report on the Sixth Five Year Plan', Fifth Session of the Fifth National People's Congress, 30 November 1982, in *Fifth Session of the Fifth National People's Congress* (main documents) (Beijing: Foreign Languages Press, 1983).
Zhao, Ziyang, 'Report on the Work of the Government', Second Session of the Sixth National People's Congress (NPC), 15 May 1984, reprinted in *Beijing Review*, XXVII:24 (1984).
Zhou, Chuandian, 'On Reforming the Management System at Grassroot Levels', *Hongqi* (Red Flag), no. 7 (April 1981).
Zhou, Enlai, *Selected Works*, vol. I (Beijing: Foreign Languages Press, 1981).
Zhou, Guo (ed.), *China and the World (3)*, Beijing Review Foreign Affairs Series (*Beijing Review*, 1983).
Zhou, Ping, 'An important Step Forwards, Democratic Management', *Beijing Review*, XXIV: 36 (1981), pp. 14–15.
Zhu, Yuanshi, 'The Causes of the Cultural Revolution', *Beijing Review*, XXIV:37 (1981), pp. 15–20.

Index